The Church in Prophecy and History

Ron Graff

ISBN-10: 0615954146
ISBN-13: 978-0615954141

Prophecy Central
8166 Vinmar Court
Alta Loma, CA, 91701

To Barbara, my wife of 53 years;
My best friend, my best critic,
and my best encourager.

Preface

This is the first volume of a proposed series of commentaries on the matchless Book of Revelation. This vital prophetic section of the Bible is more relevant than ever in our generation. It was not meant to be a hidden mystery, but, as its very name indicates, it will *reveal* truth to those who are willing to hear.

This information was previously posted, one segment at a time, in the "Rejoicing in Revelation" section on the Prophecy Central website.

References to chapters and verses refer to the Book of Revelation. This book is purposely not divided into chapters to avoid confusion about these references. An expanded outline of the first three chapters of Revelation is listed on the Contents pages.

Special thanks are due to Dr. Doyle Book, whose life and experience result in a rare combination of knowledge and sensitivity. He has served as a missionary and professor of church history. I am indebted to him for rendering extensive help in the preparation of this book.

Read *Connecting the Dots: A Handbook of Bible Prophecy* by Ron Graff and Lambert Dolphin. It is available on Amazon.com, ChristianBook.com, and Christian bookstores.

For daily updates on current events as they relate to prophecy, the latest installments of "Rejoicing in Revelation," and for "A world of information about Bible prophecy," visit the Prophecy Central website at:

www.Bible-prophecy.com

CONTENTS

Revelation Chapter 3

Appendices

Revelation Chapter 1

Introduction and Salutation 1:1-8
Introduction 1:1-3

The first few verses are an introduction to this greatest of all prophetic books:

> *The Revelation of Jesus Christ, which God gave Him to show His servants—things which must shortly take place. And He sent and signified it by His angel to His servant John, who bore witness to the word of God, and to the testimony of Jesus Christ, to all things that he saw.* – Revelation 1:1-2

The first three words of this book in the original Greek language express the purpose of the entire work. The first word is "Revelation." It is also translated as "Apocalypse" (Gr. *apokalupsis*--disclosure, unveiling) which indicates that the information the book contains is meant to reveal truth, not conceal it. In other words, it is knowledge which can and should be understood.

One of the chief excuses people give for not studying this intriguing book is that it is too difficult to understand. Some people think that its meaning is hidden from them; that the frequent use of symbolism conceals the truth; that it is a waste of time to try to analyze these prophecies. If that were true, why would God give us this detailed information? And why would He call it a "revelation," an unveiling of truth?

When I was a boy I witnessed an important event in Idaho Springs, Colorado, the little mountain town where I grew up. It was the day of the unveiling of a statue in the town square. The image had been set up at night and was covered with a huge cloth. We had been waiting for this big event for months. Finally, the day arrived, and most of the people of the town were there for the occasion. There were speeches, musical performances, and a carnival atmosphere as we all waited for the big moment to arrive. Finally the time came, and with great fanfare, the cloth was slowly pulled away from the statue. There it stood in all its glory; and we all went wild with our applause. At last we could see with our own eyes every detail of this valuable sculpture!

The "Apocalypse" is like the unveiling of that statue, but infinitely better. It is the revelation of God's plan to bring the Earth and its inhabitants back into a harmonious state when Jesus Christ will reign over His creation in righteousness.

Because of the trials recorded in the book the word "apocalypse" has taken on an entirely different meaning to many people. It has come to mean "catastrophe," "Armageddon," and "the end of the world." The book does predict dreadful events, including wars, plagues, earthquakes, and asteroid collisions. It does warn of an evil world ruler, persecutions, and the "mark of the Beast." But it is NOT the unveiling of all these evil and dreadful things. It is the unveiling of something incredibly wonderful.

The second and third words are "Jesus Christ." The clear implication here is that Jesus Christ is the central subject of the book. Therefore, the focus should not be on the Tribulation or Antichrist or the terrible events that are described in these pages. Bad things will happen in the future, but these are preparatory to the glorious coming of Jesus Christ as King of Kings and Lord of Lords in Chapter 19. This corresponds perfectly to Jesus' own teaching in the Olivet Discourse that the coming trials are like birth pains (Matthew 24:8). An expectant mother may suffer greatly with hard labor, but when the result is a beautiful baby, she will always say that the labor was worth it.

"Jesus" is our translation of the Greek word *Iēsous* and the Hebrew word *Yeshua*, or "Joshua." It means "Jehovah saves." That is why Mary was told by the angel Gabriel to name Him Jesus, "Because He will save his people from their sins." (Matthew 1:21)

"Christ" is the third word. This is the English translation of the Greek word *christos*, or "anointed one." It is the equivalent of the Hebrew *meshiach*, or "Messiah." Numerous passages in the Old Testament predicted a Messiah, who would partake of the divine nature and be a deliverer of mankind. He was seen as one who would atone for sin, and would also deliver His people from tyranny and establish His righteous kingdom. When Jesus came to Earth as a baby His mission was to pay for our sin. When He comes the second time it will be to establish His kingdom on Earth.

The focus on Jesus Christ is seen throughout the book. Chapter 1 includes a vision of Jesus in Glory. Chapters 2 and 3 are messages from Jesus to His churches, Chapters 4 and 5 are a heavenly scene with Jesus in view to prepare the reader to know that He is righteous in all the tribulation that will follow. In Chapters 19 through the end of the book, Jesus is shown to be the Coming King.

This revealed knowledge is given from God the Father to His son Jesus. This is in keeping with what He said in John 15:15:

> ... for all things that I heard from My Father I have made known to you.

These things are to "shortly" take place. As you read through the New Testament you will notice that the writers expected Jesus to return at any time. In every age Christians have looked for His return, just as earlier believers had constantly been looking for the coming of Messiah the first time. Even in the 1st Century there were cynics who asked "where is the promise of His coming?" (2 Peter 3:3-4). Peter answered,

> But, beloved, do not forget this one thing, that with the Lord one day is as a thousand years, and a thousand years as one day. The Lord is not slack concerning His promise, as some count slackness, but is longsuffering toward us, not willing that any should perish but that all should come to repentance. – 2 Peter 3:8-9

One view of prophecy, known as Preterism (from the Latin word *praeteritus*, meaning "past.") teaches that many prophecies, especially those in the Book of Revelation, were fulfilled during the destruction of Jerusalem in AD 70 and/or the persecutions of the Roman Empire. Most adherents to this belief are "partial" Preterists because they still expect the literal return of Christ and judgment of the dead. "Full" Preterists believe that all of Revelation has been fulfilled. They believe the return of Christ and the rest of the book are allegorical.

This view was originated by Roman Catholic writers and later adopted by some Protestants. It is incompatible with a literal approach to Bible study. Their explanations about how the prophecies of Revelation were fulfilled are not at all convincing the way the Old Testament prophecies were about the life of Christ.

An angel (the Greek word *angellos* means "messenger") entrusted this revelation to John the Beloved, one of Jesus' twelve apostles. Many angels appear in the book, but one in particular seems to have been the messenger of these tidings to John. John himself was very old at this time, probably in his 90's. He was in exile on the island of Patmos because of his faith in Christ. John was the only one of the twelve apostles who, according to tradition, was not put to death for his belief in Jesus. However, one early story says that he was thrown into a boiling pot of oil and miraculously survived.

Blessed is he who reads and those who hear the words of this prophecy, and keep those things which are written in it; for the time is near. – Revelation 1:3

This is a very special promise about this prophecy. Of all of the 66 books in the Bible, this is the only one with a promise like this. It says that whoever reads this prophecy, or even hears it (since many people did not know how to read), will be "blessed." To be blessed (Greek *makarios*, "extended") means having the privilege of receiving God's favor or provisions. It is sometimes translated "made happy," but it is much more than that. It is an inner sense of well-being. Jesus started His famous "Sermon on the Mount" by giving The Beatitudes (Blessings) (Matthew 5:1-12).

If a person is to be "blessed" by reading or hearing this prophecy, it should be obvious that its contents should not cause him to be fearful or depressed. God has not given us a spirit of fear (2 Timothy 1:7). In fact, "Fear not" is a recurring theme throughout the Bible. The Twenty-Third Psalm reminds us of this whenever we say,

4

Yea, though I walk through the valley of the shadow of death,
I will fear no evil; for you are with me;--Psalm 23:4a,b

Fear is the opposite of faith. So it should be understood at the beginning of the journey through this vital portion of God's Word that it should build our faith; not cause a spirit of fear.

Revelation is meant to bring joy because of the outcome of its dramatic events. It predicts the triumph of good over evil, the restoration of the Earth to perfection, salvation of those who believe in Jesus Christ, and their deliverance from a corrupted world into one of indescribable beauty and opportunity!

Of course, readers and listeners who do not yet know Christ will want to be sure they are in a right relationship with Him. The Gospel is found repeatedly in the pages of this matchless prophecy, especially in the message to the church at Laodicea, the apostate church at the end of the Church Age. Chapters 2 and 3 will explore this in detail. But looking ahead, Jesus invited the people of that church to open the doors of their lives to Him. In that church many had a formal religious experience, but few had a personal relationship with Him:

Here I am! I stand at the door and knock. If anyone hears my voice and opens the door, I will come in and eat with that person, and they with me. – Revelation 3:20

A couple of warnings are in order here about using Revelation to do evangelism. First, be careful not to give people the wrong impression about the book. When I was in Jr. High School, and a brand new Christian, I made this mistake in a big way. I wanted to show one of my friends the seriousness of his lack of interest in Jesus. I thought it would be a good idea to read to him from Revelation about the seven vials of God's wrath. He listened, and was terrified. He could hardly say anything, but when he did, he blurted out, "If that's what the Bible teaches, I don't want to have anything to do with it!" Unfortunately, he avoided me the rest of our time together in that school. I hope that The Lord eventually sent him a more sensitive person to share the Gospel.

Another caution about using the message of Revelation wisely is to not focus primarily on the glorious future that it portrays when talking to people who despair of this life. I knew one troubled soul who committed suicide to hasten her experience of heaven!

Now, notice that the blessing is not just for those who read or listen, but for those who "keep those things which are written in it." The word used in the original Greek scroll is the verb *terero*, meaning "to guard" or "to keep." This would be the very opposite of what some Bible teachers do today when they ignore it, or, as also is the case for a growing number of fellow-evangelicals, to deny that the study of prophecy is of any benefit, and may even impede their progress in building the Kingdom.

The final thought in this key verse of the book is this, "… for the time is near." This carries forward the expression from the first verse, "things which *must shortly take place.*" As noted before, New Testament writers and Christians of every age have been expecting Jesus to return at any time. This is known as the doctrine of "imminence," a belief that Christians should live their lives in the knowledge that Jesus' return will take place suddenly and unexpectedly, and they should be ready for that glorious event!

When Jesus ascended into heaven, an angel told the watching crowd of disciples,

> *This same Jesus, who has been taken from you into heaven, will come back in the same way you have seen him go into heaven.* – Acts 1:11

The apostle Paul called this coming event "the blessed hope" (Titus 2:13). Some people like to read the end of a book before the rest to see if they even want to spend their time on it. Chapters 19 through 22 of Revelation are all about the fabulous ending of the story. It is all wrapped up in the return of Jesus. Here, in fact, are the last two verses of the Bible:

> *He who testifies to these things says, "Surely I am coming quickly."*
> *Amen. Even so, come, Lord Jesus!*
> *The grace of our Lord Jesus Christ be with you all. Amen.* – Revelation 22:20-21

Salutation 1:4-5d

John, to the seven churches which are in Asia:
Grace to you and peace from Him who is and who
was and who is to come, and from the seven Spirits who are
before His throne, and from Jesus Christ,--Revelation 1:4,5a

The original books of the Bible were handwritten on scrolls. These scrolls were made of papyrus or parchment, Papyrus was manufactured by processing the pith from the papyrus plants in a manner similar to the way modern paper is made from wood pulp. Parchment was a later improvement because it was made from more durable animal skins. Sheets of these pages were glued or stitched together, and then rolled up for storage. These rolls were called "scrolls," and they were read by unrolling a page at a time, while rolling up the previous page. The words on the pages were handwritten with great care. Chapters and verses were added much later for convenience, and are not considered "inspired" by God.

Our word "paper" is derived from the Greek word *papuros.* Our word "Bible" comes from the Greek words *ta biblia,* meaning "The books."

The writer of the book is John, one of Jesus' Twelve Apostles. He names himself at the beginning of this letter so that the readers will not have to go to the end of a bulky scroll to discover his identity. He had already stated in the first verse that Jesus was the true author of the prophecy, and that it was simply *entrusted* to John by an angel to record. John and his brother James were known as the "Sons of Thunder" (Mark 3:17) before Jesus called them to be with Him. The two of them with Peter formed a leadership "inner circle" among the disciples who were with Him at special times, such as His Transfiguration (Matthew 17:1 ff.) and prayer in the Garden of Gethsemane on the night before He was crucified (Matthew 26:36 ff.). He is often called "John the Beloved" because although he never identified himself by name in the writing of his Gospel, he did refer to himself as "the disciple whom Jesus loved" (John 13:23). At the time of the writing of this book he was the last living representative of the Twelve Apostles.

The letter is directed to *"the seven churches which are in Asia."* These were seven local congregations in the seven cities that are mentioned in Chapters 2 and 3 of the book. They were very different from one another, as is the case among churches today. Being unique, they were given differing messages about their conditions.

These messages might also apply to different local churches or even denominations of churches that exist today. Some are like the Apostolic church at Ephesus, others like the persecuted church at Smyrna, and so on.

The messages also prefigure different periods of church history. These historical periods will be analyzed when we study the messages given to each church in Revelation 2 and 3.

There is something significant about the number seven in the Bible. From the seven days of creation in Genesis (Genesis 2:1-3), through the seven angels having the seven last plagues in the Book of Revelation (Revelation 10:7; 21:9 ff.), the number is used consistently to symbolize completeness or perfection. In fact it is found 36 times in the 22 chapters of the book.

Symbolism is used frequently in this prophetic book. But symbolic language is not necessarily difficult to understand. It may deter those who are not adequately informed, but for those who follow good rules of interpretation, and take the time to study the whole book, along with the rest of the Bible, the symbols will usually become clear and very meaningful. Many of them are explained in Revelation itself, and the rest can be discovered by comparing Scripture with Scripture.

John's salutation to those who would read the letter is similar to the formula that the apostle Paul often employed. It starts with the words, *"Grace to you and peace."* These profound words encapsulate the essence of the Gospel. First, grace means "undeserved favor." This one word alone is shorthand for the whole process of salvation. God created sinless humans and placed them in a perfect environment, but in order for them to love Him of their own free will, He decided to give them the ability to choose good or evil. When they chose to disobey His will, and eat the forbidden fruit, they failed the test and broke the one simple rule the Lord had given them.

8

However, instead of forsaking His creation, God provided the most amazing solution to their sin problem. His One and Only Son would be sent to Earth to become a man in order to pay for their sin (and ours) by His own sacrificial death on the Cross. (Genesis 3:15; John 3:15; 2 Corinthians 5:14-17; Ephesians 2:8-9). And in the meantime, while waiting for that salvation to be accomplished, God provided a temporary covering for their sin. They did not deserve such love and provision, and neither do we. But that is what grace is all about.

Those who experience God's grace by receiving Christ as their Savior may then enjoy peace! The Gospel promises peace *with* God because of Christ's work (Romans 5:1), and also the peace *of* God, which passes all understanding (Philippians 4:7).

These benefits of grace and peace are a further proof that the study of eschatology (end- times) should not cause fear and distress, but should result in peace of mind.

This incomparable gift of saving grace and peace comes from God Himself. In this salutation God is seen in His triune nature: as the Father, the Holy Spirit, and Jesus Christ the Son. ***The Father*** is said to be, ***"Him who is and who was and who is to come."*** Theologians describe God as "omnipotent" (all-powerful), "omniscient" (all-knowing), and "omni-present" (everywhere-present at once). He is not limited by time the way we are. He exists in the "now." But He existed also in the past. And He will exist into eternity.

Likewise this grace and peace come from ***The Holy Spirit***. Here He is described, using the symbolism of the number seven. The wording is, **"And from the seven spirits who are before His throne."** This expression does not occur anywhere else in the Bible. Here in Revelation it occurs three more times (Revelation 3:1; 4:5; and 5:6). In all of these, the wording is "seven spirits *of God*." The meaning surely is, God the Holy Spirit, in all of His perfection.

In the third place, this salvation comes from ***God the Son: Jesus Christ***. We might have expected a different order – Father, Son, and Holy Spirit. However, in this book Jesus is central, and He is about to be displayed in the rest of this introductory chapter in ways that He had never been known before.

...and from Jesus Christ, the faithful witness, the firstborn from the dead, and the ruler over the kings of the earth. – Revelation 1:5

Continuing the description of Jesus, John gives three memorable portrayals of our Savior. This begins a very long list of names and titles for Him in Revelation. You might like to keep track of them as you study the book. One of these names is found in the very first verse (**Jesus** – "Savior"). One title was also given there (**Christ** – "Messiah").

He is **the faithful witness**. The Greek word is *martus*, and it has two important meanings in this book. The first meaning is "testimony," as in a courtroom setting, where the witness tells what he or she has seen or heard. John 1:18 says that Jesus is the only one who has truly seen God the Father, and He has told us about Him. In John 8:38 He said, "I speak what I have seen with My Father."

The other meaning of *martus* is one who gives his life *because* of his testimony. Our word for this is "martyr." In every age there have been many Christians put to death for their faith. In most cases they could have lived if they had been willing to deny their belief in Jesus, but they would not give up their faith! Jesus Himself was a martyr. He was crucified for telling the truth about Himself. He was willing to die in order that we might live:

> *But God demonstrates His own love toward us, in that while we were still sinners, Christ died for us.* – Romans 5:8 (Read the whole chapter for more about this).

As seen in the previous verse, His death was the fulfillment of God's gift of grace. Our first parents accepted God's forgiveness. At that point sin offerings were instituted, even though they were not made a formal law until Moses' time. We know this is true because of the offerings that Cain and Abel made. Cain's offering was not acceptable because it did not involve the death of an animal (Genesis 4). This was a constant reminder that "The wages of sin is death." (Romans 3:23).

When Jesus died on the cross, the veil of the temple was torn in two from the top to the bottom (Matthew 27:51). This symbolized the end of the need for the sacrificial system. Before His death animal sacrifices were just a "covering" for sins until the Lamb of God would make the perfect offering:

> *For it is not possible that the blood of bulls and goats could take away sins.* — Hebrews 10:4

> *For such a High Priest was fitting for us, who is holy, harmless, undefiled, separate from sinners, and has become higher than the heavens; who does not need daily, as those high priests, to offer up sacrifices, first for His own sins and then for the people's, for this He did once for all when He offered up Himself. For the law appoints as high priests men who have weakness, but the word of the oath, which came after the law, appoints the Son who has been perfected forever.* — Hebrews 7:26-28

Next, Jesus is called **the firstborn from the dead.** This is an obvious reference to His resurrection. Jesus paid for our sins by His death, but each person must accept the gift of eternal life (John 1:12; Romans 10:9-10; Revelation 3:20). His resurrection was the proof that He was who He claimed to be and His death really was acceptable to the Father. The whole long chapter of 1 Corinthians 15 is devoted to the subject of the resurrection. It gives many convincing reasons to believe it, including the fact that there were more than 500 eye-witnesses. In verse 23 Paul called Christ the "firstfruits" of the resurrection, and added that believers will also be raised at His coming.

One more impressive title is given in this verse. Jesus is said to be **"the ruler over the kings of the earth."** This is primarily a preview of His Glorious Return, which will be mentioned in verse 7, and described more fully in Chapter 19. When He comes to Earth again, it will be as "King of Kings and Lord of Lords" (Revelation 19:11-16).

In one sense Jesus already rules over the kings of the Earth, and in another way He is not yet "King of Kings" in the way He will be at His second coming. You might remember that during His temptation, the Devil offered to give Him the earthly kingdoms if He would just worship him (Matthew 4:9-10). He could make that offer because on our sin-corrupted planet, evil is thriving. That is why the Devil is called the "god of this world" (2 Corinthians 4:4), and the "prince of the power of the air" (Ephesians 2:2). There is no comparison between the evil empires of this world system and the future righteous kingdom Jesus will establish. On the other hand, as God the Son, He is still sovereign over His creation. God does set a limit of what He will allow. Psalm 75:7 says, "But God *is* the Judge: He puts down one, and exalts another."

Jesus had told his disciples that the Kingdom of Heaven was "at hand" (Matthew 4:17). He knew his offer to be King at His triumphal entry would be rejected. Nevertheless, He will come in great glory in the future to establish it (Luke 21:25-31; 22:18, 30). In Acts 1:6 the disciples asked Him, "Lord, will You at this time restore the kingdom to Israel?" He told them they couldn't know the time, but when the Holy Spirit would come, He would enable them to be witnesses to the whole Earth.

Evidently the Kingdom was not to be established at that time. He would not yet reign on Earth, and the disciples would not yet reign with Him, but they would spread the message of the Kingdom, even as He had been doing.

That is why Jesus taught us to pray "Your kingdom come. Your will be done on earth as [it is] in heaven" (Matthew 6:10). We still pray that way because even though His Kingdom does already exist in Heaven, and He is our King already, the Kingdom still has not yet been established here on Earth.

Jesus told Pilate, "My kingdom is not of this world. If My kingdom were of this world, My servants would fight, so that I should not be delivered to the Jews; but now My kingdom is not from here" (John 18:36-37).

Born-again Christians are citizens of the Kingdom of Heaven (Philippians 3:20). However, we are also citizens of our earthly nations. That's why Jesus told His disciples,

> *"Render therefore to Caesar the things that are Caesar's, and to God the things that are God's."*– Matthew 22:21

While we are here, we are ambassadors, representing Christ and His Kingdom:

Now then, we are ambassadors for Christ, as though God were pleading through us: we implore you on Christ's behalf, be reconciled to God. – 2 Corinthians 5:20

During this time, we establish outposts of the Kingdom in our homes, churches, missions, and other Christian enterprises. We seek constantly to gain new members of the Kingdom by following Christ's example of ministering to people's needs and giving them the Gospel. There is much "Kingdom work" to do now even though it has not yet been fully established on Earth.

Dedication 1:5e-8

To Him who loved us and washed us from our sins in His own blood, and has made us kings and priests to His God and Father, to Him be glory and dominion forever and ever. Amen. – Revelation 1:5e-6

These words form a dedication of the book to the Lord Jesus Christ. It would be better if this section came at the beginning of a new paragraph since it begins a new thought. This is the problem of man-made chapter and verse divisions.

This section is a "doxology." In many churches doxologies are recited or sung. They are usually scriptural passages that give glory (Greek *doxos*) to God.

Jesus is called, ***"Him who loved us."*** What could be a better thing to say about anyone? I have presided at funerals for people who were known to very affectionate. It is not unusual to hear one person say, "We were best friends. She really loved me." Afterwards another person might say, "She loved me, and I thought we were best friends." Another would say, jokingly, but sincerely too, "I know she loved me the most."

If this can be true of fallible human beings, just imagine how much more it can be said about God the Son, when the Bible assures us that "God is love" (1 John 4:16).

The timeless children's song declares,

Jesus loves me! This I know,
For the Bible tells me so;

Another great musical reminder of this truth is the chorus of an old hymn,

Out of the ivory palaces,
Into a world of woe,
Only His great eternal love
Made my Savior go.

John 15:15 records that Jesus told the disciples that He no longer called them servants, but friends. On the night before Jesus was crucified, He washed His disciples' feet. John affirmed that Jesus "loved them to the end" (John 13:1). This love relationship is so deep that the apostle Paul taught that the church is called the Bride of Christ (Ephesians 5:25-27, 32).

Of course, God the Father loves us also. According to the matchless words of John 3:16:

For God so loved the world that He gave His only begotten Son, that whoever believes in Him should not perish but have everlasting life.- John 3:16

The result of Jesus' great love is that He has **washed us from our sins in His own blood.** This kind of imagery is not common in a love story. But unfortunately, the only way that the hero of this amazing true drama could save the object of His love was by dying in her (our) place! As mentioned earlier in this verse, Jesus was the "firstborn from the dead." His primary purpose in coming to Earth the first time was to be a sacrifice for sin. John the Baptist called him *"The Lamb of God, who takes away the sin of the world"* (John 1:27). He paid the price, *"once for all when He offered up Himself"* (Hebrews 10:27).

Jesus Himself said,

Greater love has no one than this, than to lay down one's life for his friends. — John 15:13

And the apostle Paul gave us this theological perspective:

Let this mind be in you which was also in Christ Jesus, who, being in the form of God, did not consider it robbery to be equal with God, but made Himself of no reputation, taking the form of a bondservant, and coming in the likeness of men. And being found in appearance as a man, He humbled Himself and became obedient to the point of death, even the death of the cross. Therefore God also has highly exalted Him and given Him the name which is above every name, that at the name of Jesus every knee should bow, of those in heaven, and of those on earth, and of those under the earth, and that every tongue should confess that Jesus Christ is Lord, to the glory of God the Father. – Philippians 2:5-11

As a result of Jesus' love and sacrifice for us, He **has made us kings** (literally: *"a kingdom"*) **and priests to His God and Father.** *While the* focus is still on Jesus, this part of the dedication to Him names us as the beneficiaries of His work. As a result of the great salvation He has provided, He has given us vital Kingdom work to do (Colossians 1:3). We are kings in the sense that one day, when He establishes His Kingdom on Earth, we will reign with Him (1 Corinthians 6:2; 2 Timothy 2:12).

Another great privilege that is ours as a result of His death is the work of the priesthood. As mentioned in the previous verse, when Jesus died on the cross, He provided the one perfect sacrifice for sin. The veil to the Holy of Holies in the Temple was miraculously ripped in two, symbolizing that the old sacrificial system was no longer unnecessary. Not only that, but as Peter would later explain, the role of the priesthood was expanded to include all true believers:

You also, as living stones, are being built up a spiritual house, a holy priesthood, to offer up spiritual sacrifices acceptable to God through Jesus Christ. – 1 Peter 2:5

But you are a chosen generation, a royal priesthood, a holy nation, His own special people, that you may proclaim the praises of Him who called you out of darkness into His marvelous light; – 1 Peter 2:9

Why is this so special? In the Old Testament, under the Mosaic Law, the priests were intermediaries—standing between the people and God. The people would give the priests their requests. Then the priests would intercede for them in prayer. And only once each year, the High Priest alone entered the Holy of Holies to make atonement for his own sins and for the sins of the people (Hebrews 9:7). But now, all who have placed their faith in Jesus have this direct access! Furthermore, as priests, all of us have the privilege and responsibility of interceding for the needs of others:

> *Let us therefore come boldly to the throne of grace, that we may obtain mercy and find grace to help in time of need.* – Hebrews 4:6

Did you wonder about the phrase, "to His God and Father"? Is that an indication that Jesus is not God? Not at all! In this passage God the Father calls Jesus "My Son." In the first chapter of Hebrews the Father calls the Son "God!"

> *But to the Son He says:*
> *"Your throne, O God, is forever and ever;*
> *A scepter of righteousness is the scepter of Your kingdom.* – Hebrews 1:8

The Father also says in that chapter that the Son is the Creator, and the "express image" of His (the Father's) person (Hebrews 1:1-12).

Whole books of theology have been written to show that the Father, the Son, and the Holy Spirit are three equal persons in the Holy Trinity. One early statement (called The Athanasian Creed) expressed it this way: "The Father is God, the Son is God, and the Holy Spirit is God, and yet there are not three Gods but one God."

Who can fully understand God and His ways?

> *"For My thoughts are not your thoughts,*
> *Nor are your ways My ways," says the* LORD.
> *"For as the heavens are higher than the earth,*
> *So are My ways higher than your ways,*
> *And My thoughts than your thoughts."* – Isaiah 5:8-9

God is not limited by our physical universe, which is something He created. We have some understanding of our three-dimensional world, but we cannot hope to fathom the complexity of our multi-dimensional God, who is utterly beyond His created universe.

No illustration of the Trinity is perfect to our limited understanding, but here is my favorite. Suppose we lived in a two-dimensional world and had no concept of the third dimension. Everything would look like lines and points to us. Even a circle would look like a line, but it might get dimmer on the ends to show that it curved away from our point of view. Now, suppose a sphere should pass through our flat world. At first, when it touched our plane it would appear as a dot. As it entered further through the plane it would become a line, and the line would grow longer until it was half-way through. Then the line would gradually shrink, and finally disappear.

Inhabitants of such a world could not understand what had happened nor could they conceive of the true shape of the sphere.

Neither can we fully understand our Great God. But we can join with John and countless others since his time who have echoed this doxology to both the Father and the Son, ***To Him be glory and dominion forever and ever. Amen.***

Glory is a vital subject in the Bible. It occurs many times in Revelation. At this point we will just begin the discovery of what glory means in God's Word. It starts with God revealing something about Himself to His creatures. He displays His glory. His creatures then acknowledge His greatness by honoring Him and praising Him. They give Him glory. This partial revelation of Himself sometimes took the form of light, as in the case of the pillar of fire and pillar of cloud that accompanied the Children of Israel (Exodus 13:21-22 and 16:10). 1 John 1:5 declares that "God is light." His first creative act was to say, "Let there be light" (Genesis 1:2). The Gospel of John, also written by the same author as Revelation, begins with a beautiful summary of God, of creation, of life, and of light. It also introduces the creative power as "the Word." Then the Gospel reveals this:

And the Word became flesh and dwelt among us, and we beheld His glory, the glory as of the only begotten of the Father, full of grace and truth. – John 1:14

17

Toward the end of Revelation "The Word of God" occurs as one of the many names of Jesus. And on the journey there will be many other occurrences of "glory" in the book.

Continuing the dedication of Revelation, John said:

Behold, He is coming with clouds, and every eye will see Him, even they who pierced Him. And all the tribes of the earth will mourn because of Him. Even so, Amen. – Revelation 1:7

The whole book of Revelation is like a movie thriller, complete with supernatural heroes and villains, sci-fi scenarios, and unbelievable special effects. Verses 7 and 8 could be considered a trailer for the movie. It is just a little preview of the fantastic conclusion of this age and the beginning of the next! Notice that even in this preview, the good overcomes the bad and there is a happy ending.

Behold is the dramatic translation of the Greek word for "look." We will see it many times in this book, whenever there is something that needs special attention. **He is coming!** This is the central message of the entire Revelation. Not only was Jesus a living example of all that a human could be; and the only one who was sinless and powerful enough to pay for our sin; and was raised from the dead to prove that He was who He claimed to be; but, wonder of wonders, He is coming back to Earth again!

There are many reasons why it is essential for our living Savior to physically return to this privileged planet.

He is coming again to complete His role as Messiah. Old Testament passages predicted that Messiah would come to deliver God's people from evil government and establish a righteous kingdom (Isaiah 9:6-7; Jeremiah 23:5; etc.). However, some of the messianic prophecies indicated that He would be a "suffering servant" (Psalm 22; Isaiah 53; etc.). It is now clear that He had to suffer first to deal with the sin problem, and later He will reign. He did offer to reign (John 12) but He knew He would be rejected. So He came the first time to proclaim the Gospel–the "Good News"–and to be a sacrifice for the sins of the world, but He is coming a second time as King of Kings (Revelation 19:11-16). This first chapter of

Revelation describes His dramatic appearance as the righteous judge and mighty warrior (verses 12 through 16).

He is coming again to replace the evil world systems with His righteous kingdom. In the book of Daniel a series of dreams and visions depicted the flow of world empires from the time of Babylon until the end-times when Jesus will come to destroy evil kingdoms and establish His own righteous one (Daniel Chapter 2; Chapters 7 through 9; Chapters 11 and 12).

He is coming again to fulfill His promise to His followers:

"Do not let your hearts be troubled. You believe in God; believe also in me. My Father's house has many rooms; if that were not so, would I have told you that I am going there to prepare a place for you? And if I go and prepare a place for you, I will come back and take you to be with me that you also may be where I am." – John 14:1-3

This aspect of Christ's Second Coming is a separate event from His Glorious Return at the end of the Tribulation period. It is called the Rapture, and is described in 1 Thessalonians 4:13-18 and 1 Corinthians 15: 50-58. The most obvious difference between the Rapture and the Glorious Return is that in one, believers meet Jesus in the air and are taken to where He is, and in the other, Jesus comes to Earth, bringing believers with Him. There is strong evidence in the book that the Rapture occurs before the Tribulation.

When Jesus returns to Earth at the end of the Tribulation, it will be **with clouds**. John had been among the disciples on the Mount of Olives on the day that Jesus ascended into heaven:

Now when He had spoken these things, while they watched, He was taken up, and a cloud received Him out of their sight. And while they looked steadfastly toward heaven as He went up, behold, two men stood by them in white apparel, who also said, "Men of Galilee, why do you stand gazing up into heaven? This same Jesus, who was taken up from you into heaven, will so come in like manner as you saw Him go into heaven." – Acts 1:9-11

In the 14th chapter of Revelation Jesus is seen in the clouds when He initiates judgment on the Earth, and in the 19th chapter it is said that the heavens will open for Him to return to fight the Battle of Armageddon.

By some method, unknown in John's days, it is said that when Jesus returns, *every eye will see Him!* Today we can picture this because of satellite television signals and the Internet. It is likely that the world's attention will be drawn for days or weeks to Israel, where the evil world dictator will be gathering representatives from all over the Earth to fight this epic battle. The cameras will be in place, and when Jesus appears, it will be made visible to people everywhere. It is likely that even the poorest of people will have an inexpensive mass-produced smart phone or some other means of viewing this phenomenal event.

The expression, **even they who pierced Him**, would be a reference to the inhabitants of Jerusalem during the siege by all nations against God's holy city. At that time many of the inhabitants of Jerusalem will realize that they misunderstood who Jesus was. When He returns in glory, they will believe that He is their Messiah!

> *"And I will pour on the house of David and on the inhabitants of Jerusalem the Spirit of grace and supplication; then they will look on Me whom they pierced. Yes, they will mourn for Him as one mourns for his only son, and grieve for Him as one grieves for a firstborn. In that day there shall be a great mourning in Jerusalem."*--Zechariah 12:10-11

This mourning by God's chosen people in Jerusalem will be a good thing. It is a sign of repentance that will lead them to salvation in that day (Romans 9, esp. vv. 25-27).

And all the tribes of earth will mourn because of Him. While the people of Jerusalem are delivered from their enemies, they will mourn <u>for</u> their pierced Messiah but the nations all over the Earth that have sent their soldiers to die in this battle will mourn *because* of Him.

Will all of this really happen? Revelation gives this double affirmative: **Even so, Amen.** "Even so" comes from the Greek word *nai*, "yes," "assuredly so" (as in "Let your yes be yes"--2 Corinthians 1:18). This affirmation is followed by "amen," meaning "so be it!" Therefore we had better believe it!

"I am the Alpha and the Omega, the Beginning and the End," *says the Lord, "who is and who was and who is to come, the* *Almighty."* – Revelation 1:8

I am is the personal name of God that was revealed to Moses. Before Moses' time God revealed Himself as *Elohim*, the plural form of the Hebrew word *El*, meaning "strong one:"

> *Then Moses said to God, "Indeed, when I come to the children of* *Israel and say to them, 'The God of your fathers has sent me to you,' and they* *say to me, 'What is His name?' what shall I say to them?"*
> *And God said to Moses, "I AM WHO I AM." And He said,* *"Thus you shall say to the children of Israel, 'I AM has sent me to you.'"* -- Exodus 3:13-14

Who was speaking here in Revelation? It is God, of course. It might have been the Father, giving His endorsement of this prophecy. Some think that it was Jesus, who could make the same claims about His eternal existence and power. Or it could refer to the whole Trinity, especially since the prophecy was said to be, in verses 4 and 5, from the Father, the Spirit, and the Son.

The Alpha and the Omega refers to the first and last letters of the Greek alphabet. As you have probably noticed by the reference to original Greek words in the text, the book was written in Greek. The world government of the 1st Century was centered in Rome, and was known as the Roman Empire. However much of the culture of the time was shaped by the previous empire, Greece. The Greek language was the trade language of that period of history. A similar expression, "from A to Z," means "from the beginning of a subject to the end of it, and everything in between." Therefore, only the One True God could make such a claim.

Some important manuscripts omit the words, *The Beginning and* *the End*, but this expression is just another way of saying "the Alpha and the Omega." This brings up the question of the reliability of Scripture. It is safe to say that a great many more manuscripts of the Bible have been found than those of any other ancient book. In addition, more scholarship has gone into "textual criticism"–the study of the variations in the text–than for any other book. In the process there are many minor differences in the words used and different opinions as to whether or not a certain phrase, like this one, belongs to the original work.

Textual variations lead some people to doubt that the Bible is trustworthy, but the more people learn about this process, the greater confidence they have in God's Word. The scribes were incredibly careful when they copied Scripture. They were much more cautious than modern scholars are about proofreading our writing, and if errors were found they discarded the page and started over. It is thought that most added words were notes made in the margin by students, and mistakenly included in later copies. Sometimes a scribe would make an inadvertent substitution of one word for another that had the same meaning.

The bottom line on this subject of variations in the text is this: *no known alternative reading of any part of the Bible would change any of the major doctrines of Christianity.* Even though there are minor variations in later copies, it is reasonable to believe that the whole Bible was "inerrant in the original manuscripts:"

> *All Scripture is given by inspiration of God, and is profitable for doctrine, for reproof, for correction, for instruction in righteousness, that the man of God may be complete, thoroughly equipped for every good work.* – 2 Timothy 3:16-17

Says the Lord (God), "who is and who was and who is to come, the Almighty." This final identification of the speaker could also apply to the Father, who is often called the Almighty (Greek *pantokrator*– "ruler over all"), the Son, who "is to come," or the entire Trinity. In any case, it is so good to know that God reveals the future and gives it His stamp of approval.

THE PERSON OF JESUS CHRIST   1:9-18
(The things which you have seen)

This begins the first of three major divisions of this Revelation of Jesus Christ. It is a vision of Jesus that is quite different from the way His followers had pictured Him before. They had correctly thought of Him as the Son of God, the long-awaited Messiah, the Savior of mankind, the perfect human, the greatest teacher in human history, their best friend, their King, and, in many other ways, the most amazing of all people. To them He was infinitely loving, forgiving, and wonderful.

He called Himself "meek" (Matthew 11:29). That expression is misunderstood in our days, but the original listeners knew that the Greek word for "gentle." did not mean weakness. To be gentle one must first have great strength. A gentle person is careful how that strength is used.

He claimed equality with God in a variety of ways, including some of his descriptions of Himself. He said, "I AM the light of the world" (John 8:12), "I AM the bread of life" (John 6:35) and "I AM the resurrection and the life" (John 11:25).

Jesus has been the subject of more paintings, more poems, and more books than any other person in history. People have tried to summarize His greatness with masterpieces like "One Solitary Life," and "The Incomparable Christ." But no one has stated His greatness and His fame better than the apostle John, the writer of Revelation, at the end of his Gospel:

> *And there are also many other things that Jesus did, which if they were written one by one, I suppose that even the world itself could not contain the books that would be written. Amen.* – John 21:25

Still, in addition to all that was known about the Lord Jesus, the things that John saw next, and described for us, are totally beyond any concept that people had accepted before that time. There will be new and shocking information about Jesus in this section. But first, we need to learn about the background of this new material.

Preparation for the vision   1:9-10

I, John, both your brother and companion in the tribulation and kingdom and patience of Jesus Christ, was on the island that is called Patmos for the word of God and for the testimony of Jesus Christ.--Revelation 1:9

The writer identifies himself as *"I, John."* It would not have been necessary to include the personal pronoun, "I," (Greek *ego*), but by doing so, John emphasized the fact that this vision could be trusted since it came through him. He was by now a very old and highly respected person, and the last of the original apostles. He had also written the Gospel of John and three letters or epistles: First, Second, and Third John.

However, when he identifies himself as "your brother," he shows the humility of a true Christian, not lording it over others because of his age or his position, but speaking to them as a brother--a member of God's family. What he wants to share with them is something that every family member should know.

He also speaks as a ***companion in the tribulation*** that most of them were enduring at the end of the 1st Century.

The word used for tribulation *(Greek thlipsis)* also means "persecution." Much of the material in Revelation is about suffering for the cause of Christ. Persecution and martyrdom are prominent themes, in Chapters 2 and 3, where the history of the Church Age is depicted. Also, during the Tribulation Period, starting with the 5th chapter, a growing number of believers will be put to death for believing in the Word of God.

Christians had been persecuted since the beginning of the Church Age. In Acts Chapter 4 Peter and John were threatened by authorities for preaching about Jesus. In Acts 5 Peter and other apostles were imprisoned for their faith. In Chapters 7 and 8 a young man named Stephen was arrested for sharing the Gospel, and he became the first Christian martyr. Another young man, a Pharisee named Saul, gave permission for the event, but this Saul was witness to a special revelation of the Lord Jesus on the road to Damascus (Acts 9), and he eventually became the apostle Paul. Paul himself suffered great persecution (Acts Chapters 13 to 15; 2 Timothy 3:11; 2 Corinthians 11:23-26). He was imprisoned for his missionary work while Nero was Emperor of Rome (Acts Chapters 23 through 28), and according to tradition he was beheaded. (Nero set fire to Rome and accused the Christians of causing the destruction.)

Tradition also taught that ten of the original twelve apostles were put to death--by sword, crucifixion, and beheading. Judas killed himself after betraying Jesus. And, according to Tertullian (AD 160-225), the Emperor Domitian tried to kill John by throwing him into a cauldron of boiling oil, but it had no effect on him. Jesus might have alluded to John's escape from death in John 21. In verses 18-19 of that chapter Jesus gave Peter an idea of how he would have met a martyr's death. Peter then asked about John's future:

> *Jesus said to him, "If I will that he remain till I come, what is that to you? You follow Me."*
>
> *Then this saying went out among the brethren that this disciple would not die. Yet Jesus did not say to him that he would not die, but, "If I will that he remain till I come, what is that to you?"* – John 21:22-23

John also told the readers of this prophecy that he was a companion with them in the **kingdom and patience of Jesus Christ**, Revelation focuses on the Kingdom (Kingdom of God, Kingdom of Heaven)--See the earlier discussion about verse 5 where this issue is explained. Here is a quick review of that section: Jesus is King, and those who belong to Him are citizens of His heavenly kingdom. However, the Kingdom is still "in heaven," and we are taught to pray that it might come to Earth. This prayer will be answered when Jesus returns as King of Kings. In the meanwhile, we do have Kingdom work to do, including evangelism and discipleship. And we are ambassadors to the world while we are here.

John and his fellow-believers experienced the **patience of Jesus**. Jesus had demonstrated the utmost patience in His own suffering, and is still incredibly long-suffering in regard to the establishment of His kingdom on Earth.

This vision was given while John was in exile **on the island that is called Patmos**. Since tradition says John survived the boiling oil, he was banished to the little barren volcanic island of Patmos in the Aegean Sea near Asia Minor where the Seven Churches addressed in Chapters 2 and 3 of Revelation were located (This is modern Turkey). Like most other major religious revelations, this great vision was given to John in the setting of a wilderness experience.

John's "crime" was his faith in Jesus Christ and his determination to share that knowledge with others. He said he had been sent to Patmos *for the word of God and for the testimony of Jesus Christ.* Again, "testimony" is the Greek word *martus*, from which we get the word "martyr."

> *I was in the Spirit on the Lord's Day, and I heard behind me a loud voice, as of a trumpet,*--Revelation 1: 10

A fascinating aspect of Revelation is the way this prophecy was given by God to John.

He wrote, *I was in the Spirit...* It was evidently assumed that Christian readers at the end of the 1st Century would understand this special state of mind. The work of the Holy Spirit includes the concepts of divine revelation, inspiration, and illumination.

The writer of Hebrews said this:

> *God, who at various times and in various ways spoke in time past to the fathers by the prophets, has in these last days spoken to us by His Son,*--Hebrews 1:1-2a

Here are some of those "various ways": Direct conversation (Genesis 2:15-17; Exodus 33:11), a burning bush (Exodus 3), thunder (Job 37:5), a "still small voice" (1 Kings 19:5-12), etching on stone tablets (Exodus 31:18), talking animals (Numbers 22:28-30), dreams--their own (Daniel 7) or other people's (Daniel 2), visions (like a dream, but while one is awake--Genesis 15:1; 1 Samuel 3; Isaiah 1; Acts 101-15), announcements by angels (Daniel 10; Luke 1:26-38), voice from heaven (Matthew 3:17), even the proverbial "handwriting on the wall"(Daniel 5). But the most clear and memorable of all God's communication was the life, the work, and the words of Jesus Christ!

Revelation

In this case God spoke by way of a vision (Revelation 9:17) that included some of these other methods as well. John was prepared for reception of a vision by being "in the Spirit."

The Holy Spirit was active throughout the Old Testament, "filling," or "coming upon" various people for certain purposes (Exodus 35:31; 1 Samuel 16:13; Psalm 51:11). He began a new, permanent intimacy with believers after the death of Christ. Jesus had predicted His arrival and indwelling. He said the Holy Spirit would be "another Helper" (John 14:15-18--Greek *parakletos* --"companion, comforter") who would assist them in many ways, including the ability to accurately remember what Jesus had taught them (John 16:5-11).

When a person accepts Christ, the Holy Spirit takes up residency in him (Romans 8:9-11). Being "in the Spirit" is referred to elsewhere as being "filled with the Spirit" (Ephesians 5:18) and "walking in the Spirit" (Galatians 5:25). This is the privilege of every true Christian: to surrender himself or herself to the direction and empowerment of God's Holy Spirit. There is no thought here of entering a trance by use of drugs, hypnosis or other occult practices. John was simply in the right frame of mind for this relation by being filled with the Spirit. The revelation itself came as a vision rather than a dream.

The Holy Spirit is also instrumental in two other aspects of understanding God's Word. These aspects are called Inspiration and Illumination.

Inspiration

All Scripture is given by inspiration of God, and is profitable for doctrine, for reproof, for correction, for instruction in righteousness, that the man of God may be complete, thoroughly equipped for every good work. -- 2 Timothy 3:16-17

The key word in this verse is "inspiration." The Greek word is *theopneustros*--"God-breathed." The word "Scripture" meant the recognized books of the Bible (Acts 17:11, 1 Corinthians 15:3, etc.), which at that time would normally mean the Old Testament. Notice however, that in 1 Peter 3:15-16 the apostle Peter equated Paul's epistles with "the rest of the Scriptures."

Peter also described the process of inspiration in this way:

For prophecy never came by the will of man, but holy men of God spoke as they were moved by the Holy Spirit. – 2 Peter 1:21

The word "moved" is the present participle of the Greek verb *phero*. Its meaning is "carried along." Peter, being a fisherman, might well have pictured this as the external power he experienced when his boat was carried on the crest of a wave. As a preacher, it would have applied to what happened to him on the Day of Pentecost, when the Holy Spirit was first given to believers (Acts 2), and he was able to deliver such a powerful message that about 3000 people believed in Christ!

This would be a good place to mention the concept of *"dual authorship"* in the Bible. All of the books in our Bible, which were generally accepted by the Early Church and confirmed by godly and scholarly church leaders at the councils of Hippo Regius in 393, and Carthage in 397, are literally considered "God's Word." The original manuscripts of each book were believed to be inerrant (without error).

At the same time, one may see that the different human authors had their own vocabulary and style, and therefore did not merely write words dictated to them.

By contrast, many "New Age" authors claim to have "channeled" the words of extraterrestrial beings, which they call "ascended masters." If this is true, the spirits behind their writings are demonic ("fallen angels"-- Revelation 12:4; "doctrines of demons"--1 Timothy 1:4). Such people are not truly authors. They are merely stenographers. Their writing was dictated to them by another being.

Returning our thoughts to the work of the Holy Spirit, He has revealed divine truth to certain people, has foretold future events, and has enabled them to accurately record these revelations. At the same time, He was able to use the unique personalities of the human writers to express their message.

Therefore, the Bible has "dual authorship." God is the primary author, and by His Holy Spirit He communicated the exact content of these writings through various methods as mentioned above.

Illumination

The Holy Spirit also illuminates the Bible. Since He lives within us, He enables us to understand the Word and apply it to our lives. The Bible contains mysteries, parables, allegories, and other revelations that may not be understood by those who do not have the Spirit. Here are some passages that teach this truth:

"I still have many things to say to you, but you cannot bear them now. However, when He, the Spirit of truth, has come, He will guide you into all truth; for He will not speak on His own authority, but whatever He hears He will speak; and He will tell you things to come. He will glorify Me, for He will take of what is Mine and declare it to you. All things that the Father has are Mine. Therefore I said that He will take of Mine and declare it to you. – John 15:12-15 (Jesus)

> *But as it is written:*
> *"Eye has not seen, nor ear heard,*
> *Nor have entered into the heart of man*
> *The things which God has prepared for those who love Him."*
>
> *But God has revealed them to us through His Spirit. For the Spirit searches all things, yes, the deep things of God. For what man knows the things of a man except the spirit of the man which is in him? Even so no one knows the things of God except the Spirit of God. Now we have received, not the spirit of the world, but the Spirit who is from God, that we might know the things that have been freely given to us by God.*
>
> *These things we also speak, not in words which man's wisdom teaches but which the Holy Spirit teaches, comparing spiritual things with spiritual. But the natural man does not receive the things of the Spirit of God, for they are foolishness to him; nor can he know them, because they are spiritually discerned. But he who is spiritual judges all things, yet he himself is rightly judged by no one. For "who has known the mind of the LORD that he may instruct Him?" But we have the mind of Christ.* – 1 Corinthians 2:9-16 (Paul)

Interpretation

Another important related issue is the matter of interpretation. God revealed this information by the Holy Spirit, He inspired his chosen servant John to record it, and He gave us the Spirit to help us understand it. The issue now becomes, how will we choose to look at the book? Peter gave some good advice about this:

> *And so we have the prophetic word confirmed, which you do well to heed as a light that shines in a dark place, until the day dawns and the morning star rises in your hearts; knowing this first, that no prophecy of Scripture is of any private interpretation.*--2 Peter 1:19-20

Without going into great detail, there are several ways that people have interpreted Revelation. The *Preterist* view was mentioned in the first verse of this commentary. Preterists relate most of the book to the events of the 1st Century, revolving around the destruction of Jerusalem in AD 70 and/or the persecutions by the Roman Empire.

Another school of interpretation is the *Historicist* view. This school of thought tries to relate the various parts of Revelation to key events in history. The results vary from teacher to teacher and from age to age, always trying to make it mean something that doesn't fit.

Then there is the *Idealist* point of view. They don't even try to connect the narrative to historical or future events. To them it is just a pool of mythical events that have some spiritual application.

Our approach, and that of most people who take the Bible literally, is the *Futurist* view. We accept what the vision claims for itself--that it is about future events. (For a good discussion of these views, see the introduction to *The MacArthur New Testament Commentary* for Revelation 1-11.)[1]

The vision was given to John **on the Lord's Day**. This, of course is Sunday, and it is now common for us to refer to Sunday in this way, but this is the only place in the Bible where the expression is found. Most Christians worship the Lord on Sundays, but Jewish people observe the Sabbath on Saturdays.

Christianity was originally a Jewish sect, since Jesus and all of His disciples were Jewish. Jesus taught on the Sabbath (Mark 1:21), and He caused controversy by healing on the Sabbath (Matthew 12:10-12; Mark 3:1-4). In the early days of the spread of the Gospel Christians apparently observed the Sabbath, especially in their missionary work, where, for example, it was Paul's custom to find the Jewish people first (Romans 1:16), and spend at least three Sabbaths reasoning with them (Acts 17:2) before sharing the Gospel with the Gentiles.

However, right from the beginning, Sunday was special to Christians because it was on that day of the week that Jesus was raised from the dead. All four Gospels mention that His resurrection was on the first day of the week (Matthew 28:1; Mark 16:2, 9; Luke 24:1; John 20:1). John also recorded the fact that it was on that first day of the week, *while the disciples were gathered together,* that Jesus appeared to them (John 20:19).

Later, when the apostle Paul was ministering to new believers at Troas, the people met on the first day of the week, behind closed doors, to share a meal and to hear his final message there (Acts 20:7).

As Gentile believers became more numerous, and Jewish opposition grew, the church became more independent, while not denying their roots in Judaism.

The Jerusalem Council decided that Gentile converts did not need to be circumcised (Acts 15). Circumcision was a special sign of the covenant between God and His Chosen People, the Jews (Genesis 17:9-14), and, for that matter, so was the Sabbath (Exodus 31:13; Ezekiel 20:12). In his instruction to Gentile converts, Paul told them that they did not need to be circumcised the same way as their Jewish brethren (Colossians 2, esp. v. 11). And he added this about festivals and Sabbaths:

> *So let no one judge you in food or in drink, or regarding a festival or a new moon or sabbaths, which are a shadow of things to come, but the substance is of Christ.* – Colossians 2:16-17

By the time John penned Revelation, nearly a generation later, it was common to refer to Sunday as the Lord's Day.

Today practicing Jews still observe the Sabbath, which is Saturday. When we visit the hotels in Israel, we notice that the food served on the Sabbath is prepared in advance, and some of the elevators are set to automatically stop at every floor so that the devout will not have to even push a button!

There are also some Christian Groups, such as Messianic Christian congregations, that do observe the Sabbath.

One other thought needs to be considered on this matter. Some commentators think that, in the context of this vision, the "Lord's Day" might mean "The Day of the Lord." This would mean the Day of Judgment spoken of by various Old Testament prophets (example: Joel 3:14) and New Testament writers (example: 2 Peter 3:10). The answer to this is that this introductory section is talking about the church, even though some judgment will be involved, not the end of this age. Furthermore, the Greek construction would not be translated that way. As others have explained, *kuriake hemera* is "Day of the Lord," but *hemera kuriou* is "The Lord's Day." It is interesting that Revelation doesn't use the expression "Day of the Lord," even at the Battle of Armageddon or the creation of the New Heaven and New Earth.

The actual vision begins with a startling sound. John says, ***I heard behind me a loud voice, as of a trumpet.*** This is the first of many loud (Greek *megas*--"great") sounds that will punctuate the headlines of this story. The literal meaning for the word for trumpet (Greek *salpiggos*) is "war horn." It symbolizes the calling of God's people to action. With all of the other Old Testament symbolism in this picture, it would probably have sounded like a shofar, or ram's horn. It produces a very loud and unforgettable sound!

However, the sound was not a trumpet, but a voice "like a trumpet." When John looked, he saw that the voice emanated from his Savior and his beloved friend. But this is not the way he might have expected to see the gentle shepherd; the loving, patient teacher whom he knew so well.

In his Gospel John had written these most-memorable words:

For God so loved the world that He gave His only begotten Son, that whoever believes in Him should not perish but have everlasting life. For God did not send His Son into the world to condemn the world, but that the world through Him might be saved. – John 3:16-17

Jesus came the first time to fulfill the prophecies that Messiah would be a suffering Savior. But He is coming again, and even as John wrote about His first coming, he felt compelled to warn that He was coming again--this time as Judge of those who do not believe:

He who believes in the Son has everlasting life; and he who does not believe the

Son shall not see life, but the wrath of God abides on him. – John 3:36

Would Jesus' voice be so loud? Consider this: His was the supernatural voice that brought the universe into being! God the Son was the very creator of our world, and He did it by His voice. The record of each day's work of creation began with "Then God said..." (Genesis 1). The New Testament affirms in several places that it was Jesus who created all things (John 1:1-4; 1 Corinthians 8:6; Colossians 1:15-17; Hebrews 1:2-3).

Such a clear and powerful voice! It demands our attention for what comes next.

Presentation of the vision   1:11-18
The Revelation to John   1:11-16
The Golden Stands   1:11-12

Saying, "I am the Alpha and the Omega, the First and the Last," and, "What you see, write in a book and send it to the seven churches which are in Asia: to Ephesus, to Smyrna, to Pergamos, to Thyatira, to Sardis, to Philadelphia, and to Laodicea." – Revelation 1:11

Jesus declared, *"I am the Alpha and the Omega."* This is the second of four occurrences of this expression in Revelation. The first two are found in this first chapter of the book. The first was in 1:8, where it was apparently God the Father speaking, but possibly God the Son, or the whole Trinity. In this verse the claim is made by Jesus Himself. In the last two chapters of this vision there a similar shift--from God the Father in 21:6 to God the Son in 22:13. All of this just underscores the reality that the Three Persons of the Trinity share the same divine attributes of the One True God.

This, by the way, is another of the many names for Jesus in this book. If you are keeping track, it is followed by an eighth appellation, *The First and the Last.* This is another way of saying the same thing. "The First" comes from the Greek word *protos*, which was derived from the preposition *pro*--"before." In more recent times, when scientists discovered the atom, they named the first and most basic element of the atom the "proton." It is no wonder then that the apostle Paul was inspired to write this description of Jesus:

> *He is the image of the invisible God, the firstborn over all creation. For by Him all things were created that are in heaven and that are on earth, visible and invisible, whether thrones or dominions or principalities or powers. All things were created through Him and for Him.* **And He is before all things, and in Him all things consist.** *And He is the head of the body, the church, who is the beginning, the firstborn from the dead, that in all things He may have the preeminence.* – Colossians 1:15-18

The Greek word for "last" is also interesting. It is *eschatos*, from which theologians have named the entire discipline of "eschatology," the study of "last things"

When I was a young teenager, just before I accepted Christ as my Savior and Lord, I would sometimes go out at night and lie on the grass, looking up at the sky. Like millions of people before me, I would try to imagine how far the universe extended. At the edge of the universe, was there some kind of boundary that held it all in? With or without a boundary, what was beyond that? How could there be a limit to it? On the other hand, how could there *not* be a limit? Try as I might, I was never satisfied with the limited knowledge I had about the subject.

Today astronomers tell us how many millions of light years wide they think the universe is. It is so much bigger than I could have ever imagined, but the same problem is still there. How could it have any boundary, but then again, how could it not?

The same dilemma applies to God Himself. How could He possibly be eternal–have always existed, before He ever created the Universe? On the other hand, how could the One True God *not* be eternal? If He were not, and something else caused Him to come into existence, wouldn't that earlier "something" be the True God?

God is infinite and eternal. Our problem understanding this just causes us to fall back to God's own explanation given in our notes on verse

6 above. In Isaiah 5:8-9 God says His thoughts and ways are just much higher than ours!

The words of the wonderful hymn, "Immortal Invisible" by Walter Chalmers Smith express a proper acceptance of God's incomprehensible attributes:

> Immortal, invisible, God only wise,
> in light inaccessible hid from our eyes,
> most blessed, most glorious, the Ancient of Days,
> almighty, victorious, thy great name we praise.

Next Jesus tells John, ***And what you see...*** The information about to be given to him is a "vision," and "seeing" all of these things will involve many of his other senses as well. He should then **write in a book** all of the detail he will be given. In John's time a book would normally be a scroll.

He was then told to **send it to the seven churches which are in Asia.** How the book would be sent is not described, but when the apostle Paul wrote his letters, he often mentioned that a trusted accomplice would travel to the recipients and deliver it by hand. Once the original was delivered, handwritten copies would be made and distributed to other churches.

The churches in Asia were familiar to John because he had evidently presided over them before his banishment

The number "seven" is used again (cf. 1:4)–this time to indicate that the messages would apply to all the churches, since seven is symbolic of completion. In the coming verses there are also seven golden lampstands and seven stars associated with these churches.

Since the Book of Revelation is a book of prophecy, the symbolic meaning of these messages in the first two chapters is to foretell the history of the Church Age. This prophecy applies to seven periods of church history.

However, the seven churches did actually exist in Asia. There were individual collections of Christians in seven actual cities, each with their strengths and (usually) weaknesses. In the 1st Century all of the believers in any given city were considered part of that city's church. So the vision will address the church in each of the cities just as Paul's epistles had done many years earlier (The church at Corinth, the church at Colosse, etc.).

One can also find in these seven churches the general characteristics of various types of churches that have existed in each time period, and still exist today. This would mean that there are still "apostolic" type churches today, like the one in Ephesus; churches with many martyrs, like the one in Smyrna; and so on.

Now the churches are named: *to Ephesus, to Smyrna, to Pergamos, to Thyatira, to Sardis, to Philadelphia, and to Laodicea.* There are messages for each of these in the next two chapters.

Then I turned to see the voice that spoke with me. And having turned I saw seven golden lampstands, -- Revelation 1:12

John wrote, *Then I turned to see the voice that spoke with me.*

The word for voice is *phōnē*, meaning "sound." The word has come into our language in many forms, all having to do with hearing. Words like microphone, phonetics, and telephone are very common, and it appears the word will be prominent in the future as well, because of the importance of "smart phones."

The great voice of the Jesus the Creator was like a trumpet in verse 10. Here it is like a human voice, and in the next sentence it will be described as the sound of many waters. The supernatural and futuristic aspects of Revelation would require any human author to use similes like these and other symbolic language. Properly understood, the nearly endless symbolic expressions in the book should shake us free from our limited ways of thinking.

John identified the first thing that he noticed at this point: *I saw seven golden lampstands.*

This vision is not of the seven-branched lampstand in the Temple, but of seven individual stands, suitable for holding the oil lamps that were used for light by nearly everyone in those days. Oil lamps were more practical than candles, which would burn out too soon. They could be carried by a person to light his way, or placed on a safe lampstand in the home.

The lampstands were gold, showing that they were not ordinary furnishings of a home, but costly, ornate fixtures in a public place.

What did these lampstands symbolize? Here is an example of the fact that we mentioned earlier, that many of the symbols in Revelation are explained in the book itself. Revelation 1:20 equates the seven lampstands to the seven churches that were about to receive important messages from the Lord.

Jesus told His followers, who comprise His church, that they are the light of the world (Matthew 5:14-16). But that light is a reflected light, because He also boldly claimed that He *is* the light of the world (John 8:12). Light is a most amazing spiritual picture of truth and salvation. Since Christ indwells true Christians (Galatians 2:20), they should allow His light to emanate from them. Together, as a church (Greek *ekklesia*—"called-out", "an assembly") they are to be a light to the dark world around them.

Gold is often symbolic of deity, as in some of the articles in the Temple. So the light that comes from the church is from God.

The Glorified Savior   1:13-16

And in the midst of the seven lampstands One like the Son of Man,– Revelation 1:13a

Up to this point, John had noticed only the seven golden lampstands. But now he realized there is an important person standing there ***in the midst of the seven lampstands*** ! The Greek word for "in the midst" is *mesos*, meaning "middle" or "among."

John wasn't sure about who this person was at this point in the vision, but He would soon realize that it was the Lord Jesus Himself. How appropriate for Him to be right in the middle of His church! He promised it would be so:

And Jesus came and spoke to them, saying, "All authority has been given to Me in heaven and on earth. Go therefore and make disciples of all the nations, baptizing them in the name of the Father and of the Son and of the Holy

Spirit, teaching them to observe all things that I have commanded you; and lo, I am with you always, even to the end of the age." Amen. – Matthew 28:18-20

The apostle Paul expressed just how close Jesus is to those who believe in Him:

I have been crucified with Christ; it is no longer I who live, but Christ lives in me; and the life which I now live in the flesh I live by faith in the Son of God, who loved me and gave Himself for me. – Galatians 2:20

If we were in John's shoes, we would have had the same difficulty recognizing Jesus here because he appeared very different from the gentle Savior John had known so well. However, he did see a resemblance to Christ because he described Him as **one like the Son of Man** (Greek: *houios anthropos*). The Gospels call Jesus "the Son of God" in many places, but He is also "The Son of Man." In fact, this was Jesus' favorite title for Himself, and He used it often (Matthew 8:20; 12:40; 24:27; Mark 10:45; Luke 6:5; John 3:13-14, etc.--about 80 times!).

Why was His humanity so important? It comes from an Old Testament concept of the "Kinsman-Redeemer." The law had provided that a close relative could pay for the debt of a family member to release him from slavery (Leviticus 25:48, 49). This was the theme of the beautiful and romantic book of Ruth, where Boaz became Ruth's redeemer (Ruth 3:9-14). Thus it was thought that Messiah would redeem believers.

In Philippians, Paul explained the awesome reality of Jesus becoming man to die for our sins!

Let this mind be in you which was also in Christ Jesus, who, being in the form of God, did not consider it robbery to be equal with God, but made Himself of no reputation, taking the form of a bondservant, and coming in the likeness of men. And being found in appearance as a man, He humbled Himself and became obedient to the point of death, even the death of the cross. – Philippians 2:5-8

In Romans he explained why Jesus had to be a man in order to pay for man's sin. Adam's sin corrupted the human race and passed on to each person a propensity to do evil. The apostle had already established this sad fact where he wrote,

For all have sinned and fall short of the glory of God. – Romans 3:23

Then he gave the good news:

But God demonstrates His own love toward us, in that while we were still sinners, Christ died for us. – Romans 5:8

Finally he showed that since sin was a failure of mankind, a righteous human being would need to pay the price.

Therefore, as through one man's offense judgment came to all men, resulting in condemnation, even so through one Man's righteous act the free gift came to all men, resulting in justification of life. For as by one man's disobedience many were made sinners, so also by one Man's obedience many will be made righteous. – Romans 5:18-19

. . . clothed with a garment down to the feet and girded about the chest with a golden band. His head and hair were white like wool, as white as snow, and His eyes like a flame of fire; – Revelation 1:13b-14

John wrote that in his vision, Jesus was no longer an "ordinary" person, but one who was totally majestic and awesome. After the resurrection, Jesus was already changed. He was in perfect condition, even though He had been crucified just three days earlier. He could conceal His identity or reveal it as he did to Mary, and later to the disciples on the Emmaus Road (John 20:15-16; Luke 24:30-31). He could walk through the walls of the Upper Room to appear to the disciples (John 20:26), and could rise into the heavens without a spacecraft (Acts 1:9-10). Paul explained that after the resurrection we also will have an incorruptible body:

So also is the resurrection of the dead. The body is sown in corruption, it is raised in incorruption. It is sown in dishonor, it is raised in glory. It is sown in weakness, it is raised in power. It is sown a natural body, it is raised a spiritual body. There is a natural body, and there is a spiritual body. – 1 Corinthians 15:42-44

This glorified Jesus was **clothed with a garment down to the feet.** In the 1st Century people normally wore robes. But the robes of certain dignitaries were distinctive. They might be colored or embroidered. Kings, judges, priests and Pharisees were recognized by their special attire. On the other extreme, prophets would often have robes that were plain and coarse, befitting their messages of warning.

Jesus would be entitled to wear any of these uniforms. He is prophet, priest, and king! However, His role as judge might be the most significant in this vision. He is portrayed in so many ways in this book, but here He is seen most definitely as the Judge--first of His church in the next two chapters, and then of the world in its end-time condition. As the Righteous Judge, He commends and rewards those who do what is right, but condemns and punishes those who practice evil.

John commented on the belt or sash of this particular robe. Jesus was **girded about the chest with a golden band.** The Greek word for "band" is *zōnēn*–"belt." It was very wide, extending upward to his chest. This description causes some commentators to prefer the image of a priest, since the priestly attire often had this kind of girdle. Wide belts of this sort could hold money or other personal items, and might even be referred to as one's purse (Mark 6:8). It was gold, which could symbolize royalty, so that other commentators view this as a kingly vision. But gold is used in many places throughout the Scriptures to symbolize God (as in the Tabernacle and the Temple). And it is God who has the right and responsibility to judge the church and the world.

Next John recorded that **His head and hair were white like wool, as white as snow.** White like wool is an appropriate description of the grey-white hair of an elderly, wise person. The pictures we see of English and Early-American magistrates and legislators usually show them in their white wigs. For many, it was just the fashion of the day, but it was understood that it made them look older and wiser.

However, there was no such fashion in the 1st Century. Jewish and Christian readers would undoubtedly have thought about an earlier end-times vision by Daniel that was strikingly similar to this one.

"I watched till thrones were put in place,
And the Ancient of Days was seated;
His garment was white as snow,
And the hair of His head was like pure wool.
His throne was a fiery flame,
Its wheels a burning fire;--Daniel 7:9

That vision was of "The Ancient of Days," a description of God Himself as the Eternal One. As already mentioned in this first chapter of Revelation, the attributes of God are freely ascribed to Jesus as well, because He is God the Son.

In Daniel's vision the robe was "white as snow," while in John's vision the hair was also described this way. In the Bible, this is a description of purity and holiness (Psalm 51:7; Isaiah 1:18).

The Son also appears in Daniel 7 as separate from the Ancient of Days:

"I was watching in the night visions,
And behold, One like the **Son of Man,**
Coming with the clouds of heaven!
He came to the Ancient of Days,
And they brought Him near before Him.
Then to Him was given dominion and glory and a kingdom,
That all peoples, nations, and languages should serve Him.
His dominion is an everlasting dominion,
Which shall not pass away,
And His kingdom the one
Which shall not be destroyed. – Daniel 7:13-14

As a side note here, the most interesting and significant connections exist between the Old Testament book of Daniel and this Book of Revelation Christ. Daniel is often called "The Apocalypse of the

Old Testament." John was certainly aware of the contents of Daniel before he ever received this vision. But he was not reciting the words of Daniel or even commenting on them. This was a fresh, separate "unveiling" of the same truths revealed to Daniel hundreds of years earlier, and it makes both of the books even more credible.

When two people have virtually the same vision, it behooves them to ask themselves if there is some spiritual message there of special importance. I have not had much personal experience with such dreams, but I will share one that I knew must have been from the Lord. In high school, soon after I had met Barbara, my wife to be, but before we had ever even dated, we both had the same dream one night. I was president of the Youth for Christ club that had a weekly meeting after school on Wednesdays. I dreamed that we were having a "backwards meeting." It was my responsibility to plan themes for each week's meeting to keep it interesting. So I thought that the dream could just have been a random idea.

I mentioned it to my sister, Joan, before we both went to school the next day. While a number of club members were setting up for the meeting, my sister came to me with surprising news. Evidentially, Barbara had dreamed the same thing! Joan got us together. I told Barbara the first half of my dream, and she told me the second half! We all thought it was amazing, but didn't know what it meant. We decided that maybe someday we would plan a "backwards meeting" for the group.

In those days we had a special speaker each week, provided by the YFC leadership in the area. I had not met him before, but, as usual, I found out who he was, then introduced him to the group. To our complete surprise, the first thing he said was, "Let's do something different today. Let's all turn our chairs around, and I will speak to you from the back of the room--just for fun!"

Barbara, Joan, and I all looked at each other in disbelief. We never did understand why the speaker did it, except to get focused attention. But we did sense that the Lord wanted Barbara and me to pay attention to each other. We recently celebrated our 53rd anniversary.

But back to a more important matter, the Book of Daniel will be referenced often in this study of Revelation. Here is another section of Daniel that is very similar to this verse in Revelation

I lifted my eyes and looked, and behold, a certain man clothed in linen, whose waist was girded with gold of Uphaz! His body was like beryl, his face like the appearance of lightning, his eyes like torches of fire, his arms and feet like burnished bronze in color, and the sound of his words like the voice of a multitude. – Daniel 10:5-6

Now I have come to make you understand what will happen to your people in the latter days, for the vision refers to many days yet to come." – Daniel 10:14

The next thing John noticed was Jesus' eyes. He wrote *and His eyes like a flame of fire.* This is definitely a picture of judgment. This expression is found again in Chapter 2, verse18 where Jesus corrects the corrupt church at Thyatira; and also in Chapter 19, verse 12 when He returns to fight the Battle of Armageddon.

Sometimes people describe the look of anger this way. As the righteous judge Jesus has "righteous indignation" against those who have rebelled against His loving and gracious gift.

The concept of His burning eyes is reminiscent of Paul's teaching that Jesus will judge the works of believers, and only what is good will remain. Whatever is useless--wood, hay and stubble--will be consumed by the fire (1 Corinthians 3:11-15).

Throughout the Bible, God is depicted as fire in various ways. Some of these are: The burning bush (Exodus 3:2-4); The Pillar of Fire in the wilderness (Exodus 13:21); a consuming fire (Hebrews 12:29); and Tongues of fire at Pentecost (Acts 2:3).

His feet were like fine brass, as if refined in a furnace, and His voice as the sound of many waters; He had in His right hand seven stars, out of His mouth went a sharp two-edged sword, and His countenance was like the sun shining in its strength. – Revelation 1:15-16

His feet were like fine brass. The bronze feet are an additional picture of judgment, since bronze was the material of the Altar of Sacrifice

(Exodus 27:1-4), and of the serpent in the wilderness, one of God's most graphic judgments of sin. (Numbers 21:5-9; John 3:14-18).

Again, these symbols are very similar to Daniel's vision that we just cited above (Daniel 10:6).

The Greek word for "fine brass" (*chalkolibano*) is found only here. It is a compound word combining "brass" and "incense." It is thought that the idea being conveyed is that the color is not just the orange of brass, but mixed with yellow like frankincense. It could depict a mixture of brass and gold, and is translated here as "fine" brass.

John continued to describe the brass feet, *as if refined in a furnace.* Refining metals usually requires the use of a large, very hot furnace. Smaller quantities of some metals can be melted in a heavy pot over a kitchen fire.

When we were kids, we would sometimes melt small pieces of lead in this way to make toy soldiers. In those days most people didn't know it was bad to be exposed to lead. It was fascinating to watch a bar of cold, hard metal gradually melt in the pot like an ice cube does. It then became a little blob of liquid. It always had some impurities in it, so the surface would be dull. We could "refine" it by using a cold spoon to skim the impurities off the top. It would then be shiny and pure. We could see our reflections in it. Then we carefully poured it out into the molds to finish the project.

Peter had this refining process in mind when he explained that the trials believers must endure (which sometimes could be discipline) would produce a purified faith.

> *In this you greatly rejoice, though now for a little while, if need be, you have been grieved by various trials, that the genuineness of your faith, being much more precious than gold that perishes, though it is tested by fire, may be found to praise, honor, and glory at the revelation of Jesus Christ,*--1 Peter 1:6-7

This is certainly a picture of Jesus standing as judge in the midst of His church. In His messages to them He mentions certain things they are doing right, but with most of them He finds serious faults that need to be corrected. His judgment is not meant to destroy them, but to correct them if they are willing to change.

Even in our secular judicial system, the purpose of judgment, especially of lesser crimes, is to bring about improvement. Prisons were once called "penitentiaries," meaning a place of penitence or repentance. They have not always done such a good job of making this happen, but the hope is--and in some cases it turns out this way--that the prisoner will change his mind about breaking the law, and, when he is released, he will be a good citizen.

In Hebrews there is a wonderful explanation of the Lord's discipline:

> *And you have forgotten the exhortation which speaks to you as to sons:*
>
> *"My son, do not despise the chastening of the LORD,*
> *Nor be discouraged when you are rebuked by Him;*
> *For whom the LORD loves He chastens,*
> *And scourges every son whom He receives."*
>
> *If you endure chastening, God deals with you as with sons; for what son is there whom a father does not chasten? But if you are without chastening, of which all have become partakers, then you are illegitimate and not sons. Furthermore, we have had human fathers who corrected us, and we paid them respect. Shall we not much more readily be in subjection to the Father of spirits and live? For they indeed for a few days chastened us as seemed best to them, but He for our profit, that we may be partakers of His holiness. Now no chastening seems to be joyful for the present, but painful; nevertheless, afterward it yields the peaceable fruit of righteousness to those who have been trained by it.*
> – Hebrews 12:5-11

Discipline in the home is not punishment, but teaching. In the field of education, different subjects are called "disciplines." And in the church, those who are learners are called "disciples."

In the light of this lofty purpose of judgment or discipline, it is both startling and comforting when John portrays Jesus this way: ***and His voice as the sound of many waters.*** The harsh trumpet-voice mentioned in verse 10 has changed to something like a mighty river, a waterfall, or the sound of the ocean's waves reaching the shore. Those who hear these sounds usually understand the power behind them, but they are nevertheless drawn to them, and learn to find a sense of security in their constant roar.

He had in His right hand seven stars. The meaning of this symbol is interpreted in the vision itself. In verse 20 of this same chapter we are told that they are the angels of the seven churches. The word "angel" (Greek *aggelos*) literally means "messenger." Therefore the messengers to these churches might be their pastors. This will be considered in greater detail when we get to that point.

Why are they called "stars"? The word star (Greek *aster*) is used in many ways in the Bible. Right here in Revelation it is used as a description of Jesus; of important people--like the twelve Patriarchs of Israel; of angels; of fallen angels or demons; and of asteroids or meteors. Stars make good symbols for many reasons. They are beautiful. They are fascinating. And, as in this verse, they are used for navigation or direction.

Perhaps the description of Jesus that is most difficult to picture is this: **out of His mouth went a sharp two-edged sword.** This expression naturally brings to mind this verse about God's Word:

> *For the word of God is living and powerful, and sharper than any two-edged sword, piercing even to the division of soul and spirit, and of joints and marrow, and is a discerner of the thoughts and intents of the heart.* – Hebrews 4:12

It is obvious that Jesus faithfully taught God's Word, but, most amazingly, in John's Gospel, he actually called Jesus "the Word," who spoke the Creation into being, and later became flesh and dwelt among us! (John 1:1-3; 14; cf. Genesis 1)

Jesus has the authority to declare what is right and true, and what must therefore be done. And He has the power to cause whatever is spoken to come to pass.

Jesus will be described with a sword in His mouth in the message to the church at Pergamos (Revelation 2:12). Finally, at the Battle of Armageddon His only weapon will be the sharp sword out of His mouth (Revelation 19:15, 21). The ultimate power of the judge is the ability to put the offender to death (if necessary).

In addition to all the other striking aspects of this vision, John said that **His countenance was like the sun shining in its strength.** Just as a person dare not look directly at the Sun, a glance at the face of Jesus was so brilliant that, according to the next verse, John fell at Jesus' feet like a dead man.

John had actually seen Jesus in a similar way when he was invited to join his brother James and Peter for a most unusual occasion, the Transfiguration of Christ.

> *Now after six days Jesus took Peter, James, and John his brother led them up on a high mountain by themselves; [2] and He was transfigured before them. His face shone like the sun, and His clothes became as white as the light.* – Matthew 17:1-3

It is interesting that even though the other three Gospels all recorded the Transfiguration, John did not include it in his account of Jesus' life. This is probably best explained by the fact that John's Gospel was written much later than the other three (known as the "synoptic" Gospels), and he knew that the episode was already well-reported. His Gospel usually gave additional information not found in the others.

The reaction of John   1:17-18

> *And when I saw Him, I fell at his feet as dead. But He placed his right hand on me saying to me, "Do not be afraid. I am the First and the Last. I am He who lives and was dead, and behold, I am alive for evermore. Amen. And I have the keys of Hades and Death.* – Revelation 1:17-18

John wrote, **When I saw Him, I fell at his feet as dead.** Like other people in the Bible who received such visions (Isaiah 6:5; Ezekiel 1:28), he was terrified!

But He placed his right hand on me. John was revived by the glowing vision of Christ, who touched him and identified Himself with several meaningful descriptions. One of the most amazing things about the earthly life of our Savior was the way he mingled with people and freely touched them, even though they might be diseased and sinful. He touched

John with the same hand that was holding the seven stars. The right hand of any dignitary is considered a place of honor (Matthew 25:31-34). Just a touch by Jesus was all John needed to go on. It is a sensation that Christians of all ages have experienced when they needed it most. In the words of Bill Gaither's famous chorus,

> He touched me, oh He touched me
> And oh the joy that floods my soul
> Something happened and now I know
> He touched me and made me whole.

Jesus continued to tell John, **"Do not be afraid."** Fear is a natural survival instinct. It is one of the most negative and uncomfortable of feelings. It is sometimes considered the opposite of faith and courage, and therefore to be avoided. But there are times when fear is helpful. One notable example is "the fear of the Lord" which the Book of Proverbs calls, "the beginning of wisdom" (Proverbs 1:7). Such fear is explained as "reverence," because if a person truly reveres God, he will be afraid of the consequences of disobeying Him.

The Greek word for fear is *phobos*, and it is incorporated in many words in our own language. (claustrophobia, hydrophobia, etc.--A very long list is available on the Internet at www.phobialist.com.)

On the other hand, when one trusts the Lord, there is no need to fear. Some have noted that the Bible adjures us so many times not to be afraid that a different verse could be chosen each day of the year to remind us of this fact. Paul says that God has not given us a spirit of fear (2 Timothy 1:7). The greatest antidote to fear is to abide in God's presence and to follow His direction. Then we can say, as the Psalmist did,

> *Even though I walk through the darkest valley,*
> *I will fear no evil, for you are with me;--*Psalm 23:4

Years ago, when I was planting a church in Southern California, and was working as a "tentmaker" in my father's construction business, I learned something about overcoming fear. We occasionally had to modify propane tanks. A welder was required to do the job, but if the tank had already been used, it was not safe to cut into it with an acetylene torch until it had been properly neutralized or decontaminated. We paid to have that process done, but a welder would still not be willing to believe that it was safe unless I would stand right next to him while he did the welding. It made sense. He knew that I would not take the chance if we had not done the job correctly!

God reminded Joshua that he could be strong and courageous because He was with him (Joshua 1:9). Jesus encouraged His disciples in the same way when he gave them the Great Commission:

> *Then Jesus came to them and said, "All authority in heaven and on earth has been given to me. Therefore go and make disciples of all nations, baptizing them in the name of the Father and of the Son and of the Holy Spirit, and teaching them to obey everything I have commanded you. And **surely I am with you always**, to the very end of the age." –* Matthew 28:18-20

Again, Jesus said, **I am the First and the Last.** See the notes on verse 11.

Then Jesus said, *"I am He who lives,"* affirming His resurrection. In this chapter the narrative alternates between John's descriptions of the awe-inspiring Christ, and Jesus' own words. In verse 5 John had already described Him as *"the firstborn from the dead."* Throughout the book the concepts established in one place are often reinforced in other portions of the vision.

He added, *"and was dead."* That fact should be obvious, but He emphasized it to counter the idea of some skeptics that He didn't really die on the cross. Such doubters say that he just "swooned" during the crucifixion and was resuscitated later by His disciples to deceive the people. This error has persisted to our own time with such theories as "The DaVinci Code," which claims that He went on to wed Mary Magdalene and live in seclusion with his family. Of course, doubters cannot explain how He could have survived when He suffered so greatly, and was pierced with a spear so that blood and water came out (John 19:34). Medical professionals say this condition was caused by a broken heart.

In the Bible "death" never means annihilation. Instead, it means "separation." Physical death is the separation of the physical body from the non-physical aspects of a person. In 1 Thessalonians 5:23 Paul said, *"Now may the God of peace Himself sanctify you completely; and may your whole* **spirit, soul, and body** *be preserved blameless at the coming of our Lord Jesus Christ."*

Some theologians think that soul and spirit are the same. It is true that in some places in the Old Testament the two words seem to be used interchangeably. However, considering the story of Creation and the types of living organisms on our planet, it makes more sense to see them as separate. When the Lord created plants their physical bodies had the basic functions of life, including nutrition, elimination, growth, and reproduction. When He created animals, they had all of these functions plus the aspects of personality: intellect, emotion, and will (think about your pets). They had both body and soul. Then the Lord created the first human by a special act. Humans would have had a body and soul, like other animals, but God gave them a spirit so they would be, in that special sense, "like" God. Jesus said "God is spirit" (John 4:24).

> *Then God said, "Let Us make man in Our image, according to Our likeness; let them have dominion over the fish of the sea, over the birds of the air, and over the cattle, over all the earth and over every creeping thing that creeps on the earth." –* Genesis 1:27

> *And the* LORD *God formed man of the dust of the ground, and breathed into his nostrils the breath of life; and man became a living being. –* Genesis 2:7

The word "breath" in Genesis 2:7 (Hebrew *neshamah*) also means "spirit."

So, physical death is separation of the body from the soul and spirit. There is also spiritual death, separation of our human spirit from God because of sin:

> *And you He made alive, who were dead in trespasses and sins, –* Ephesians 2:1

When a person is "born again" (John 3:3), his spirit is reconciled with God (2 Corinthians 5:17-21).

A third and even worse separation is the "second death," which is mentioned four times in Revelation (2:11; 20:6, 14; 21:8). The second death means eternal separation from God. This is what will happen to a person who dies physically while he is still dead spiritually.

Jesus died physically on our behalf, and it could be said that He tasted spiritual death when our sins momentarily separated Him from His Father, and He cried out, *"My God, My God, why have You forsaken Me?"* (Matthew 27:46).

Yes, Jesus was dead, but in victory He declared, *"and behold, I am alive for evermore."* His goal was to provide eternal life for us (John 3:16), and we know that He succeeded because of His resurrection, which He had predicted:

> *"A little while longer and the world will see Me no more, but you will see Me. Because I live, you will live also.* – John 14:19

Amen is like a spiritual punctuation mark in the Bible. It means "So be it!"

Furthermore, Jesus said, a*nd I have the keys of Hades and Death.* Hades is the name of the place of departed spirits. It is seen as the enemy of the church (Matthew 16:18). Since Christ's ascension (Ephesians 4:8-10), it is the temporary abode of unbelievers who have died and await their final judgment (Revelation 6:8; 20:13-14). The concepts of hell and hades will be explored when we get to these passages.

THE PRESENCE OF JESUS CHRIST IN THIS AGE
1:19-3:22
(The things which are)

Insight about the Church   1:19-20

Write the things which you have seen, and the things which are, and the things which will take place after this. -- Revelation 1:19

Verse 19 is the *key* to the book. The three parts of Revelation are: 1- What you have seen--*The Person of Jesus Christ--Revelation 1:9-18* 2- What is now--*The Presence of Jesus Christ in This Age – Revelation 1:19-3:33* 3- What will take place later--*The Program of Jesus Christ For The Future--* Revelation 4:1-22:21

Jesus told John to **Write.** In verse 10 the process of divine inspiration was considered. Once a servant of the Lord was given inspired information, it would then need to be written and carefully preserved. The Holy Scriptures are all written books. The Greek word for "scripture" is *graphe.* It means "sacred book." It is found in the New Testament, but is not used in Revelation. However the vision is called "a book" in Chapter 1, verse 11, and in several verses of the last chapter (22:7, 9, 10, 18, 19). Our English word "scripture" comes from the Latin word *scriptura,* which in turn is a translation of the Greek *graphe.*

John was expected to write **the things which you have seen.** It was not supposed to be John's own ideas about the future, but specifically the revelation that he was seeing. The most valuable testimony is an eye-witness account (1 Corinthians 15:6).

John was to write what he had seen so far, and then the rest of the vision--thirty or more pages in one of our typical printed Bibles. It might have been that he could stop and write every once in a while as he received the message, but if not, the Lord would certainly bring every bit of it back to his memory as he wrote.

Then he was to write **and the things which are,** referring to the messages to the Seven Churches in Chapters 2 and 3. As mentioned earlier, these were short letters to seven very different churches that actually existed in Asia, in the area known today as Turkey. They reflect the strengths, weaknesses, and the Lord's will for each church.

Because of their variety, most churches that exist today could identify with one of these seven types of congregations. Because of that, sensitive Christians might find valuable lessons in these messages that apply to their own current circumstances.

Since Revelation is a book of prophecy, it is completely reasonable to see these seven churches in another way as well. In fact, this should be the primary way of viewing them. That is, each church stands for a period of time in the history of the church, from the Day of Pentecost (Acts 2) when it formally began, until the future date of the Rapture (1 Thessalonians 4:13-18; 1 Corinthians 15:50-58). This will be discussed this more in Revelation 3:10; and 4:1).

John would also be expected to write **the things which will take place after this.** This is the major part of the vision, revealing the main events of the seven-year Tribulation period, the Campaign of Armageddon, the earthly reign of Christ and the New Heaven and New Earth (Chapters 4 through 22).

The Greek for "what will take place" is *ginomai*, which means "to come into being." This hints at the fact that God has ultimate control of the future, as discussed under verse 5 of this chapter.

The Greek *meta tauta* is translated "after these things." This is a normal expression for transition both in John's Gospel and in Revelation. *Meta* is a Greek preposition that can have many meanings, depending on the context. One of its normal meanings is "with" and another is "after." When it is used with the pronoun *tauta*--"this, these," it signifies the beginning of a new segment of time. Its first use here in Revelation is to identify the third major section of Revelation. The history of the Church Age is outlined in the messages to the Seven Churches in Chapters 2 and 3. Chapter 4 starts with these very words, *meta tauta*, to begin telling what will happen after the Church Age.

> **The mystery of the seven stars which you saw in My right hand and the seven golden lampstands: The seven stars are the angels of the seven churches, and the seven lampstands which you saw are the seven churches.** – Revelation 1:20

At this point **the mystery of the seven stars which you saw in My right hand and the seven golden lampstands** is explained. The Greek word *musterion*, means "anything hidden." In the New Testament it generally refers to a truth not revealed in the Old Testament, but now made known.

Jesus employed this word in Mark 4:11 in connection with parables–stories designed to transmit truth to those who will receive it and hide it from non-believers.

The word "mystery" is mostly used by Paul, especially in relation to the church (Ephesians 1:9-11; Ephesians 3--whole chapter, esp. vv. 3,4,9; Ephesians 5:32--including the Rapture: the end-point of the Church Age--1 Corinthians 15:51); temporary blindness for Israel (Romans 11:25); and the Gospel being taken to the Gentiles (Romans 16:25--26; Ephesians 6:19; Colossians 1:26-27; 4:3; 1 Timothy 3:16).

In Chapter 3 of our book, *Connecting the Dots: A Handbook of Bible Prophecy*, Lambert Dolphin and I show how this word "mystery" is used to convey the vital truth that the church, which is a major part of God's plan, was not revealed in the Old Testament. The church evangelizes the world during the period of the blindness of Israel. However, there is a definite beginning and end of the Church Age and those who do not distinguish between Israel and the church cannot understand prophecy.

John did not use the word "mystery" in his gospel or epistles, but he wrote it 4 times in Revelation: in this verse, where it most definitely applies to the church; and in 10:17; 17:5 and 17:7--where it describes the conclusion of certain aspects of the end-times.

The next expression is the first of many places in Revelation where the book defines its own symbolism. It explains: ***The seven stars are the angels of the seven churches.*** This simplifies the vision considerably but we must still choose between two possible meanings of the word "angel". The primary use of the Greek word *aggelos* is "messenger." In the Bible it generally conveys the idea of supernatural messengers. In various parts of Revelation the word is used for both human messengers and that separate class of created beings called "angels." Angels are spirit beings, but they can take on human or other forms when they appear to men. There is much to discover about these creatures, but the discussion of good and bad angels will be saved for later portions of this commentary.

In the context of the Seven Churches, it seems most logical that the angels are human messengers, or the pastors of the churches.

The last part of this verse is another explanation of an earlier symbolic expression. It says, ***and the seven lampstands which you saw are the seven churches.***

The word "church" (Greek *ekklesia*, meaning "assembly") was a common word in Jesus' day for any gathering of people. It was used especially to designate a public meeting, or what might be called today a "town hall" meeting. Jesus endowed the word with His own special significance when He announced that He would form His "church" (Matthew 16:15-19). *Ecclesia* is formed from two words (*ek*, "out of" and *kalleo*, "to call"). Therefore such an assembly is "called out" for some special purpose. This is an excellent description of Christ's church, since each member of it has been "called" by God (Romans 1:6-7; 8:28-30; 1 Corinthians 1:2, 24-26; 2 Timothy 1:9). This calling brings to mind our Lord's careful personal selection of each of His disciples. He said *"The Son of Man has come to seek and to save that which was lost"* (Luke 19:10). Paul said plainly, *"There is none who seeks after God"* (Romans 3:11), but Jesus loves us and initiates the relationship with us.

The seven lampstands were first mentioned in verse 12. This verse (20) specifically explains the symbolism. Each lampstand represents one of the seven churches of Asia that are about to receive special messages from the Lord. The image of light is used universally for the concepts of truth, beauty, security, and whatever is good. Light dispels the darkness, which in turn is symbolic of falsehood, and evil. Jesus taught this principle in His Sermon on the Mount:

> *"You are the light of the world. A city that is set on a hill cannot be hidden. Nor do they light a lamp and put it under a basket, but on a lampstand, and it gives light to all who are in the house. Let your light so shine before men, that they may see your good works and glorify your Father in heaven.* – Matthew 5:14-16

Revelation Chapter 2

Instruction to the Church   2:1-3:22

There is a definite pattern to these letters to the Seven Churches. First, each church is named. Then, normally, there are five segments in each letter:

1 – Connection: Jesus reveals Himself to them in different ways that are appropriate to the content of their epistle. The imagery in the first five messages is taken from the descriptions of Christ that were introduced in Chapter 1.

2 – Commendation: There is normally a commendation or approval in each letter. Laodicea is the exception. The Lord cited something that each of the other churches did well. This made it easier for the readers to accept the criticism that usually came next. When someone special says nice things about you, it makes you want to live up to his or her expectations. It also makes it easier to accept the mistakes that you make along the way and learn to do better.

I have two special treasures that I will always keep and cherish. One is a box of love notes from my wife Barbara when we first started dating in high school. I would drop a note in her locker each day, and she would do the same for me. The other collection is a paper treasure box hand-made by my daughter with dozens of tiny pieces of paper inside, each with a good memory of being together, like buying donuts or catching frogs in the field.

To every church Jesus says "I know your works." The Gospels and the rest of the New Testament abundantly prove that salvation is by faith in Jesus Christ–not by works (Ephesians 2:8-9). However, those who have received that incredible salvation are expected to demonstrate their new life in Christ by doing good works by the power of Jesus and the Holy Spirit who indwells them, (Ephesians 2:10; Titus 3:5,8; Galatians 2:20; Philippians

4:15; Ephesians 5:15-33).

Isn't it sobering to realize that Jesus knows all about us? In our generation there is growing concern about the incredible amount of information Google collects about each one of us. But Jesus literally knows everything! What a difference that should make in our lives.

3 – Complaint: In each letter there is usually also a warning or rebuke (except Smyrna and Philadelphia). Our first reaction to criticism is usually negative. In Chapter 1, verse 15 it was shown that discipline is meant to be a good thing. Good parents must correct his children as they grow and make mistakes. Otherwise they will have a miserable life, and probably die young.

In this portion of each message, or in the critique section, this commentary will discuss some of the ways these churches were actually prophetic previews of the different periods of church history.

4 – Critique: In most of the letters there is more information given about their situation. This section usually calls for repentance or some change of action in the church.

5 – Counsel: At the end of each message there are some final encouragements and promises. These benefits were promised to individuals in each of these churches who were overcomers. The message as a whole was to the entire church, but in every church, in every different age, there are those who believe and obey, and there are those who ignore the truth. Some special blessing is promised to each individual who remains true to the Lord in spite of the problems of their day. In John's first Epistle he explained the concept of being an overcomer:

> *For this is the love of God, that we keep His commandments. And His commandments are not burdensome. For whatever is born of God overcomes the world. And this is the victory that has overcome the world—our faith. Who is he who overcomes the world, but he who believes that Jesus is the Son of God? – 1* John 5:3-5

A final thought in each letter is, "He who has an ear, let him hear what the Spirit says to the churches." This is another reminder about the responsibility of each individual to heed these instructions. The emphasis on "hearing" is carried over from the promise of a blessing in Chapter 1, verse 3, to everyone who reads the book, or even hears it.

To Ephesus   2:1-7 (Apostolic Church – AD 33 to AD 100)

"To the angel of the church of Ephesus write,

'These things says He who holds the seven stars in His right hand, who walks in the midst of the seven golden lampstands: "I know your works, your labor, your patience, and that you cannot bear those who are evil. And you have tested those who say they are apostles and are not, and have found them liars; and you have persevered and have patience, and have labored for My name's sake and have not become weary. Nevertheless I have this against you, that you have left your first love. Remember therefore from where you have fallen; repent and do the first works, or else I will come to you quickly and remove your lampstand from its place—unless you repent. But this you have, that you hate the deeds of the Nicolaitans, which I also hate.

"He who has an ear, let him hear what the Spirit says to the churches. To him who overcomes I will give to eat from the tree of life, which is in the midst of the Paradise of God.""'
– Revelation 2:1-7

This first message is to Ephesus, the preeminent congregation of the region. It applies to the members of that particular church in Asia, but it is a prophetic overview of the first major period of Christianity, usually called the Early Church, or the Apostolic Period. Christianity was literally a "world-changing" new faith, based in Judaism and founded on the Old Testament Scriptures, but offering a "New Covenant" (Matthew 26:28; Hebrews 9:15), a resurrected Savior (John 11:25; Acts 1:22; 4:2), a miraculous and explosive beginning on the Day of Pentecost (Acts 2), the Gospel ("Good News"–1 Corinthians 15), and zealous missionaries, willing to die for their faith in Christ (Book of Acts). Only about 20 years after the resurrection of Christ, His followers were being described as "these who have turned the world upside down" (Acts 17:6).

However, by the time Revelation was given to John, another 40 or more years had passed. If we look back forty years in our own generation we can understand how many great changes can take place in that length of time. The church was still growing, but it had lost its original zeal–its "first love"--for the Lord Jesus Christ.

In Chapter 1, verse 20 it was suggested that *"the angel"* is probably the pastor of the church. There are no biblical examples of angelic beings serving as teachers or leaders of a church. The structure of the Early Church was considerably less complicated than it is today. Every true Christian was considered a disciple ("learner").

At a certain point, Jesus' original 12 disciples were designated "apostles" (Matthew 10:1-2--Greek *apostelos*, meaning "one sent forth on a mission"). Matthias was chosen after Judas' death to take his place as an apostle (Acts 1:26), and Paul was chosen by Jesus later as an additional apostle to the Gentiles (Romans 11:13). A few other leaders, like Barnabas, Silas, and Timothy, were called apostles in a more limited sense as pioneer missionaries.

By the time Paul wrote the Epistle to the Ephesians (approx. AD 62), he named certain offices or positions of ministry in the church:

And He Himself gave some to be apostles, some prophets, some evangelists, and some pastors and teachers, for the equipping of the saints for the work of ministry, for the edifying of the body of Christ, – Ephesians 4:11-12

The structure of the verse shows that "pastor-teacher" should be taken as one position. Pastor means "shepherd," and his chief purpose is to spiritually "feed the sheep." That is also what a teacher does.

Actually, the primary word in the New Testament for leadership of the church is "elders." Qualifications are given for holding this office (Titus 1:5-9 and 1 Timothy 3:1-7, where similar qualifications for "overseer" or bishop are given). The word is often used in the plural, indicating that a church might have more than one leader. There are two passages in the New Testament that strongly indicate that elders, shepherds (pastors), and overseers (bishops) are all the same office:

> *From Miletus he sent to Ephesus and called for the **elders** of the church. And when they had come to him, he said to them: "You know, from the first day that I came to Asia, in what manner I always lived among you...*
>
> *Therefore take heed to yourselves and to all the flock, among which the Holy Spirit has made you **overseers**, to **shepherd** the church of God which He purchased with His own blood."* – Acts 20:17-18, 28

> *The **elders** who are among you I exhort, I who am a fellow elder and a witness of the sufferings of Christ, and also a partaker of the glory that will be revealed: **Shepherd** the flock of God which is among you, serving as **overseers**, not by compulsion but willingly, not for dishonest gain but eagerly;* – 1 Peter 5:1-2

Notice in passing that when the Early Church was growing rapidly, another kind of leaders–deacons–were added to help with all the physical work of caring for the poor and needy (Acts 6).

This letter is addressed to **the church in Ephesus.** Ephesus was the greatest city of the entire Roman province of Asia. It was in a most-desirable location, where the Cayster River reached the Aegean Sea. With an excellent harbor and a commanding position on trade routes into Asia, it grew to be a major commerce center.

Ephesus was also important because of its world-famous Temple of Diana (Artemis), one of the seven wonders of the ancient world. The temple was larger than a football field and had 127 columns, each at least 40 feet tall and many of them adorned with carved images. It was dedicated to the worship of Diana, the multi-breasted mythological goddess. The worship of Diana was grossly immoral.

There is important information in the Book of Acts about the founding of the church in Ephesus. Have you noticed that in the New Testament the reference to a body of believers in any city is" *the* church" (singular)? In those days there were no denominations or rival congregations. There were no church buildings, so most segments of the church in any city were like our "small groups" today, meeting in people's homes. For that reason, as mentioned above, almost all of the epistles ("letters") in the New Testament were addressed to one church in each city—in this case, the church of Ephesus.

Acts 18:18-21 tells of Paul's first visit to Ephesus. He couldn't stay at that time, but he left a godly husband/wife team--Aquila and Priscilla--to start the work. While they were there, a highly educated and eloquent Jewish speaker named Apollos came from Alexandria in Egypt. He knew about John the Baptist, but not about Jesus, so Aquila and Pricilla taught him about the life and work of the Savior (Acts 18:24-28).

Paul then returned to Ephesus and invested three years there (Acts 19-20, see 20:31), apparently the longest of any of his ministries. He was able to use Ephesus as a base to reach out to the rest of the area. After two years the church had made a tremendous impact:

> *And this continued for two years, so that all who dwelt in Asia heard the word of the Lord Jesus, both Jews and Greeks.* – Acts 19:10

Amazing things happened in Ephesus during those years. Many mighty miracles were done in Jesus' name. Evil spirits and sorcerers opposed the work, and there was a huge uprising in the city when the silversmith's business of making idols of Diana began to decline because so many people were coming to Christ.

Later, Paul's associate Timothy served the church there (1 Timothy 1:3), and later still, according to church traditions, the apostle John lived and ministered there.

Connection

These things says He who holds the seven stars in His right hand, who walks in the midst of the seven golden lampstands: – Revelation 2:1b-c

Jesus, the true source of this message describes Himself this way: ***These things says He who holds the seven stars in His right hand, who walks in the midst of the seven golden lampstands.*** The meaning of these words was explained in Chapter 1, verses 12-16 and 20. Perhaps this image was a reminder to the leaders of the church at Ephesus that even though Ephesus was the "mother church" of the area, and the most prominent, that the other churches were also important, and Jesus was the true head of His whole church.

Commendation

> *"I know your works, your labor, your patience, and that you cannot bear those who are evil. And you have tested those who say they are apostles and are not, and have found them liars; and you have persevered and have patience, and have labored for My name's sake and have not become weary."* –
> Revelation 2:2- 3

Jesus said, *I know your works.* The omniscient Son of God is never so preoccupied by the maintenance of His universe that He fails to keep track of what each of us is doing. In this portion of the letter that fact should be an encouragement, because He is commending them for their good works. As mentioned before, our salvation does not depend on good works, but they are still very important. He taught His disciples that if they love Him they will keep His commandments (John 14:15). He said about other people, "By their fruits you shall know them" (Matthew 7:20). And in a parable about good works, He said the master will tell the faithful one, "Well done, good and faithful servant" (Matthew 25:21). See the additional notes on good works in Chapter 2, verse 26, and Chapter 3, verse 1.

The apostle Paul reinforced the importance of doing good things in many of his writings, including Ephesians 2:8-10, where he said we were "created unto good works," and in 1 Corinthians 9:25 and 2 Timothy 4:8, where he taught that those who are faithful will receive crowns for their service. Here in Revelation Chapters 2 and 3 it will be revealed that crowns will be given to believers. Then, Chapter 4 indicates that those crowns will be given to the Lord as a proof of our love.

Truthfully, people who think they are children of God, but who realize that they do not live in a way that produces good works, should take a new, honest look at whether or not they are "born again" (John 3:1-8). In Revelation 3:20 the simple but definite step one must take to accept Christ as Savior will be explained.

Jesus also commends the Ephesians for **your labor, your patience.**

Believers of this period endured great hardships without giving up their faith. Christianity was considered false by the majority of Jewish people who had been blinded because of their unbelief (Romans 11). Those who followed Christ often had to do so against the wishes of their families. Jesus warned His followers that this would happen (Matthew 10:34-39). Opposition to early Christianity became so strong that believers were scattered and many were imprisoned and even killed. Before he was converted, Saul of Tarsus (who was renamed "Paul" after his conversion) zealously persecuted the church (Acts 9:1-2,21).

Also, during this time Caesar worship was practiced. Devotees to the Roman state religion actually claimed that Caesar was god[2]. Remember that their background religion was the Roman panoply of mythological gods, some of which were also considered human. These concepts came from the Greek religious system before the Roman era, and could actually be traced back to Babylonian origins. The letter to Pergamum will shed more light on this belief. The normal statement of devotion and loyalty to the Emperor was, "Caesar is Lord." That's why the expression "Jesus is Lord" was a test of true belief for Christians in 1 Corinthians 12:3.

The next good thing that Jesus said about the Ephesian church was, **and that you cannot bear those who are evil.** Ephesus, like one of our own large cities, was a place where many evil people could be found. From the immoral pagan religions, to the corrupt politics and illegal activities, the city was home to evil (Greek *kakos*–"inwardly rotten") people. What is most interesting here is that it wasn't the normal criminal types that are given as examples, but religious hypocrites: "false apostles" and "Nicolaitans." This is exactly the way Jesus viewed the Pharisees during His earthly ministry (Matthew 23:13-29). To Him, the worst kind of person was one who pretended to be good when his motives were evil.

The word used for "bear" means to "carry what is burdensome." Jesus commends the fact that they do not tolerate wickedness. This is interesting because He was criticized for making contact with people who were tax collectors and prostitutes. He practiced true tolerance. He was willing to befriend them for the sake of giving them the truth, but He never let them think that their wrong ideas and actions were acceptable to God (John 8:11).

A generation ago tolerance meant putting up with something or someone who has a different point of view. But today there is a new understanding of tolerance: that all beliefs and lifestyles should be accepted as equal. This is philosophically impossible since those who hold that position cannot live up to their own theory. They are intolerant of our most heart-felt belief that Jesus is "The way, the truth, and the life," and no one can come to the Father apart from Him (John 14:6).

The first example Jesus gave that they did not tolerate evil-doers was *that you have tested those who say they are apostles and are not.* In the previous verse we discussed the very limited use of the title "apostle" in the Bible. The original apostles were chosen by Christ to serve the first-generation church, but the Bible does not teach apostolic succession. It was not God's idea for the church to have a domineering hierarchy.

During the Apostolic period there were false apostles. The early church was careful to identify true apostles and reject the false. This explains the need for the apostle Paul to defend his calling as an apostle in 2 Corinthians, Chapters 11 to 13. He said that some people were "transforming themselves into apostles of Christ" (2 Corinthians 11:13).

And have found them liars. It is not explained how the church at Ephesus tested these false apostles. Some of the questions they might have asked were: Did Jesus Christ call them, and if so, is there sufficient proof, as in the case of Paul? Did the whole church have the practice of appointing new apostles? They undoubtedly followed biblical concepts of discernment, such as:

Test all things; hold fast what is good. – 1 Thessalonians 5:21

But he who is spiritual judges all things, yet he himself is rightly judged by no one. For "who has known the mind of the LORD that he may instruct Him?" But we have the mind of Christ. – 1 Corinthians 2:15-16

Then Jesus emphasized the importance of the diligence and patience of the Ephesian believers by restating His commendation in a slightly different way. ***You have persevered and have patience, and have labored for my name, and have not become weary.*** This underscores how admirable these qualities were in the Early Church, and how completely these believers had devoted their lives to the spread of the Gospel. Jesus had addressed the problem of weariness this way:

Come to Me, all you who labor and are heavy laden, and I will give you rest. – Matthew 11:28

The apostle Paul also gave encouragement on the subject:

And let us not grow weary while doing good, for in due season we shall reap if we do not lose heart. – Galatians 6:9

Complaint

Nevertheless I have this against you: That you have left your first love. – Revelation 2:4

Unfortunately Jesus already had a shocking problem with the Ephesian church. ***Nevertheless I have this against you,*** is the one major issue that He did need to raise.

Like a heart-broken lover, Jesus cried, ***that you have left your first love.*** The word "left" is *aphiémi*, meaning "to send away. It is from the preposition *apó*, "away from" and *hiēmi*, "to send." The use of this word indicates a willful decision to break the relationship. Most Christians who find themselves in this state do not accept responsibility for the problem. They often do not even remember how it happened.

How can this be? What does it mean? Imagine a husband or wife, saying for the first time, "You don't love me anymore!" When this happens in a marriage it is usually the result of a very slow process, and even if the one who still loves his or her spouse fears that their love is dying, it is a most dramatic moment when the bitter truth is finally blurted out.

If we are in some small measure capable of feeling sorry for God, this is the issue that should make us the most ashamed of ourselves. The Great Father of the universe, who is by His very nature "love" (1 John 4:7-8); who created us in His image for the purpose of being able to receive and return that love (Genesis 1:26-27); and who "so loved the world that He gave His only begotten Son, that whoever believes in Him should not perish but have everlasting life" (John 3:16); is heart-broken when His ungrateful creatures just don't love Him anymore! It happened in the Garden of Eden, before the great flood, during the Exodus, and countless other times in the Bible, so much so that He called Israel an adulterous wife (Ezekiel 16, Book of Hosea). Under the Old Covenant Israel was His wife, and under the New Covenant the church is called the "Bride of Christ" (Matthew 25:1-13; Ephesians 5:22-33).

During His earthly ministry Jesus taught that loving God was the most important thing we could do (Matthew 22:36-38). In this letter to the Ephesians, He didn't give any examples, or proof that His precious Apostolic Church had lost its first love, but they would know it was true.

There are still churches today that resemble those of the Apostolic Period. Some of them are in areas of the world where the Gospel is just now taking root and spreading like wild-fire. But there are other churches, especially in old denominations, where members are just going through the motions. The work is a burden, but they are laboring hard to maintain the status quo. They might even be valiant to preserve the purity of doctrine, but they don't really have the love or the joy of the Lord.

If the 1st Century Church could lose its first love for Christ, it is possible for any Christian to be distracted from his devotion to the Lord by the cares of the world. Jesus Himself related the Parable of the Sower, which teaches that some new Christians fail to develop deep roots, others are choked by the competing "weeds" that spring up around them, and still others grow well and bear good fruit (Matthew 13:3-8).

Critique

Remember therefore from where you have fallen; repent and do the first works, or else I will come to you quickly and remove your lampstand from its place—unless you repent. – Revelation 2:5

The good news is that, if a person or even a whole group of people in a church should lose their first love, there is a way to be restored. Jesus gave three steps to remedy this problem. First, He said, ***Remember therefore from where you have fallen!***

Many times during pastoral counseling I have heard people say about their spouse, "I never really loved him (or her)." Or they might say, "He (or she) never really loved me." Once a relationship has gone bad it is a normal human response to forget all the good times and only remember the bad ones. I always asked people who said this to be honest with themselves. I would say something like this: "Surely you were not so shallow when you decided to get married. You wouldn't have made that commitment to someone you didn't love, would you? Do you think your spouse would have agreed to marry you if she didn't love you?"

Jesus asked the Ephesians to remember what a wonderful experience it was when they first turned the burden of their sins over to the lover of their souls! They had to have been "on top of the world" when that happened! They just needed to recapture that sense of wonder and appreciation they felt when they first gave their hearts to Him.

Often we have to "decide" to remember things. There is so much buried in our minds after decades of living! There are hundreds, or even thousands of people's names permanently written in the storage banks of our amazing memories. But we often need to instruct our mind to remember a person and then wait for a while. Often, in the middle of some other thought, that person's name pops into our heads! This also happens when old friends or relatives get together and talk about the "good old days." Memories about events one had not thought about for ages come flooding back with surprising clarity.

If any sincere Christian will just take the time to remember how Jesus found him in great need, and forgave him of his sins, then brought

68

him into His great family, and became his truest friend, his heart will surely be softened, and he will want to return to that wonderful state of mind.

The next thing Jesus said would be necessary for the Ephesians to be restored to their first love was to **repent.** The Greek word *metanoeó* comes from the preposition *meta*, which in this case means "change" and the verb noieó, "to think." Therefore the process of repentance, which most people rightly understand is a call to changing one's evil ways, actually means "a change of thinking." Many people will change their behavior when reprimanded, but unless they also change their way of thinking, they will make the same mistake over and over.

Some people think that a Christian never needs to repent since his sins have been forgiven, but John was most definitely writing to believers when he penned this wonderful promise:

> *If we confess our sins, He is faithful and just to forgive us our sins and to cleanse us from all unrighteousness.*--1 John 1:9

The word "confess" also needs to be explored. It is *homologeo*, from *homou*–"together" and *lego*–"to say." It means "to say the same," or, "to agree." It is much more than simply admitting that we have done something wrong. If we would say the same thing God does about our sin, we would utterly hate it and desire never to do it again.

How can we get to this point? We might allow the Holy Spirit to show us how vile our thoughts are, and how selfish our actions have been. We might write our sins on a sheet of paper. At first we would admit to one or two things, then, as we continued to be honest, we would begin to write things we would never want the rest of the world to know:

> *"The heart is deceitful above all things,*
> *And desperately wicked;*
> *Who can know it?"* – Jeremiah 17:9

I have had these moments of agony and tears. As terrible as it is to have a glimpse of the way the Lord sees my sin, the relief and cleansing it brings is beyond description.

There is a third prescription Jesus gave for restoring their first love. He said, *and do the first works.* What was it like for you when you first gave your heart to Christ? Perhaps your priorities were changed. Your new friends were probably committed disciples of Christ. You probably could hardly wait to go to the next Bible study. You wanted your old friends to find what you had discovered about Jesus. You loved to worship the Lord.

If you have drifted away from that wonderful "first love," it is possible to regain it, but you will need to return to the sincere simplicity that you once had when you were first born again.

Or else I will come to you quickly and remove your lampstand from its place—unless you repent. Would Jesus really remove the church at Ephesus, with all of its history? In the Old Testament God allowed the Ark of the Covenant to be captured when the leaders of Israel had become corrupt. He also allowed Eli the priest and his two sons to die in a battle. Just as this happened the wife of one of his sons gave birth to a child, and she called him "Ichabod," meaning "inglorious," because she said, "The glory has departed from Israel" (1 Samuel 4: 22).

In the course of time, God did allow the unrepentant church to be removed. In fact the whole city of Ephesus ceased to exist, and even its ruins are unimpressive today.

> *But this you have, that you hate the deeds of the Nicolaitans, which I also hate.–* Revelation 2:6

Jesus mentioned something else favorable about the Ephesians at this point. He said," *But this you have, that you hate the practices of the Nicolaitans."* This is a little surprising since Christianity elevates love to the highest of virtues. But, of course there is such a thing as "righteous indignation," (Ephesians 4:26-27), and Jesus Himself drove out the moneychangers from the Temple when He saw them defiling it with their greed (Matthew 21:12-13).

The name Nicolaitans is found in the Bible only here and in verse 15 of this same chapter. Some commentators assume that it referred to the followers of some heretic named Nicolas. However, the only Nicolas mentioned in the Bible was a godly person, chosen to be one of the first deacons in Acts 6. It is more likely that the name *Nikolaités*, coming from two Greek words *nikaó*–"to conquer" *and laos*–"people," referred to an element in the church that wanted to dominate the people. This is probably a reference to the false apostles mentioned earlier, and their tendency to establish a ruling class over the rest of the people in the church.

I have known a number of pastors who acted like little dictators in the church. They evidently never believed what Jesus taught–that whoever would be greatest in the Kingdom would need to be a servant to all (Matthew 20:25-28). John himself had written about this kind of egotist in his third epistle:

> *I wrote to the church, but Diotrephes, who loves to have the preeminence among them, does not receive us.. – 3 John 9*

Historical Fulfillment (Apostolic Period)

Jesus is the only head of the church. He did give them apostles, and over time, as seen in the Book of Acts and in the epistles to the churches of the 1st Century, a few other leaders were added to their simple organizational structure. (See the notes about pastors and other ministries in verse 1 of this chapter.)

Peter, the natural leader of the Early Church (John 21:16, Acts 2:14) instructed other leaders to not "lord it over" other believers since Christ is the Chief Shepherd of His church (1 Peter 5:2-4). Another picture of the church in the New Testament is that it is a body with many different parts, all functioning together for the good of the whole person, and controlled by its head, who is Jesus Christ Himself (I Corinthians Chapters 12 to 14; Ephesians 1:22-23; Ephesians 4:1-16. Romans 12:4-8).

Then Jesus added another unusual statement: **which I also hate.** Expression of hatred from the Lord, or from His people, is rare in the Bible. In the strict sense, Jesus even taught us to love our enemies instead of hating them (Matthew 5:43-44). But the word is sometimes used in a comparative sense, like Jesus' instruction to "hate" one's family–meaning to love less than their love for Him (Luke 14:26). In Amos there is instruction to hate what is evil:

Hate evil, love good;
Establish justice in the gate.
It may be that the LORD God of hosts
will be gracious to the remnant of Joseph. – Amos 5:15

This is followed by an expression of God's own hatred of their religious activities that were not sincere:

"I hate, I despise your feast days,
And I do not savor your sacred assemblies." – Amos 5:21

God does not hate evil-doers; He only hates the evil that they do.

Counsel

"He who has an ear, let him hear what the Spirit says to the churches. To him who overcomes I will give to eat from the tree of life, which is in the midst of the Paradise of God." – Revelation 2:7

He who has an ear, let him hear. Who should be able to understand this teaching? Someone with a mystical sixth sense? Someone who has an enlightened guru to explain it? No! If a person has a working ear, he should be able to hear. These truths are being revealed to those who are willing to hear. Still, there are many, who really do not want to know the truth:

You search the Scriptures, for in them you think you have eternal life; and these are they which testify of Me. But you are not willing to come to Me that you may have life. – John 5:39-40

Since Jesus was speaking, why did He say, **what the Spirit says to the churches**? He was indeed speaking, but the entire vision came to John by way of the Holy Spirit. See our notes on Chapter 1, verse 10, where John said that he was "In the Spirit."

In each of the letters Jesus promises a blessing **to him who overcomes.** See the notes from Chapter 2, verse 1 about the fact that every true Christian is an overcomer. However, the trials that each church faces will tend to sort out the true believers from the false.

The promise to true believers in this church is this: He **will give the right to eat from the tree of life.** The original tree of life was in the Garden of Eden. However, Adam and Eve ate from the forbidden fruit on the tree of the knowledge of good and evil instead. God banned them from the garden and set a guard to keep them from entering, presumably because He did not want them to eat from the tree of life and experience eternal existence in their sinful state (Genesis Chapters 2 and 3).

When Jesus added, **which is in the paradise of God,** He was probably referring to the same place He had in mind when he told the thief on the cross, "Today you will be with Me in Paradise" (Luke 23:42). The word comes from the Persian language's description of a garden. Theologians say that it might be a portion of Hades, the place of the departed dead, until the future judgments, when believers will go to Heaven and non-believers will go to Hell. Jesus' story of Lazarus and the rich man (Luke 16:19-31) give some credence to this concept, but the word "Paradise" is not used in that story.

The apostle Paul spoke of someone (possibly himself) who was caught up to the third heaven, which he equated with Paradise. It was a place of indescribable wonder (2 Corinthians 12:1-4). It is thought that the "third" heaven is beyond the first one–our skies, or the atmosphere around the Earth; and beyond the second one–outer space and the physical universe. The third heaven is God's own abode, which is beyond time and space.

Paul went on to assure us that for a Christian to be absent from the body is to be present with the Lord (2 Corinthians 12:6-8).

I once heard the story of a little boy who was trying to understand this concept. He simplified it greatly by saying, "Well, wherever Jesus is, that will be Heaven to me."

The Tree of Life might be in that intermediate place now, so that overcomers might partake and never die again.

When we get to the last chapter of Revelation we will consider the thought that the Tree of Life will be located on the New Earth (Revelation 22:2).

To Smyrna 2:8-11 (Persecuted Church – AD 100 to AD 312)

> ***"And to the angel of the church in Smyrna write,***
>
> ***'These things says the First and the Last, who was dead, and came to life:***
>
> ***"I know your works, tribulation, and poverty (but you are rich); and I know the blasphemy of those who say they are Jews and are not, but are a synagogue of Satan. Do not fear any of those things which you are about to suffer. Indeed, the devil is about to throw some of you into prison, that you may be tested, and you will have tribulation ten days. Be faithful until death, and I will give you the crown of life.***
>
> ***"He who has an ear, let him hear what the Spirit says to the churches. He who overcomes shall not be hurt by the second death."'"*** – Revelation 2:8-11

Next, the Lord Jesus said, ***"And to the angel of the church in Smyrna write..."*** This second letter is to Christians in the beautiful city of Smyrna, about 40 miles north of Ephesus. It was another very important center of commerce and culture in Asia Minor. It boasted an excellent harbor on a gulf of the Aegean Sea. The city was also located on the Hermus River.

It was a very old city, dating back to around 3000 BC. At one time the Hittites lived there. It was destroyed by the Persians in 545 BC, but was rebuilt during the period of the Greek Empire. Alexander the Great had laid the plans for the city, but it was built by his generals after his death.

By the time this prophecy was written, the city was a center for the cult of Rome and the worship of multiple Greek/Roman deities. It was especially noted for its practice of Caesar worship. (See note above under verse 2 of this chapter.)

"Smyrna" comes from the word myrrh. This was an expensive reddish resin from trees of the genus Commiphora in North Africa and the Arabian Peninsula. Myrrh was one of the gifts of the Magi, along with gold and frankincense (Matthew 2:11). The gifts were symbolic of the person and work of our Savior. Gold, a common biblical symbol of deity, speaks of His preexistence as God the Son, frankincense, a valuable incense often used in prayer, was emblematic of His sinless humanity and His priestly role, and myrrh, usually used for embalming, prefigured His death on our behalf (John 19:39).

The main thoroughfare of the city was called "The Golden Street." At one end it had the Temple of Zeus and at the other end, the Temple of Cybele. Along the way there were also temples for Apollo, Aphrodite, and Asclepius.

The Bible does not record the beginning of Christian faith in the city, but it was probably closely connected to the growth of the church in Ephesus.

Today the city is known as Izmir, and it is the third most populous city in Turkey, with more than 3 million inhabitants. The name is actually derived from the Greek words beginning this letter: *eis Smirnin,* meaning "to Smyrna." Notice the similarity of sound if you drop the I: zmir/ "Smyrna" / "myrrh."

There are still churches today in Izmir. At one time it was called "Smyrna of the Infidels" by devout Muslims because of its significant Christian population.

As we read on, we will see that this church is prophetic of the second period of church history: the Persecuted Church. This persecution had already begun in John's days, but it would increase more and more until the time of the conversion of Emperor Constantine.

Connection

"These things says the First and the Last, who was dead, and came to life;" – Revelation 2:8b-d

Jesus identified Himself to this church with these words: ***These things says the First and the Last.*** As with most of these letters, Jesus referred back to the vision John saw and reported in Chapter 1. Making this claim again, He emphasized His deity, because only the One True God could be the First and the Last. See the notes on 1:11.

Then Jesus added this–another description from Chapter 1:*Who was dead, and came to life.* See the notes on 1:17 where the biblical concepts of human life and death were considered. Death means separation. Physical death is separation of the body from the soul and spirit. Spiritual death is separation of the human spirit from God, who is Spirit. And eternal death is the dreaded state of dying physically while still spiritually dead. This is what happens to those who do not accept Christ as Savior.

While the death of Christ was payment for our sins, His resurrection is the infallible proof that what He taught was true and what He did for us was acceptable to the Father.

Commendation

"I know your works, tribulation, and poverty (but you are rich); and I know the blasphemy of those who say they are Jews and are not, but are a synagogue of Satan." – Revelation 2:9

To each of the churches Jesus reminds them: *"I know your works."* See notes about works on Chapter 2, verse 2. First among their outstanding qualities was the way they handled *"tribulation."* The Greek word *thlipsis*, the word for "persecution," is from a root meaning "compression." It describes persecution from the point of view of the pressure that is experienced by those who are hated, injured, and killed by their enemies.

When Jesus, in His Sermon on the Mount, said *"Blessed are those who are persecuted for righteousness' sake,"* (Matthew 5:10), another Greek word for persecution was used. That word is *dióko*, which is the verb that basically means "to pursue." This describes persecution from the point of view of the one who is causing the trial.

Difficulties are normal for Christians, and God often allows them in order to build our character and refine our faith (James 1:2; 1 Peter 1:6):

Yes, and all who desire to live godly in Christ Jesus will suffer persecution. – 2 Timothy 3:12

The Book of Job gives great insight about why God allows trials. Satan, the "accuser" questioned Job's motives for living a godly life, claiming that he was faithful to the Lord only because of the blessings he received. God allowed the enemy to test him, knowing that Job was strong enough to prove his faith. In the process, Job was greatly blessed and Satan's plan to destroy him was thwarted.

The apostle Paul indicated that the same testing process is at work in our lives as well:

> *No temptation has overtaken you except such as is common to man; but God is faithful, who will not allow you to be tempted beyond what you are able, but with the temptation will also make the way of escape, that you may be able to bear it.* – 1 Corinthians 10:13.

The Greek word used in this verse is *peirasmos,* which can mean "trial," or "temptation."

Historical Fulfillment (Persecution Period)

By the time of this Revelation the persecution of the church had already begun. According to traditional history, all of the original apostles had been martyred except for John. Most Christians had been driven out of Jerusalem and were faithfully witnessing to people of the far-flung areas to which they fled. They usually experienced opposition from Jewish people wherever they went as well as resistance from believers in idolatrous religions. This persecution would be especially serious during this particular time because of the cruelty of Roman Emperors, who saw the church as an enemy, since Christians would not bow to them.

The most famous martyr of the period would be Polycarp, the Bishop of Smyrna, who was burned alive for his faith there in about AD 153. The period of the Persecuted Church would continue until the time of Emperor Constantine's conversion in AD 312.

Amazingly, the church continued to grow through these persecutions. One of the Church Fathers named Tertullian (AD 160 –225) made the now-famous statement, "The blood of the martyrs is the seed of the church."

Persecution of Christians has been a factor in all periods of church history. It has gone in cycles, and it happens to be very intense in our own days. With more than 100 million persecuted Christians in the world, it is a growing problem, especially in Communist and radical Islamic countries. Believers are being driven out of the Middle East in such numbers that some predict there will be no openly Christians there in the future. Even in the United States there is a noticeable rise in opposition to Christians, especially if they take a stand on the moral issues of the day.

Even before the 9/11 attacks, Harvard professor Samuel P. Huntington wrote the book, *The Clash of Civilizations and the Remaking of World Order*. In it he predicted there would be a "clash of civilizations" between three great cultures (the Western, Asian, and Islamic). He predicted a massive conflict between the West and Islam caused by Islamic militarism.

In Jesus' other major sermon recorded in the New Testament, the *Olivet Discourse*, He predicted that persecution would grow worse during the Tribulation that is still future.

"Then they will deliver you up to tribulation and kill you, and you will be hated by all nations for My name's sake.--Matthew 24:9

Most of the terrifying events of the Tribulation are building up during this present time, which Jesus called "The beginning of birth pains" (Matthew 24:8). Ethnic wars, terrorism and anti-Christian philosophies contribute to an ever-growing toll of suffering and death. This subject will be considered more in Revelation Chapter 6.

And poverty describes the second problem that this church faced with such courage. Smyrna was a prosperous city, but for Christians poverty was a by-product of persecution. Like the Jews in Europe during World War II, who were persecuted by the Nazis, the Christians in Smyrna probably lost everything else before losing their very lives for the Gospel.

However God the Son confidently asserted, ***"but you are rich."*** No modern reality show could match the tremendous courage these faithful believers had or the heartache that they endured. In the Sermon on the Mount Jesus had taught this:

> *"Do not lay up for yourselves treasures on earth, where moth and rust destroy and where thieves break in and steal; but lay up for yourselves treasures in heaven, where neither moth nor rust destroys and where thieves do not break in and steal. For where your treasure is, there your heart will be also.* — Matthew 6:19-21

He also had said,

> *For what profit is it to a man if he gains the whole world, and loses his own soul? Or what will a man give in exchange for his soul?* — Mark 8:36

Their third problem in Smyrna was **the blasphemy of those who say they are Jews and are not.**

To "blaspheme" is to speak against someone. It was used to describe those who defame God, but it would also apply to those who disparage other people. It was likely that these trouble-makers were really Jewish by birth, but they did not represent the purpose of the Chosen People. They were not true to their own Scripture or they would have tried to reason with the Christians who had such Jewish roots themselves.

Jesus, who knew the hearts of these persecutors, said they **"are a synagogue of Satan."** Actually all false religion is energized by Satan. This will be shown most dramatically later in this Revelation.

Complaint

There is no reprimand for this church, since it was constantly purified by the rigors of persecution. To put it simply, only a strong, dedicated Christian would be willing to die for Christ. A hypocrite would quit the church long before he would risk losing his life.

Critique

Do not fear any of those things which you are about to suffer. Indeed, the devil is about to throw some of you into prison, that you may be tested, and you will have tribulation ten days. Be faithful until death, and I will give you the crown of life. – Revelation 2:10

In spite of the situation at Smyrna, the Savior says, **Do not fear.** How can a person not be afraid when there is such a real and imminent threat? The sacrifice of brave soldiers throughout the course of human history is surely one of the most amazing aspects of the way our Creator designed us. When it is necessary to face certain death in order to protect our loved ones, there arises in the human spirit a heroic determination to die if necessary to promote the greater good.

How much more courage and determination people have when they know that God is with them! This is the supernatural peace that passes understanding (Philippians 4:7). The apostle Paul said that it was the fruit of the Holy Spirit (Galatians 5:22-23).

David demonstrated this God-given courage many times. How else could he have offered to fight Goliath when he was just a young man, and all of Israel's soldiers were afraid to stand against the giant? In the Psalms he explained his faith in the Lord:

> *In God I have put my trust; I will not be afraid. What can man do to me?* – Psalm 56:11

> *Yea, though I walk through the valley of the shadow of death,*
> *I will fear no evil;*
> *For You are with me;*
> *Your rod and Your staff, they comfort me.* – Psalm 23:4

Daniel exhibited this same supernatural courage when he was thrown into the lions' den (Daniel 6), and his three friends were willing to face the fiery furnace rather than worship a false god (Daniel 3).

Persecution takes many forms, so the Lord Jesus included all of them when He told them not to fear *"any of those things which you are about to suffer."* Paul, who was no stranger to persecution and suffering, said something remarkable to the believers at Philippi:

> *For to you it has been granted on behalf of Christ, not only to believe in Him, but also to suffer for His sake,*--Philippians 1:29

The fascinating thing about this verse is that it claims that suffering for Christ is actually a gift and a privilege. It is something that has been granted or given to them: first to believe in Christ, but also to suffer for His sake. Godly people can actually give thanks for the experience, because it draws them even nearer to Jesus, and it proves to others who witness it how real their belief is.

Indeed, the devil is about to throw some of you into prison. There are many names for Satan in the Bible. One of the most common descriptions is the devil (Greek *diabolos*, meaning "the accuser"). He and his demons are always trying to destroy believers. One of his most effective tactics is to ruin our reputation or our confidence by accusing us of wrong-doing. In the case of persecution, he is behind the drama that turns people against the saints.

I recently read a novel called "Safely Home" by Randy Alcorn. I recommend it to you because, even though it is a novel, it describes the terrible-but-true conditions that Christians face in China. The main character in the story begins each day wondering if this will be the day that he might need to die or reject his faith. And he wonders if, when that time comes, he will have the courage to stand for the Lord Jesus. He and his family live in utter poverty because Christians cannot have the better jobs. He has to meet in secret places with other believers in the middle of the night because house churches are illegal. He is thrown into prison and forced to do slave labor, but he doesn't lose his faith. It is a story of the great victory that untold numbers of Chinese Christians have experienced.

There was a purpose for the trials that the church of the second period of church history would endure: **That you may be tested.** As noted earlier, these trials were a refining process. The pure faith that was produced by going through persecution was a powerful proof to all who heard about it that Christianity was true! People who were looking for a belief system that was real could not resist the attraction of such purified conviction.

Christians throughout the remainder of time would draw inspiration from the faithfulness of the saints from this second period of church history. However, the Lord would set a limit to its duration: ***And you will have tribulation ten days.***

The word "day" is used in various ways in most languages, and in the Bible also. It can mean day-time, or a 24-hour period of time, but it might also mean a long period of time. Later, Daniel's prophecy of "seventy weeks" will be shown to mean seventy "sevens" of years. And Peter wrote,

> *But, beloved, do not forget this one thing, that with the Lord one day is as a thousand years, and a thousand years as one day.* — 1 Peter 3:8

Many commentators have suggested that these ten days foretold the ten periods of Christian persecution under various Roman emperors. Here is a list of these well-known attacks against Christians:

Nero – AD 64-68
Domitian – AD 90-95
Trajan – AD 104-107
Aurelius – AD 161-180
Severus – AD 200-211
Maximus – AD 235-237
Decius – AD 250-253
Valerian -- AD 257-260
Aurelian – AD 270-275
Diocletian – AD 303-312

The first period of persecution was during the apostle Paul's time in the Early church, and the second period affected the apostle John, resulting in his exile to the Island of Patmos where this Revelation was given to him.

The last of the ten persecutions ended when Constantine became emperor and was converted to Christianity.

This means that there was some overlapping between the first two periods of church history. There were certain congregations or even denominations in every age that would identify with one of these seven churches. This is especially true of Smyrna since there have been pockets of persecution in every generation.

The seriousness of the danger to Christians in Smyrna is underscored by the next thing Jesus said: *"Be faithful until death."* Most Christians are not called upon to give up their lives for Christ, but a great many have made that sacrifice. The New Testament teaches the reality of spiritual warfare. It was seen in Jesus' own temptation (Matthew 4), His public teaching (Matthew 5:10-12), and his private instruction (Luke 21:32-33; John 21:22-23). Because of this spiritual battle, the apostle Paul gave instruction about using the Armor of God (Ephesians 6:10-20), and both Peter and James warned us to resist the devil (1 Peter 5:8-9; James 4:7).

There will be casualties in this great spiritual battle, but death is not the "bitter end" for a Child of God. Physical death, the separation of the body from the soul and spirit (See notes on Chapter 1, verse 17), will free us from the limitations of a corrupted world (Romans 7:21-24) and allow us to be "present with the Lord" forever (2 Corinthians 5:1-7).

To these faithful martyrs Jesus promised, *"And I will give you the crown of life."* Crowns are mentioned in many contexts in Revelation. Christians receive crowns (here, and 3:11). The 24 elders have crowns that they place at the Lord's feet (4:4, 10). The false messiah—the rider on the white horse—has one (6:1; 13:1); demonic creatures have them (8:7). And Jesus has many crowns when He returns as King of Kings (Revelation 14:14; 19:12-16). Crowns symbolize victory, and are usually worn by rulers.

This crown is called the *"crown of life,"* a most appropriate reward for those who die in Christ's service. It is also promised in James 1:12 for those who overcome trials and temptations. This is the only crown that is named in Revelation, but there are four others named in the rest of the New Testament. These are seen as laurel wreaths, given to the winner of various races or contests. Paul mentions an *"imperishable crown"* (1 Corinthians 9:19-24) for excellence in missionary service and self-discipline. This is a description rather than an actual name. There is the *"crown of rejoicing"* (1 Thessalonians 2:19) for winning others to Christ; the *"crown of righteousness"* (2 Timothy 4:8) for loving Christ's appearance--believing in the

Second Coming and longing for it; and the *"crown of glory"* (1 Peter 5:2-4) for humble leadership of Christ's flock.

This brings up the important question of the judgment of believers. Born-again Christians will be tested to see what we have done as a result of our sincere love for the Lord:

> *For we are God's fellow workers; you are God's field, you are God's building. According to the grace of God which was given to me, as a wise master builder I have laid the foundation, and another builds on it. But let each one take heed how he builds on it. For no other foundation can anyone lay than that which is laid, which is Jesus Christ. Now if anyone builds on this foundation with gold, silver, precious stones, wood, hay, straw, each one's work will become clear; for the Day will declare it, because it will be revealed by fire; and the fire will test each one's work, of what sort it is. If anyone's work which he has built on it endures, he will receive a reward. If anyone's work is burned, he will suffer loss; but he himself will be saved, yet so as through fire.* – 1 Corinthians 3:9-15

> *Therefore we make it our aim, whether present or absent, to be well pleasing to Him. For we must all appear before the judgment seat of Christ, that each one may receive the things done in the body, according to what he has done, whether good or bad.* – 2 Corinthians 5:9-10

Apparently rewards will be given for our proper choices. There is no punishment *as such* for our former sinful life or for our failures as followers of Christ, because all of our sins will be forgiven (Psalm 32; Isaiah 1:18; Romans 8:1-4; Psalm 103:11-12; Micah 7:19). However, we will be aware of the wasted aspects of our lives that produced no rewards. In Revelation 4 we will see that we will place our rewards at the base of the Lord's throne.

Here's the thought that should motivate us about this future judgment: When we finally see the Lord Jesus face to face, won't we be overwhelmed by His presence and be unspeakably grateful for our salvation? And won't we desire, more than anything else, to prove our love for Him? We will show our gratitude by casting our crowns at His feet. But, horrible thought, what if we have nothing to give Him?

However, every single person who has trusted Christ for salvation will enjoy eternal life and blessings with the Lord. Jesus even promised the thief on the cross, who believed at the last minute, that he would be in Paradise with Him that very day (Luke 23:43).

Missionary C.T. Studd wrote these now-famous words:

Only one life, 'twill soon be past.
Only what's done for Christ will last.

Counsel

"He who has an ear, let him hear what the Spirit says to the churches. He who overcomes shall not be hurt by the second death."
 --Revelation 2:11

He who has an ear, let him hear what the Spirit says to the churches. See the notes about this expression on the message to the church at Ephesus in verse 7 above.

He who overcomes shall not be hurt by the second death. See notes on overcomers at the beginning of Chapter 2, verse 1; and notes about the second death in Chapter 1 verse 18. Remember that 1 John 5: 5 defines an overcomer as any person who truly believes in Jesus.

To Pergamum   2:12-17 ("Married"/ Compromised Church – AD 312 to AD 476)

> *"And to the angel of the church in Pergamos write,*
>
> *'These things says He who has the sharp two-edged sword: "I know your works, and where you dwell, where Satan's throne is. And you hold fast to My name, and did not deny My faith even in the days in which Antipas was My faithful martyr, who was killed among you, where Satan dwells. But I have a few things against you, because you have there those who hold the doctrine of Balaam, who taught Balak to put a stumbling block before the children of Israel, to eat things sacrificed to idols, and to commit sexual immorality. Thus you also have those who hold the doctrine of the Nicolaitans, which thing I hate. Repent, or else I will come to you quickly and will fight against them with the sword of My mouth.*
>
> *"He who has an ear, let him hear what the Spirit says to the churches. To him who overcomes I will give some of the hidden manna to eat. And I will give him a white stone, and on the stone a new name written which no one knows except him who receives it."'"* – Revelation 2:12-17

This letter was to be given to the pastor of the church in Pergamos.
And to the angel... (See notes on "angel" in Chapter 2, verse. 1) .

Of the church in Pergamos write... Pergamos, also known as Pergamum, had a colorful history as the ruling city of a large portion of Asia Minor after the fall of the Kingdom of Thrace in 281 BC. It was controlled by kings from the Attalid family from 241 to133 BC. They were apparently good administrators, cultivating special relationships with Rome, and establishing a culture that included a university and a great library with some 200,000 books. This library was second only to the one in Alexandria. Parchment was invented there because jealous Alexandrians would not allow the shipment of papyrus to them. The city hosted the Panathenaea games, which were considered equal to the Olympic contests.

Pergamum was steeped in pagan idolatry, serpent worship, and Caesar worship. Most of the temples were located on the top of its hill. The greatest of these was the Temple of Zeus, the chief god of the Greek panoply. Other Greek/Roman temples there included those dedicated to Athena and Dionysus.

Asclepius, the god of medicine and healing was the patron god of the city. His image, with a serpent-entwined staff, was worshipped in the Asclepion, a large area in the lower part of the city where people came to bathe in its sacred pool, touch tame snakes, and hopefully be healed. The modern symbol for medicine is snakes wrapped around a pole. This imagery comes from this Greek mythological character, but the true origin of the connection between snakes and healing undoubtedly originated with the Bible's story of the fiery serpents in the wilderness. God allowed venomous snakes to bite the Israelites when they grumbled against Moses and the Lord (Numbers 21). God told Moses to fashion a brass snake and put it on a pole. When the rebels would repent and look at the serpent, the symbol of their sin, they would be healed. This story became the background for Jesus' own teaching about His crucifixion:

And as Moses lifted up the serpent in the wilderness, even so must the Son of Man be lifted up, that whoever believes in Him should not perish but have eternal life. For God so loved the world that He gave His only begotten Son, that whoever believes in Him should not perish but have everlasting life. – John 3:14-16

And I, if I am lifted up from the earth, will draw all peoples to Myself." This *He said, signifying by what death He would die.* – John 12:32-33

Pergamum was also a focal point for the newer religion of Caesar Worship. It had been chosen for the site of the Temple dedicated to Octavius in 29 BC. "Each citizen was required to offer incense to the emperor once a year and declare that Caesar was Lord."[3]

The name Pergamos, or Pergamum, comes from two Greek words. The first is *purgos*, meaning "fortified," and the second is *gamos*, meaning "married." It was indeed an unholy union of various religions and cultures with the great Roman Empire.

This city of Pergamum and the experiences of its growing Christian community are prophetic of the third age of the church, from the time of the conversion of the Roman Emperor Constantine, to the fall of the Roman Empire (AD 312-476). During this time the church became "married" to the world and was weakened considerably by its compromises with Satan's evil world system that began with the building of Babylon (Genesis 10:8-12) shortly after the Flood of Noah's time, and will come to a climax during the end-times (Revelation 17 & 18).

Constantine the Great was the first Roman emperor to convert to Christianity. In AD 312 he saw a vision of a cross in the sky and the words, "In this sign conquer." This was just before his victorious battle against Maxentius. He reversed the persecutions of the former emperor Diocletian. In 313 he and Licinius issued the Decree of Milan, which granted complete freedom to Christians throughout the empire, and religious liberty to all.

Constantine undoubtedly meant well when he issued this decree, but because of this favorable treatment people adopted Christianity in name, but most of them still clung to their worldly beliefs and lifestyles. This actually caused much damage to the church.

Connection

'These things says He who has the sharp two-edged sword:" -- Revelation 2:12b

To this church Jesus revealed Himself as he *who has the sharp two-edged sword* proceeding from His mouth. See the notes on Chapter 1, verse 16. Hebrews 4:12 calls God's Word a double-edged sword, able to divide even between soul and spirit. In the same book Jesus is considered God's ultimate Word (Hebrews 1:1-2). In John's own writings Jesus is called The Word (John 1:1, 14). If the church would follow Jesus and His Word, they would be able to separate the truth from the pagan influences that had come in like a flood.

When Jesus returns at the Battle of Armageddon His weapon of mass destruction will be His words, symbolized by a sharp sword out of His mouth (Revelation 19:15, 21).

Commendation

"I know your works, and where you dwell, where Satan's throne is. And you hold fast to My name, and did not deny My faith even in the days in which Antipas was My faithful martyr, who was killed among you, where Satan dwells." – Revelation 2:13

Jesus told the Pergamum Christians, *"I know your works, and where you dwell."* Their "good works" were primarily holding on to the truth and not giving in to the spread of evil. They also faced persecution, but not to the extent experienced by the church at Smyrna. The thing that kept them from being a powerful witness for Christ was the overpowering presence of wickedness and a spirit of compromise–combining Christian beliefs with those of false religions.

It was brave of them to live **where Satan's throne is.** The name Satan means "accuser." It is used 7 times in the Book of Revelation, four of these in the messages to the seven churches (2:9, 13, 24; 3:9), and three other times (12:9; 20:2, 7). Satan is also named in the rest of the book under a variety of other appellations: devil (Revelation 2:10; 12:9, 12; 20:2,10); accuser of the brethren (12:10); serpent (12:9, 14,15; 20:2); and dragon (12:3, 4, 7, 9, 13, 16, 17; 13:2, 4, 11; 16:13, 20:2). He is also known by many other names and descriptions in the rest of the Bible, including "Lucifer" meaning "shining one," or "light-bearer" (Isaiah 14:12); "angel of light" (2 Corinthians 11:14); "tempter" (Matthew 4:3), and others.

Did Satan actually have a throne in Pergamum? If so, why would his throne be there instead of Rome or some other great city? There was no place actually called "Satan's Throne" there. However, he did reign over the evil kingdoms of the world, and there was a temple in Pergamum that Jesus could have had in mind when He said, "where Satan dwells."

It will be helpful to take some extra time here to look at some of the extensive information that is available about Satan and false religions, both in the Bible and in human history. This part of our commentary will be a little longer than normal, but we will gain essential insight that will help us understand the rest of Revelation.

First, consider Satan's power on this planet. Do you remember Jesus' temptation just before He began His public ministry? In Matthew, Chapter 4, we read that Jesus went up on a mountain and fasted 40 days. When He had reached the physical low-point of His human endurance Satan tempted Him to turn stones into bread to satisfy his hunger. Then he tried to entice Him to leap from the high-point of the Temple to prove that He was the Son of God, because if He were, angels would surely catch Him. He resisted the evil one by quoting Scripture. This, by the way, is a powerful lesson to us about how we should respond when we are tempted. We need to remember what the Bible teaches and declare it aloud if possible.

Then Satan tempted Jesus a third time:

Again, the devil took Him up on an exceedingly high mountain, and showed Him all the kingdoms of the world and their glory. And he said to Him, "All these things I will give You if You will fall down and worship me." – Matthew 4:8-9

Jesus didn't want to rule over the sin-corrupted decaying nations of the world! He had come to bring new life, and to eventually establish a righteous world-wide kingdom on Earth. So how could Satan even be offering Him *all* the kingdoms of the world? How was that a legitimate offer?

Actually, the Bible does teach that the devil has temporary dominion over these kingdoms because of the sinful condition of mankind, and the rebellion of so many against God's own good plan for them.

First let's look at what the Bible says about Satan's earthly powers, and then we will consider how this situation developed. God created angels before He created humans. They were perfectly formed spirit beings , but like the humans God would design later, they were given the ability to choose good or evil (Jude 1:6; 2 Peter 2:4) and to love God and follow His

91

will, or to rebel against His goodness. In the case of Satan, in Isaiah 14:12ff. and Ezekiel 28:11ff, he became prideful and wanted to be worshipped like God Himself. Notice that these passages in Isaiah 14 and Ezekiel 28 were written to the earthly kings of Babylon and Tyre, but in both cases, the focus shifts to Satan, the evil spirit behind the scenes that energized them. These things could not be said of mere human kings.

According to Revelation 12, Satan and a third of the angels were cast out of heaven and thrown to Earth:

> *And another sign appeared in heaven: behold, a great, fiery red dragon having seven heads and ten horns, and seven diadems on his heads. His tail drew a third of the stars of heaven and threw them to the earth.* – Revelation 12:3-4

This chapter reveals that these "stars" were demons (fallen angels).

> *And war broke out in heaven: Michael and his angels fought with the dragon; and the dragon and his angels fought, but they did not prevail, nor was a place found for them in heaven any longer. So the great dragon was cast out, that serpent of old, called the Devil and Satan, who deceives the whole world; he was cast to the earth, and his angels were cast out with him.* – Revelation 12:7-9

Some theologians think that the time that Satan and his followers might have come to Earth was described at the beginning of Genesis:

> *In the beginning God created the heavens and the earth. The earth was without form, and void; and darkness was on the face of the deep. And the Spirit of God was hovering over the face of the waters.* – Genesis 1:1-2

The thought is that whenever God creates something it is created perfect. That's why, at the end of the creative days, God "saw that it was good," and after the sixth day He declared that everything He had made was "very good" (Genesis 1:31). But there seems to have been a lapse of time between the original creation of the universe (the heavens and the Earth) and the special work of fashioning our planet in six literal days to the way it is now.

After God created the universe, including the original form of the Earth (Isaiah 45:18), something must have happened that resulted in it becoming a dark place that was without form. This could have been caused by the expulsion of Satan and the demons to the Earth. Please note that there is no reason to believe that any pre-Adamic people existed during that time because the Bible makes it clear that Adam and Eve were the first humans.

In any case, while Adam and Eve were still in the Garden of Eden, they were affected by spiritual warfare. This is the battle between good and evil (See the notes about this conflict in Chapter 2, verse 10). Adam and Eve were allowed to be tested, but they could have resisted the temptation to sin. Unfortunately, they chose to disobey their Creator (Genesis 3). They passed on the propensity to sin to their children (Romans 5:12), and sin spread throughout the whole human race. From the time of our first parents until now, God provided a way of salvation for those who would believe in His provision of a substitute payment for sin. That is why God introduced the concept of a covering made from animal skins (Genesis 3:21). The first family practiced sacrifices (Genesis 4:1-5). The Law prescribed the details for sacrifices later (Exodus 29; Leviticus Chapters 1 through 7). And Jesus died as the sacrificial lamb to pay for sin once and for all (Hebrews 10:1-18).

Meanwhile, those who rebelled against God and rejected His provision for salvation gathered together in cities. The first city recorded in the Bible was built by Cain, the son of Adam and Eve, after he had killed his brother and been banished from the family (Genesis 4:16-17). Spiritual warfare raged until, at the time of Noah's flood, the thoughts and actions of most humans were "only evil continually" (Genesis 6:5).

Satan might have thought that he had won the spiritual battle for the souls of men, but God chose a tiny remnant of eight people--Noah and his family--to live through the Great Flood and begin populating the Earth again (Genesis Chapters 6 through 8).

Noah's family members were all true believers, and they obeyed God when He told them to move out in various directions and replenish the Earth (Genesis 9:1). However, it wasn't long after that new beginning that one of Noah's great-grandsons, Nimrod, began a new rebellion. He was a "mighty hunter before the Lord." This is understood by most commentators to mean he was the leader of a new rebellion against God's plans (Genesis 10:8-9). He established a number of cities where people could stay together to build their own religious structures instead of obeying God and worshipping only Him. Two of the cities he built were Babylon and Nineveh, both of which would become capital cities of the enemies of God's chosen people hundreds of years later (Genesis 10:10-12).

The worst part of Nimrod's influence was the promotion of false religions to take the place of the worship of the One True God. The Tower of Babel was built for astrology, and for people to try on their own to reach into the heavens (Genesis 11:1-9). This was the beginning of the occult, of idolatry, and of the perversion of the truth.

Spiritual warfare became intense once again. Over the course of time false religions grew and spread from these cities, from one generation to another, in the mythology of various people. In his fascinating book, *The Two Babylons*, Alexander Hislop, a Church of Scotland preacher in the 1800's, explained this process. The memory of Nimrod became the mythical god Marduk to the Babylonians. (If you remove the "N" from Nimrod you are left with the consonants M-R-D, which then became Marduk). Nimrod was also symbolized in the constellation of Orion the Hunter. Over the course of the next 2000 years. these mythological gods of Babylonian culture would morph into Tammuz of the Sumerians, Bel of the Chaldeans, Osiris in Egypt, the Ammonite Moloch, Adonis, Kronos and Apollo in Greece, Mars and Vulcan in Rome, Odin in Scandinavia, and more[4]!

Returning to the matter of Satan's throne, and the question of whether or not he could offer Jesus the kingdoms of the world. Jesus repeatedly referred to Satan as the "ruler of this world" (John 12:31; 14:30; 16:11). The apostle Paul called him the "god of this age" (2 Corinthians 4:4) and the "prince of the power of the air" (Ephesians 2:2). This sad condition was the result of spiritual warfare, especially in the great population centers where evil grew the most. Jesus was aware of the extent of evil when He said,

"Enter by the narrow gate; for wide is the gate and broad is the way that leads to destruction, and there are many who go in by it. Because narrow is the gate

and difficult is the way which leads to life, and there are few who find it." –
Matthew 7:13-14

Satan was obviously behind the perverted religion that began in
Nimrod's Babylon and gradually spread to the great cities of all the major
empires of world history. By Jesus' time the major empires had been the
Egyptian Empire, the Assyrian Empire, the Babylonian Empire, the Medo-
Persian Empire, the Greek Empire, and the Roman Empire. As noted
above, false mystery religions had spread from Babylon throughout the
world, changing slightly to adapt to each new culture.

Alexander Hislop, who was mentioned above, explained the
transfer of a counterfeit religious system from Babylon to other cultures all
over the ancient world. The city of Babylon was the center of false
religions. The Medes and Persians conquered Babylon in 538 BC. They
came back later, in 487 BC to destroy the city. At that time, the Babylonian
Magi relocated to Pergamum, a small city at the time, but in a strategic
location. Hislop quoted historians from the mid-19th Century, who wrote,
"The defeated Chaldeans fled to Asia Minor, and fixed their central college
at Pergamos."[5]

Incidentally, the Bible says that later, when Jesus was born, there
were some godly Magi (Wise Men). They believed the Scriptures and
followed the star that announced the Savior's birth (Matthew 2:1-12). This
means there were two kinds of Magi. This is probably best explained by
something that happened in the days of Nebuchadnezzar and Daniel
hundreds of years earlier. The original Magi were ungodly astrologers and
occultists. King Nebuchadnezzar of Babylon asked his wise men to tell him
what he had dreamed and what it meant. They were not able to tell him
what he had dreamed. God revealed the dream to Daniel and gave him the
interpretation of it. (Daniel 2). Because of this, Nebuchadnezzar made
Daniel *"ruler over the whole province of Babylon, and chief administrator over all the
wise men of Babylon."* (Daniel 2:46-49, especially v. 48) No doubt, Daniel
reformed the thinking and practices of those wise men and taught them
what the Bible had to say, including his own prophecies, which would later
become the Book of Daniel.

A group of the Magi evidently reverted to the old Babylonian doctrines. These are the ones who moved to Pergamum, while the Bible-believers moved to Persia.

Hislop wrote, "Thus the vacant seat of Belshazzar was filled, and the broken chain of the Chaldean succession renewed."[6] He went on to say that the leader of the group was the "Pontifex Maximus," the Latin name for "greatest pontiff (bridge-builder)" or chief priest.

When Attalus III, the last king of Pergamum died in 133 BC he bequeathed all of Pergamum to the Roman government.

The title "Pontifex Maximus" had been used by the head of Roman religion for some time when Julius Caesar accepted the title in 63 BC. When he became ruler of the Roman Republic in 49 BC the leadership of both the government and Roman religions were vested in the same person. This subject will be expanded later .

What was meant by Satan's throne? Where was the center of evil in the city of Pergamum? Some would suggest that it was the Asclepion, where serpents were worshipped. But the greatest symbol of pagan religion in the city was the Altar of Zeus on the acropolis above the city. It was a massive marble structure 117 ft. wide by 110 feet deep, and it was 40 feet high. Since the structure was a gigantic altar, it is thought that there were endless sacrifices offered there.

The base of the edifice is covered by high-relief friezes that depict the epic mythical battle between the Giants with serpent-legs and the Olympian gods. The site was excavated between 1878 and 1886 by German archaeologists, and the massive panels of the friezes were taken to Berlin, where a museum was built to replicate the entire structure.

Spiritually speaking, it was unwise to cart so much of this massive structure all the way to Germany and glorify it by restoring it in this way. Do Satan and his demons attach themselves to evil artifacts like these? They certainly can if they want to. And maybe it is just a coincidence, but World War I was partly fomented by Germany shortly after the Museum was built. In fairness, the other countries involved share some guilt for that "war to end all wars," but when it was over, the victors--The U.S., Britain, France and Italy–in the Treaty of Versailles--required Germany to accept responsibility for the outbreak of hostilities. It was a horrendous conflict, using deadly new weapons like machine guns, tanks, airplanes, submarines, and poison gas. Worst of all, the civilian population became a target of war. Of the nearly 17 million deaths during the fighting, about 7 million were civilians!

The foundation of the original Pergamon museum in Berlin was weak, and the whole building needed to be enlarged, so a second museum was built in 1930, and in that one the explorers also built a replica of the Ishtar Gate from ancient Babylon!

A few years after the completion of the second Pergamon Museum, Adolph Hitler sparked the beginning of World War II. Again, maybe it is coincidence, but there is evidence, like that of the History Channel's documentary *Hitler and the Occult*, that supernatural evil was a part of this horrible scenario. World War II resulted in more than 60 million deaths and marked the only use of nuclear weapons in warfare.

Much more will be said about Babylon, false religions, the occult and a final world-wide religious movement in Revelation Chapters 17 and 18.

Jesus commended the believers at Pergamum this way: ***And you hold fast to My name.*** Believers in Christ did not originally call themselves "Christians." The first name for the movement was "The Way" (Acts 9:2; 19:9, 23; 24:22). This was very appropriate since Jesus said,

> *"I am the way, the truth, and the life. No one comes to the Father except through Me."* – John 14:6

It wasn't until Christians were scattered from Jerusalem and were being persecuted that they were called "Christians" (Acts 11:26). Those who first used this name probably meant it to be an insult. Whether or not that is true, believers have always been willing to accept the name, happy to be associated with their Savior!

The name of "Jesus" is especially meaningful to all who understand who Jesus is and what He has done for them. (See "Jesus" and "Christ" in the notes on Chapter 1, verse 1.)

Jesus then added, ***and did not deny My faith.*** "My faith" would certainly mean faith, or belief, in Jesus Himself: that He was who He claimed to be, especially as Messiah/Savior; and that He accomplished what He said He would do, to die for them and rise again the third day. This "faith" could also refer to the belief system itself, that is, all that He had taught them. The goal of the persecutor is to cause the victim to deny his faith. This made it very difficult for most martyrs because they knew they could go on living and helping their needy families if they would just say that they renounced their belief in Christ. Just imagine having to make that decision. Wouldn't people understand that they didn't mean it if they recanted the faith? Wouldn't it be the most loving thing to do for the sake of their families?

The apostle Peter, who would one day be willing to die for his faith in Jesus, wrote:

Yet if anyone suffers as a Christian, let him not be ashamed, but let him glorify God in this matter. – 1 Peter 4:16

Jesus then gave a glowing example of a person who did not deny the faith... ***even in the days in which Antipas was My faithful martyr who was killed among you.*** Antipas has been one of my favorite Bible characters since my first year in at Biola. I was living in the dorms at the Biola Hotel next to the Church of the Open Door. Dr. J. Vernon McGee was pastor then, and I had enjoyed his live radio program for years before that time. He was speaking on Wednesday nights, so I naturally wanted to hear him in person. When he reached this verse, he asked, "Who was Antipas?" I didn't know, and I was trying to think of any connection. As I remember it, Dr. McGee said, "Nobody knows! There is no other record or mention of this man's name in history. But listen, friends, Jesus knew, and He was pleased with him and called him 'My faithful martyr.' That's all that really matters. Other people don't need to be impressed with your life. But oh, how wonderful it will be if Jesus is pleased with you."

Jesus concluded His commendation of the believers at Pergamum and of Antipas The Faithful, by acknowledging again that this was a most difficult place to be a Christian because it was ***where Satan dwells.*** Sometimes I think Jesus would say the same thing about where we live in Southern California in these evil days. He would probably say the same thing about wherever you live too. But the amazing thing is this, and the faithful believers at Pergamum proved it, Satan is strong, but Jesus is stronger!

You are of God, little children, and have overcome them, because He who is in you is greater than he who is in the world. – 1 John 4:4

Complaint

But I have a few things against you, because you have there those who hold the doctrine of Balaam, who taught Balak to put a stumbling block before the children of Israel, to eat things sacrificed to idols, and to commit sexual immorality. Thus you also have those who hold the doctrine of the Nicolaitans, which thing I hate. – Revelation 2:14-15

In a firm and loving way, like a good coach, Jesus told the believers at Pergamum, **But, I have a few things against you.** To the church at Ephesus there was just one problem. To those at Smyrna, there was nothing they were doing wrong. But to this church He has a "few" issues. "Few" is the normal word in Greek for a small amount, and the Lord actually names only two things.

Here is the first problem: **You have there those who hold the doctrine of Balaam.** This refers to a fascinating story from the Old Testament book of Numbers, Chapters 22 through 24, where a prophet named Balaam was hired by Balak, king of the Moabites, to curse Israel. He tried repeatedly, but God would not allow him to utter a curse against His people.

If you have time to read these chapters in Numbers, do it now. You won't know whether to laugh or cry!

Who taught Balak to put a stumbling block before the children of Israel. Balaam evidently advised Balak to involve the Israelites in worldliness and immorality (Numbers, Chapter 25). Thus Israel could be corrupted from within.

Just reading through Numbers Chapters 22 through 24, you would not discover that Balaam suggested that the Moabites use their women to lure Israelite men into immoral relationships. But in Chapter 25 you see that that is exactly what happened, and it led to the death of thousands of the men of Israel. That chapter does not mention Balaam at all, but, since it comes right after his failed attempts to curse them, it makes you wonder:

Now Israel remained in Acacia Grove, and the people began to commit harlotry with the women of Moab. They invited the people to the sacrifices of their gods, and the people ate and bowed down to their gods. So Israel was joined to Baal of Peor, and the anger of the LORD was aroused against Israel. – Numbers 25:1-3

The Bible answers this question in the book of Numbers. Moses said,

Look, these women caused the children of Israel, through the counsel of Balaam, to trespass against the LORD in the incident of Peor, and there was a plague among the congregation of the LORD. – Numbers 31:16

The result of Balaam's strategy was devastating. Jesus reminded the believers at Pergamum that some of the Israelites were persuaded **to eat things sacrificed to idols, and to commit sexual immorality.** Jesus didn't say that the people of Pergamum had actually committed the same kinds of sin, but they had plenty of opportunity to do so in their city. In any case, they were allowing false teachers to indoctrinate them with the idea that they could indulge in sinful activities and still be good Christians (2 Peter 2:15; Jude 1:11).

Truthfully, there are many in our generation who are affected by this same error. A misunderstanding of God's great grace is often taught, especially to young people. It is true that we are not saved by works (Ephesians 2:8-9; Titus 3:5), but it is also true that those who are saved by grace are "created for good works" (Ephesians 2:10; Titus 3:8).

Here is the second issue: ***Thus you also have those who hold the doctrine of the Nicolaitans, which thing I hate.*** Some commentators see this statement as another way of expressing what has already been said about the teaching of Balaam. However, the word "also" would not be necessary if it were just a continuation of the previous warning. The Greek word is the preposition *kai*, which is the normal word for "and." But even if it were translated "and" here, it would still signal a separate problem.

In our earlier study about the church at Ephesus (see the notes on Revelation 2:6), we learned that Nicolaitans were officious people who wanted to impose control over others. We saw that Nicolaitan comes from two Greek words *nikaó* – "to conquer" and *laos* – "people,"

At Pergamum this would-be hierarchy had entrenched their position by developing a "doctrine." They were now systematically "teaching" their concepts. It is evident that their lessons didn't include Jesus' explanation that whoever would be greatest in the kingdom should be servant to all (Matthew 20:25-28), or Peter' warning that was mentioned earlier against "lording it over the flock" (1 Peter 5:2-4).

Historical Fulfillment (Compromise Period)

Now, since the Book of Revelation is about prophecy, let us turn our thoughts to how these issues relate to the third period of church history. As mentioned above, in the notes on verse 12, this message fore-shadowed the events that would take place between AD 312 (Emperor Constantine) and AD 476 (the fall of the Western Roman Empire).

Because the Roman Emperor Constantine had been converted, he issued an edict to allow freedom of worship to all, including Christians. Christianity began to be the favored religion of the Empire. Great numbers of people joined the church.

It was wonderful that the persecutions ended, and there were other good things, like the churches being built in the Holy Land by the emperor's mother, Helena. These churches have preserved some of the sites of great importance. One of these is the Church of the Nativity in Bethlehem.

Unfortunately, this phase of church history had some negative consequences as well. Many of the people claiming to become Christians did not understand the Gospel and what it really meant to follow Jesus. They just added what little they did know about Him to the other religions they had before. They did not necessarily leave their old pagan religions behind. In that way the church became corrupted. It began to be "married" with Satan's evil world system.

In the previous verse while considering Satan's throne at Pergamum, it was mentioned that Attalus III, the last king of Pergamum, died in 133 BC. He bequeathed all of Pergamum to the Roman government. The priesthood of the old Babylonian religion was transmitted at that time to the head of the Roman religions, the "Pontifex Maximus." In 63 BC Julius Caesar was given this title. Then, in 49 BC he also became the ruler of the Roman Republic. After his death the Roman Emperors also assumed the title "Pontifex Maximus."

More than 400 years later, Emperor Gratian (AD 375-383), who was a Christian, decided it was no longer appropriate for the Emperor to serve as pagan religious leader, so he divested himself of the title Pontifex Maximus.[7] However, soon after he rejected the position it was assumed by Damascus I, the Bishop of Rome (AD 366-384).[8] At that point Satan was able to start introducing seeds of compromise into the church. Over time these false ideas grew to become major problems, like some aspects of monasticism, salvation by works, prayers to saints, undue emphasis on Mary, non-biblical sacraments, confession to a priest, papal infallibility, and other beliefs and practices that were later rejected by Protestants.

Theodosius I (379-395), the last Emperor over both the eastern and western halves of the Roman Empire abolished pagan worship and established Catholic Christianity as the official religion of the Roman Empire.

A few decades later, in AD 445 Emperor Valentinian III issued a decree establishing the primacy of the Bishop of Rome. This decree was first applied to Leo I, so he became the first "Pope" ("Papa") of the Roman Catholic Church. Catholics consider all the Bishops of Rome to have been Popes, but this decree marked the beginning of the papacy as we now know it.

At this point I need to explain that I am not "anti-Catholic." Catholic means "universal," and up to this historical juncture there had just been one main "trunk" for the family tree of Christianity. It was just "the church." From that point of view, all of our denominations had our origins in this same universal church.

However, starting with Constantine, there were lots of corruptions of the belief and practices in the church. These eventually led to a series of "branches" from the main trunk during this period of history.

I am also not anti-Catholic because of my personal experience with Catholic people. In my first pastorate in East Los Angeles, most of the people I met in the community were Catholics. I was eager to share the Gospel with them, and they were surprisingly open to listening! We used the "Four Spiritual Laws" in those days, and because we were quoting God's Word, Catholic people were almost always willing to hear and trust the Bible. Many of them had never heard the simple plan of salvation, but they were open to it. They might not have known what was in the Bible, but they had a reverence for it. Over the years I have become close friends with numerous Catholics, including some priests, who are dedicated followers of the Lord Jesus Christ. In our church home in Alta Loma the highest percentage of converts from other faiths came from the Catholic Church.

It is right, however, to oppose teaching that can be shown to be unbiblical, whether it is in the Catholic Church or any other denomination. From that point of view there are many serious problems in Catholic history, theology, and current directions. Historically, the longer a denomination has been in existence, the more it has drifted away from simple faith in the Word of God. The same can be said about most Christian colleges and seminaries.

Let's summarize how the church at Pergamum is a prophetic example of the third period of church history. Their two big problems were allowing the encroachment of the teaching of Balaam and the teaching of the Nicolaitans. The teaching of Balaam was designed to cause God's people to experiment with the immoral practices of the world. This was done on a grand scale after Emperor Constantine legitimized Christianity and encouraged others to join the church without understanding the true meaning of the Gospel. All kinds of false beliefs and practices were brought into the church, and the moral sensitivity of the people declined:

> *Adulterers and adulteresses! Do you not know that friendship with the world is enmity with God? Whoever therefore wants to be a friend of the world makes himself an enemy of God.* – James 4:4

The teaching of the Nicolaitans, which began in the Early Church, was put into practice by recognizing one of the several bishops ("overseers" See notes on Chapter 2, verse 1) as the head of the entire church. This was the Bishop of Rome, and from this point, the leadership of the church grew extensively until it looked, and acted, like a worldly government.

Critique

Repent, or else I will come to you quickly and will fight against them with the sword of My mouth. – Revelation 2:16

Jesus' then gave a stern warning to **repent.** As mentioned before, for five of these seven churches the Lord had some complaint. He told each of them to repent. They needed to have this change of direction in their lives, brought about by a change of thinking about the issues. See the notes on this in Chapter 2, verse 5. To recap that that discussion: repentance involves confession, and confession is agreeing with God about the sins that were committed (1 John 1:9).

A command from Jesus to repent seems very harsh, but it is actually a privilege. Instead of punishing them directly for their mistakes, He was giving them an invitation to get back into a place of blessing. The privilege of repentance is:

An opportunity to make a change before it is too late.

An opportunity to clear one's conscience--to deal with guilt and fear.

An opportunity to begin again with renewed hope.

But what if an errant Christian will not repent? In that case, Jesus warns, *or else I will come to you quickly.* It is really significant that these words are used as a threat, when they are also given as the longed-for climax of the entire book. Look at the last two verses of Revelation:

He who testifies to these things says, "Surely I am coming quickly."
Amen. Even so, come, Lord Jesus!
The grace of our Lord Jesus Christ be with you all. Amen – Revelation
22:20-21

If we know we are doing what is pleasing to Him, we will look forward to His return. But, like a child who has been disobedient, we might dread that day.

Christ's coming is a key concept in Revelation. It is mentioned by Jesus Himself, and occurs in different forms at least 25 times in the book. In fact, the return of Christ is a major theme in the Bible. Nearly every book in the New Testament mentions it. Paul called it "the blessed hope"!

Looking for the blessed hope and glorious appearing of our great God and Savior Jesus Christ,--Titus 2:13

Some teachers in our generation claim that if people believe that Jesus is coming to reign on the Earth during the Millennium it would actually cause them to lose interest in helping the poor and needy. Their theory is that these people just focus on the world getting worse and worse, and all they want to do is to survive until He comes. Actually, there are some people who do have this outlook, but they don't get it from a balanced reading of the Bible! The apostle Paul certainly did not see it that way. Read the whole chapter of Titus 2 to see how the return of Christ motivates us to live now with a purpose.

Currently there is a considerable debate about the Kingdom of God. Is Jesus reigning on Earth now? What does it mean to pray, "Your kingdom come. Your will be done on Earth as it is in heaven" (Matthew 6:10)? Here is an excerpt from our free online book, *2012: The Year the World Didn't End* to help us understand these vital issues.

Kingdom Work

During this trying time Jesus is incredibly active, using us to win converts to His Kingdom until He returns as King over all (Revelation 11:15-17; 19:11-16).

Jesus had told his disciples that the kingdom was "at hand." (Matthew 4:17). He knew his offer to be King at His triumphal entry would be rejected. Nevertheless, He will come in the future (Luke 21:25-31; 22:18, 30). In Acts 1:6 they asked Him, "Lord, will You at this time restore the kingdom to Israel?" He told them they couldn't know the time, but when the Holy Spirit would come, He would enable them to be witnesses to the whole Earth.

Evidently the Kingdom would not yet be [fully] established at that time. He would not yet reign on Earth, and the disciples would not yet reign with Him, but they would spread the message of the Kingdom, even as He had been doing.

That is why Jesus taught us to pray "Your kingdom come. Your will be done on Earth as [it is] in heaven." (Matthew 6:10). We still pray that way because even though His Kingdom does already exist in Heaven, and He is our King already, it still has not yet been established here on Earth.

Jesus told Pilate, "My kingdom is not of this world. If My kingdom were of this world, My servants would fight, so that I should not be delivered to the Jews; but now My kingdom is not from here" (John 18:36-37).

Born-again Christians are citizens of the Kingdom of God:

For our citizenship is in heaven, from which we also eagerly wait for the Savior, the Lord Jesus Christ,--Philippians 3:20

We are also citizens of our earthly nations:

Tell us, therefore, what do You think? Is it lawful to pay taxes to Caesar, or not?"

But Jesus perceived their wickedness, and said, "Why do you test Me, you hypocrites? Show Me the tax money."

So they brought Him a denarius.

And He said to them, "Whose image and inscription is this?"

They said to Him, "Caesar's."

And He said to them, "Render therefore to Caesar the things that are Caesar's, and to God the things that are God's." When they had heard these words, they marveled, and left Him and went their way. – Matthew 22:17-22

While we are here we are ambassadors, representing Christ

and His Kingdom.

> *Now then, we are ambassadors for Christ, as though God were*
> *pleading through us: we implore you on Christ's behalf, be reconciled*
> *to God.* – 2 Corinthians 5:20

During this time, we establish outposts of the Kingdom in our homes, churches, missions, and other Christian enterprises. We seek constantly to gain new members of the Kingdom by following His example of ministering to their needs and giving them the Gospel.

Many "New Evangelicals" in their emphasis on meeting the needs of the poor and needy have steered away from concern about prophecy. They correctly notice that some who are expecting the Lord's imminent return have such a pessimistic view that things will just get "worse and worse," that they neglect the other biblical instruction about environmental responsibility and humanitarian assistance.

However, the conflict between good works and prophecy is not an "either/or" question, but it requires a "both/and" solution. We should be aware that these are the end-times, but because of that we should be occupied with Kingdom work now. He taught this directly in the parable about using what has been given to us while we are waiting for the Kingdom to be established. He said, "Do business [KJV- "occupy"] till I come." (Luke 19:13, Luke 19:8-26)   As always, [Christian action] requires the balanced approach that involves teaching the "whole counsel of God" (Acts 20:27). [9]

Returning now to this warning to those who would not repent, Jesus said, ***and will fight against them with the sword of My mouth.*** See the notes on Chapter 1, verse 16, and Chapter 2, verse 12, where God's Word is shown to be a double-edged sword, and Jesus Christ, the Living Word, wields unlimited power when He speaks.

Counsel

"He, who has an ear, let him hear what the Spirit says to the churches. To him who overcomes I will give some of the hidden manna to eat. And I will give him a white stone, and on the stone a new name written which no one knows except him who receives it." — Revelation 2:17

He who has an ear, let him hear what the Spirit says to the churches. See notes about this expression in Chapter 2, verse 7. Again, the responsibility is on the reader or listener to make use of what has been said.

For notes on the expression, *to him who overcomes.* See Chapter 2, verse 1 about the fact that every true Christian is an overcomer. Overcoming at Pergamum would mean standing against the false teaching of Balaam and the Nicolaitans.

To the overcomers in Pergamum Jesus gave this promise: *"I will give some of the hidden manna to eat."* Manna was God's miraculous provision for the Israelites in the wilderness. It was fresh, perfect food that could be gathered every day except on the Sabbath. For their Sabbath needs a double portion was given the day before.

The story of Balaam and the temptation of the Israelites took place while God's Chosen People were travelling through the wilderness on the way to the Promised Land. It was during this same journey that God provided the manna. The Lord always provides for us just at the time we need it the most (1 Corinthians 10:13).

Jesus indicated that spiritual food that was even more necessary than our "daily bread." He told the tempter,

"It is written, 'Man shall not live by bread alone, but by every word that proceeds from the mouth of God.'" – Matthew 4:4

What is the "hidden" manna that Jesus promised? The spiritual bread was the Word of God. It might be that the church at Pergamum was not getting enough of God's Word because of the encroaching hierarchy.

Jesus Himself was the Word that became flesh and dwelt among us (John 1:14). He had also revealed Himself as the "Bread of life:"

> *Therefore they said to Him, "What sign will You perform then, that we may see it and believe You? What work will You do? Our fathers ate the manna in the desert; as it is written, 'He gave them bread from heaven to eat.'"*
>
> *Then Jesus said to them, "Most assuredly, I say to you, Moses did not give you the bread from heaven, but My Father gives you the true bread from heaven. For the bread of God is He who comes down from heaven and gives life to the world."*
>
> *Then they said to Him, "Lord, give us this bread always."*
>
> *And Jesus said to them, "I am the bread of life. He who comes to Me shall never hunger, and he who believes in Me shall never thirst.* – John 6:30-35

I will give him a white stone. Many different ideas have been suggested about the meaning of "white stone." One thought was the ancient custom of giving a black stone to someone found guilty in court, or a white stone to someone who is acquitted. Another concept came from athletic contests where a white stone was awarded to victors. In any case, it is a trophy and a keepsake to remind the overcomer of his or her struggle and of the Lord's help.

Furthermore, Jesus revealed this about the trophy: *And on the stone a new name written which no one knows except him who receives it.* We cannot know what this means because it is secret, like a love letter. The name will undoubtedly be different for each believer, and it will be a term of endearment.

My favorite teacher in Junior High had a pet name for each student in his classes. He called me "RG." His name for others was "Sport," "Blondie," "Speedy," etc. This made us feel special. Another example of this comes to mind: I had a special name for each of my children-- something no one else would call them.

When I was a young Christian we used to sing a popular chorus by C. Austin Miles about this new name:

There's a new name written down in glory,
And it's mine, O yes, it's mine!

Each one of us is unique to our Creator and Savior. When we see Him He will reveal to each of us a loving special name that will be meaningful to us forever.

To Thyatira   2:18-29
Middle Ages of the Church--476-1517)

"And to the angel of the church in Thyatira write,
'These things says the Son of God, who has eyes like a
flame of fire, and His feet like fine brass: "I know your works,
love, service, faith, and your patience; and as for your works,
the last are more than the first. Nevertheless I have a few
things against you, because you allow that woman Jezebel,
who calls herself a prophetess, to teach and seduce My
servants to commit sexual immorality and eat things sacrificed
to idols. And I gave her time to repent of her sexual
immorality, and she did not repent. Indeed I will cast her into
a sickbed, and those who commit adultery with her into great
tribulation, unless they repent of their deeds. I will kill her
children with death, and all the churches shall know that I
am He who searches the minds and hearts. And I will give to
each one of you according to your works.

"Now to you I say, and to the rest in Thyatira, as
many as do not have this doctrine, who have not known the
depths of Satan, as they say, I will put on you no other
burden. But hold fast what you have till I come. And he who
overcomes, and keeps My works until the end, to him I will
give power over the nations—

'He shall rule them with a rod of iron; They shall be
dashed to pieces like the potter's vessels'—as I also have
received from My Father; and I will give him the morning
star.

"He who has an ear, let him hear what the Spirit says
to the churches."'" — Revelation 2:18-29

We come now to the shocking letter to Thyatira. It gives valuable insight into the condition of the 1st Century Church.

And to the angel of the church in Thyatira write. As in each of these letters, the message is addressed to the angel ("messenger") of the church. See the notes about this, and how it probably means the pastor of the church, in Chapter 2, verse 1.

Thyatira was on the Roman road in a valley between Pergamum and Sardis alongside of the Lycus River. There are many suggestions about the meaning of the name, but Greek authorities say it is of "uncertain origin." We do know that it had older names, like Pelopidas and Semiramis.[10]

Semiramis is especially interesting because this was the name of the prototype goddess of the Babylonians, who was said to have been the wife of Ninus, another name for Nimrod, the Biblical character who was discussed earlier in our study of "Satan's throne" in Pergamum. See the notes on Chapter 2, verse 13. The ancient Babylonian religion, with its astrology, sorcery, and idolatry had been the source of most other major false mythologies and beliefs, and had transferred its leadership to the city of Pergamum, just a few miles Northwest of Thyatira.

Religious shrines in Thyatira included the temple of the ancient Lydian sun-god, Tyrimnos, and another one dedicated to Sambethe.[11] Inscriptions found there refer to many trade guilds, including bronze-smiths, wool and linen-workers, dyers, tanners, leather-workers, and others.[12]

Thyatira is mentioned in Revelation as one of the Seven Churches (Revelation Chapters 1 and 2), and once in the Book of Acts. It was the hometown of Lydia, a business woman in Philippi. She was the first recorded convert to Christianity in Europe:

Therefore, sailing from Troas, we ran a straight course to Samothrace, and the next day came to Neapolis, and from there to Philippi, which is the foremost city of that part of Macedonia, a colony. And we were staying in that city for some days. And on the Sabbath day we went out of the city to the riverside, where prayer was customarily made; and we sat down and spoke to the women who met there. Now a certain woman named Lydia heard us. She was a seller of purple from the city of Thyatira, who worshiped God. The Lord opened her heart to heed the things spoken by Paul. And when she and her household were baptized, she begged us, saying, "If you have judged me to be faithful to the Lord, come to my house and stay." So she persuaded us. – Acts 16:11-15

This letter is the longest of all the messages to the Seven Churches even though the church was the smallest of the seven. It was full of valuable information, not only about the condition of the local church at Thyatira in the 1st Century, but it was also prophetic of the fourth period of church history. It previews a long, morally dark phase of Christianity, from about the time of the fall of the Western Roman Empire in AD 476 until the time of the Reformation, which began in 1517. During this time unfortunate historical events, such as the inquisitions and the Crusades demonstrated the deepening lack of spirituality of the church. This period was also the time when indulgences were sold, making people believe they could pay money to have their sins removed. This led to the posting of Luther's 95 Theses on the door of the Wittenberg church and the beginning of the next period of church history, the Reformation.

Connection

"These things says the Son of God, who has eyes like a flame of fire, and His feet like fine brass." — Revelation 2:18b-d

Surprisingly, the description **Son of God** occurs only once in the entire Revelation! Jesus called himself "Son of Man" in Chapter 1, verse 13 (see the notes there). That title emphasized His humanity, his coming as a Kinsman-Redeemer, to redeem us from the penalty of our sin. But here he reminds the church that He is the very Son of God! He will come as the Righteous Judge to those who ignore His warnings.

These descriptions: ***Who has eyes like a flame of fire, and His feet like fine brass,*** are pictures of judgment. See notes on Chapter 1, verse 14. This is a valuable reminder, not only to the early church, but to the "politically correct" church of our own generation, that we are the Bride of Christ, and are to be kept pure for Him (Ephesians 5:25-27).

The apostle Paul confronted the Corinthian Christians, when they thought they were just being "tolerant," that they must excommunicate the flagrant sinner who was ruining their testimony (1 Corinthians 5:1-12).

Peter said this about the church maintaining its purity:

For the time has come for judgment to begin at the house of God; and if it begins with us first, what will be the end of those who do not obey the gospel of God? – 1 Peter 4:17

Jesus gave us the perfect formula for dealing with sin in the church.

"Moreover if your brother sins against you, go and tell him his fault between you and him alone. If he hears you, you have gained your brother. But if he will not hear, take with you one or two more, that 'by the mouth of two or three witnesses every word may be established.' And if he refuses to hear them, tell it to the church. But if he refuses even to hear the church, let him be to you like a heathen and a tax collector. – Matthew 18:15-17

Commendation

"I know your works, love, service, faith, and your patience; and as for your works, the last are more than the first". – Revelation 2:19

As has already been seen, the tone of this letter is pretty negative, but even this church at Thyatira received a mild commendation for doing some things right. The omniscient Son of God told them, *I know your works.* The New Testament is very clear that a person can be saved only by grace through faith in Jesus Christ, and that this salvation does not depend on good works (Ephesians 2:8-10). Those who are born again are redeemed by the precious blood of Jesus Christ (1 Peter 1:18-19).

At Thyatira, and in countless other churches during the past 2000 years, many members hoped that their good deeds would outweigh their bad deeds in the Day of Judgment. This is especially true where a culture of tolerance for immorality existed. Professing Christians who knew that their habits were not pure might try to compensate by doing good things. In His Sermon on the Mount Jesus gave a dreadful warning to those who try to act like Christians without knowing Him personally:

"Not everyone who says to Me, 'Lord, Lord,' shall enter the kingdom of heaven, but he who does the will of My Father in heaven. Many will say to Me in that day, 'Lord, Lord, have we not prophesied in Your name, cast out demons in Your name, and done many wonders in Your name?' And then I will declare to them, 'I never knew you; depart from Me, you who practice lawlessness!' – Matthew 7:21-23

On the other hand, in a church like Thyatira, where false teaching and immorality were taking their toll, there would naturally be some–or possibly many–who oppose the mistakes that were being made. Their good works would be true and acceptable offerings to the Lord to demonstrate their devotion to Him and their care for others. The point is, Jesus knew what they were doing, and He also knew their hearts. Let's look at these good works.

There are four words for **"love"** in the Greek language. C.S. Lewis showed that three of them belong to a category he called "Need-loves." They are based on our emotional need to receive affection from others. Lewis called the other category "Gift-love." This is God's love, a sacrificial love that comes from His very nature, and may be replicated by Christians because of their relationship with Him. He illustrated it this way:

> "Need-love says of a woman 'I cannot live without her'; Gift-love longs to give her happiness, comfort, protection–if possible, wealth."[13]

The three words in the "Need-love" category are: *storge*–"familial affection," *philos*–"friendship," and *eros*–"romantic love". The one word in the "Gift-love" category is *agape*. Jesus endowed this word with special meaning. It came from a common verb, *agapao*–"to love, to wish well". It was not used often as a noun, but He began to use it to express God's unconditional love:

> *For God so loved the world that He gave His only begotten Son, that whoever believes in Him should not perish but have everlasting life.* – John 3:16

Jesus taught that this was the kind of affection that we should display to others because of His work within us.

Beloved, if God so loved us, we also ought to love one another...
We love Him because He first loved us. – 1 John 4:11, 19

He gave us the "Great Commandment" to love God with all our being, and to love our neighbor as ourselves (Matthew 22:35-40). By doing so, we would automatically fulfill all of the requirements of the Law. He also elevated it to the highest virtue for His disciples by giving them a "New Commandment" to love one another as He had loved them (John 13:34-35).

The Greek word used for **service** is *diakonia*. This is also the basis for the biblical office of deacons. They were the special godly assistants to the apostles that were chosen in Acts, Chapter 6 to meet the needs of the widows and others in the church. Most churches have deacons to oversee this kind of ministry, but all Christians are expected to serve others (Matthew 20:25-28).

Faith is the same as "belief." It is essential for salvation (John 1:12; Hebrews 11:6). It is also the virtue that trusts God in the midst of trials (1 Corinthians 10:13; 1 Peter 1:6-9). Godly members of the church at Thyatira exercised this faith as they tried to be overcomers: standing against the false teaching and declining morality of the majority.

The fourth example of their good works is **your patience.** This word is also translated "perseverance," and "endurance." It was not easy for the godly remnant in this environment to stay true to God's Word and resist the evil changes that were taking place.

And as for your works, the last are more than the first. Jesus' summary of the faithfulness of the remnant was, that in spite of the increasing falsehood around them, they were the real thing, and they were more active than ever in standing for the truth.

Others in Thyatira, who were slipping into false teaching, might have also been doing more good works than ever in the false hope, as mentioned above, that they will be saved by their good deeds.

Complaint

Nevertheless I have a few things against you, because you allow that woman Jezebel, who calls herself a prophetess, to teach and seduce My servants to commit sexual immorality and eat things sacrificed to idols. – Revelation 2:20

Considering the Lord's encouraging words to the church at Thyatira in the previous verse, a visitor in those days might have thought that this was a great church. With all their good works, it probably was a beehive of activity, a place where people cared about each other; and maybe even a good place to enlarge one's network of helpful and influential people.

However, Jesus told them," *Nevertheless I have a few things against you.*" In the original Greek text the word for "few" or "a small amount," which was used in the message to the previous church, is missing. It could be translated, "Nevertheless I have things against you." This is a similar complaint, but is more serious here. The smaller problem that was brewing in Pergamum had actually become a big problem at Thyatira.

The weakness of this church was one of toleration: *because you allow* someone to teach falsehood and lead others into the practice of immorality. Remember that part of the commendation to the Ephesian church was that they did *not* tolerate false teachers masquerading as apostles. See the commentary on Chapter 2, verse 2. Jesus, of all people, was willing to associate with sinners and was criticized for doing so. But He spent time with them only to show them His love, help them find the truth, and teach them how to leave their sinful ways behind.

The meaning of "toleration" has changed during our lifetime. It originally meant acceptance of a person in spite of his or her beliefs and practices. Now, in the age of political correctness, it means accepting the notion that each person's beliefs and practices are of equal validity.

During the "Jesus People" revival in the 1970's, Calvary Chapel was tolerant about hippies' appearance and mannerisms, but not about their addictions and false ideas. They sincerely welcomed them into their services, and gave them the much-needed truth of the Gospel.

Satan always urges people to doubt the truth about Christ. Every church and every Christian can expect to be tempted, often by false teachers or immoral friends, to not be "so narrow" in their thinking. Godly young people are often bullied by their peers for being "too holy," and are not included among the popular crowd. Christian business people might be driven out of the competition in their field by others who don't have the same high view of ethics.

When false teachers appear and tell believers that it is acceptable to mix worldly values with their Christian beliefs, there are always some folks who are glad to have the excuse to concoct their own religion. We can relate to this in our generation because of the moral issues we face. Many Christians have decided that abortion and homosexuality are compatible with Christianity. They might know that the Bible says otherwise, but to them, that is no longer the deciding factor.

Our young people are being told that all belief systems are equal, and it doesn't matter what they believe as long as they are sincere. Each person who adopts this ridiculous philosophy has to reject Jesus' bold statement that He is the way, the truth, and the life, and that no one can come to the Father except through Him (John 14:6).

Once people have bought into this false teaching they think they can design their own belief system and no one can say it is right or wrong. Then, if they believe in a god at all, he conforms to what they want to believe. They will say things like, "My god would never allow anyone to go to hell." "My god would want a gay couple to be married if they want, because love is from God."

God has given us His Word and the help of the Holy Spirit to discern what is true. We need to be like the Bereans, about whom Paul said,

These were more fair-minded than those in Thessalonica, in that they received the word with all readiness, and searched the Scriptures daily to find out whether these things were so. – Acts 17: 11

Jesus identified the source of false teaching. He called her **"that woman."** He also names her, but the expression "that woman" indicates that she was very well known by the entire congregation in Thyatira.

Jesus called her **Jezebel.** This was the name of an Old Testament queen who was an incredibly wicked person. She was the wife of King Ahab, who also was exceptionally evil:

> *Now Ahab the son of Omri did evil in the sight of the LORD, more than all who were before him. And it came to pass, as though it had been a trivial thing for him to walk in the sins of Jeroboam the son of Nebat, that he took as wife Jezebel the daughter of Ethbaal, king of the Sidonians; and he went and served Baal and worshiped him.* – 1 Kings 16:30-31

Jezebel was responsible for introducing Israel to the worship of Baal. During her reign the prophet Elijah was directed by God to call for a show-down between Baal and Jehovah. This fascinating story is found in 1 Kings 18. The 450 prophets of Baal were not able to get a response from their false god, but when Elijah called on the Lord, He sent a fire from heaven to consume the offering on Mt. Carmel. After this event Elijah killed all the false prophets.

Enraged, the evil Jezebel sought to capture and kill Elijah, but God protected him. It was prophesied that Jezebel would die a horrible death and be eaten by dogs. This prophecy was fulfilled exactly as given (1 Kings Chapters 19 through 21 and 2 Kings 9).

According to the 1990 U.S. Census, women are almost never named Jezebel and it is an equally uncommon last name. It seems unlikely that Jezebel was the actual name of the false prophetess in Thyatira. This name is symbolic of immorality and idolatry. But Jesus gave her the hateful name because of what she was doing to His church! Just as Jesus had renamed Simon, calling him "Peter" or "rock" to symbolize the strong character he would develop, Jesus gave this woman the most derogatory name possible to symbolize her evil role and perhaps her destiny.

It is significant that the antagonist in this story is a woman because of the prominence of goddesses in all of the pagan systems of mythology, all the way from Semiramis in the Babylonian system to Venus in the Roman panoply of gods. Semiramis was mentioned above as one of the earlier names of the city of Thyatira. Her story gave rise to the Sumerian goddess Asherah and Ishtar, the Babylonian goddess of fertility. In Egypt she was known as Isis, In Greece she inspired the creation of Aphrodite and Artemis, and in Rome, she became Venus and Diana.

In our culture goddess worship is a growing concept, especially in Wicca and the occult, New Age teaching, and environmentalism.

The ultimate expression of this goddess imagery will be considered in the 17th chapter of Revelation where an adulterous woman is sitting on the scarlet beast. This is symbolic of the final evil empire during the Tribulation period (Revelation Chapters 13 to 18).

Jesus depicted the Jezebel of Thyatira as she *"who calls herself a prophetess."*

Some commentators think that she was the local pagan seer who served at the shrine of the Sybil Sambethe, just outside the city walls. Sybil was Greek for "prophetess." There were numerous shrines of this sort all over the Roman Empire, and The Greek Empire that preceded it. A PBS documentary described the most famous of these, the Oracle of Delphi in Greece:

> People came from all over Greece and beyond to have their questions about the future answered by the Pythia, the priestess of Apollo. And her answers, usually cryptic, could determine the course of everything from when a farmer planted his seedlings, to when an empire declared war.[14]

It is likely that this woman was a professing Christian and a part of the local church at Thyatira. There were legitimate prophetesses in the New Testament. Phillip's four daughters served the church in that way (Acts 21:8-9). The fact that she "called herself" a prophetess is an indication that she did not deserve the title, but just appropriated it to herself, and by her forceful personality gained the attention of many in the church.

Bible prophecy is the only kind of revelation that has a perfect record of fulfillment. These prophecies are from God, who knows everything about the future. This Book of Revelation is a perfect example of this most-trustworthy type of prophecy.

There is a *gift of prophecy* according to the Bible. It is described in 1 Corinthians Chapters 12 and 14. It is the God-given ability to know certain things supernaturally, but it is to be used according to strict rules, including

THE CHURCH IN PROPHECY AND HISTORY

the approval of other people who have the same gift. Such prophecies are produced by the power of the Holy Spirit, but they are not considered "the Word of God" in the same way the Scriptures are. One example of this was the prophecy about the apostle Paul, not to go to Jerusalem or he would end up a prisoner in Rome (Acts 21:11-12). It was fulfilled, but not in the exact way Paul's friends had pictured it (Acts 21:30-33).

Some Christian prognosticators (like Nostradamus and St. Malachy) might or might not have had the gift of prophecy.

Other religions sometimes have prophecies too, but they don't have a good record of fulfillment, except in the case they were borrowed from the Bible (like many Islamic prophecies).

There are also *many other kinds of prophecies:* palm-reading, astrology (horoscopes), psychics (like Benjamin Crème), and occultic and New Age channelers (like Alice Baily and Edgar Casey). These are either the result of careful analysis and future projections, or they are messages from evil spirits. Demons cannot actually predict the future, but they have knowledge that a normal human would not have.

The Lord Jesus described what this prophetess did in this way: ***to teach and seduce My servants.*** Teaching is the primary way that biblical knowledge is passed on (2 Timothy 2:2). The Greek word for "teach" is used 220 times in the New Testament, mostly for instruction about the Scriptures: God's written Word. Teaching the truth is a wonderful thing. But teaching what is false is the worst kind of evil:

> *"But whoever causes one of these little ones who believe in Me to stumble, it would be better for him if a millstone were hung around his neck, and he were thrown into the sea.* – Mark 9:42

False teaching is often a mixture of the truth with wrong application. In the case of Jezebel, the fruit of her teaching led to immorality and spiritual unfaithfulness.

There is a prohibition in the New Testament against women teaching men (1 Timothy 2:12), but in many cases they taught other women and children more effectively than the men would have.

Jesus also accused this prophetess of seducing His servants. The Greek word translated seduce here is *plano,* which has the meaning "to lead astray." This suggests that any effort to mislead people is a type of seduction. But in this situation Jesus' followers were not only led into spiritual unfaithfulness, they were also enticed **to commit sexual immorality.**

The word for sexual immorality is the Greek *porneuo*, which means "to commit fornication." It is derived from the word *pernao*--"to sell off," meaning, in this context, the surrendering of sexual purity.

Most people in Thyatira belonged to one of the trade guilds. They were like our labor unions, but in their pagan meetings, members were expected to engage in immoral revelry to their patron god or goddess.

The prophetess might have been teaching that it is acceptable for Christians to compromise with the world system, in order to keep their status in their profession. In the process they would have to lead a double life.

Moral leniency had been an issue in the Corinthian church decades before this time. In 1 Corinthians 6:12-20 the apostle Paul had written very pointedly about a sexual problem there. He taught that true Christians should avoid immorality and consider their bodies to be temples of the Holy Spirit.

In addition to sexual immorality, these weak Christians of Thyatira were guilty of eating **things sacrificed to idols.**

This did not necessarily mean eating food that had been offered to idols and then sold in the marketplace. The apostle Paul discussed this matter in 1 Corinthians 8. In pagan religions more animals were sacrificed than could be used in their ceremonies and support of their priesthood, so the extra meat was sold at a discount in public markets. Paul said that it was not intrinsically sinful to eat meat that was offered to an idol since a grounded Christian would know that there was no real god behind the idol. However, he said that if eating it would cause a weaker Christian to stumble—because he didn't yet understand that there is only one true God— he would not eat it either.

In the case of the Christians at Thyatira there was a different reason not to eat this sacrificial meat. In the context of this story about Jezebel, to do so would be to participate in the immoral rituals of their false worship. Earlier it was seen that the church at Pergamum had the same problem (see Chapter 2, verse 14).

Historical Fulfillment (Middle Ages)

These issues were actually prophetic about the fourth period of church History--from about 476, the fall of the Western Roman Empire, until 1517, the beginning of the Protestant Reformation.

First, review the complaint that Jesus had against the church at Thyatira:

Nevertheless I have a few things against you, because you allow that woman Jezebel, who calls herself a prophetess, to teach and seduce My servants to commit sexual immorality and eat things sacrificed to idols. – Revelation 2:20

This criticism was appropriate for the church in the Middle Ages. Honest consideration must be given to the mistakes that were made, one generation after another, that gradually corrupted Christianity. Let us enter this discussion prayerfully, and ask the Holy Spirit to guide our thoughts.

There are two opposite ways of looking at this period. We can always try to find the good in every situation. Or we can usually discover something that is bad. If one could know the whole truth, he could see an element of both good and evil in most events. God and Satan are engaged in spiritual warfare constantly (Ephesians 6:10-20), and there is no doubt that the Lord will win in the end (John 12:31; 16:8-11; Revelation 20:1-10). There are times when goodness obviously prevails, as in the era of the Great Awakening in America's early colonies. Sadly, there are times when malice rules the day, as at the height of the Holocaust during World War II. In that example, the prejudice and cruelty stand out as a horrific reminder of man's depravity, but at the same time, compassion and self-sacrifice emerge in stories of heroes like Corrie ten Boom and Oskar Schindler, who risked their own lives to save a few of God's Chosen People.

In His message to the church at Thyatira, the Lord first mentioned their good works: their love, service, faith, and patience (v. 19 above). But then He exposes the serious mistakes they were making. The same thing can be said about the church's history during the Middle Ages, also known as the Medieval Period. This era covered approximately 1000 years, from the fall of the Western Roman Empire in 476 to the beginning of the Reformation in 1517.

The church's story during these centuries is full of errors, false teaching, and even immorality. But at the same time there are countless accounts of individuals and groups within the church who were brilliant, incredibly devout, and true to the teaching of the Bible. Let us keep in mind that the long list of detours made during this time weakened, the True Church but did not destroy it (1 Corinthians 12:12-26 ; Colossians 1:17-20) because Jesus, the Head of the Church, controlled those who were faithful to Him. He had promised, "I will build My church, and the gates of Hades shall not prevail against it" (Matthew 16:18). Just as it was in the church at Thyatira, there is always a remnant of faithful believers. We study their writings, celebrate their evangelistic efforts, and applaud their charitable work. As the original church morphed into the "Roman Catholic Church" some of these heroes stayed behind in other branches of the Early Church, such as the Coptic Church or the Assyrian Church of the East. Others stayed in the Catholic tradition and did their best to remain faithful in spite of the changes. At the end of this era, reformers like Martin Luther and John Calvin started new denominations to jettison some of the grievous concepts that had been adopted by the Catholics.

The shocking story of Jezebel, the false prophetess at Thyatira, is a preview of the changes that would affect the church during this fourth period of church history. The major issues will be listed here, but even in brief summaries, this will be a long section. It is all very important though, in terms of what happened to the church during the Middle Ages and the Dark Ages, and what might happen to it during the Tribulation Period.

Major Changes in the Church before the Middle Ages Began

Priesthood, Confessional, Calling Priests "Father"

During the 2nd Century some of the Early Church Fathers began to teach that bishops ("overseers" from the Greek *episkopos*) could function in a priestly role. They took upon themselves the authority to grant forgiveness of sins to those who repent and confess their failures. This is a clear example of the "doctrine of the Nicolaitans" that was studied above under the message to the church at Pergamum. Those who wanted to ascend above the laity in the church were beginning to add importance to their role by adopting priestly functions that were not meant to be a part of Christianity.

How do we know the church did not need an ordained priesthood? Priests were a very important part of the Old Testament sacrificial system. And that system was always a preview of the complete sacrifice of the Lord Jesus for our sins.

When Jesus died on the Cross, one of the amazing events that accompanied His death was the tearing of the curtain to the Holy of Holies in the Temple?

> *Then the sun was darkened, and the veil of the temple was torn in two. And when Jesus had cried out with a loud voice, He said, "Father, 'into Your hands I commit My spirit.'" Having said this, He breathed His last.* – Luke 23:45-46

This was proof that we would no longer need a priest to offer prayers or sacrifices for our sins. This was explained by the writer of the Book of Hebrews:

> *For Christ has not entered the holy places made with hands, which are copies of the true, but into heaven itself, now to appear in the presence of God for us; not that He should offer Himself often, as the high priest enters the Most Holy Place every year with blood of another— He then would have had to suffer often since the foundation of the world; but now, once at the end of the ages, He has appeared to put away sin by the sacrifice of Himself. And as it is appointed for men to die once, but after this the judgment, so Christ was offered once to bear the sins of many. To those who eagerly wait for Him He will appear a second time, apart from sin, for salvation.* – Hebrews 9:24-28

> *By that will we have been sanctified through the offering of the body of Jesus Christ once for all.*
> *And every priest stands ministering daily and offering repeatedly the same sacrifices, which can never take away sins. But this Man, after He had offered one sacrifice for sins forever, sat down at the right hand of God, from*

that time waiting till His enemies are made His footstool. For by one offering He has perfected forever those who are being sanctified. – Hebrews 10:10-14

Another thing the Old Testament priests did was to offer prayers for the people. The priest was the mediator between the people and God. But that is no longer necessary, because, as Paul explained to Timothy,

For there is one God and one Mediator between God and men, the Man Christ Jesus. – 1 Timothy 2:5

Raymond E. Brown, a Roman Catholic scholar admitted,

"When we move from the Old Testament to the New Testament, it is striking that while there are pagan priests and Jewish priests on the scene, no individual Christian is ever specifically identified as a priest. The Epistle to the Hebrews speaks of the high priesthood of Jesus by comparing his death and entry into heaven with the actions of the Jewish high priest who went into the Holy of Holies in the Tabernacle once a year with a offering for himself and for the sins of his people (Hebrews 9:6-7).

"But it is noteworthy that the author of Hebrews does not associate the priesthood of Jesus with the Eucharist or the Last Supper; neither does he suggest that other Christians are priests in the likeness of Jesus. In fact, the once-for-all atmosphere that surrounds the priesthood of Jesus in Hebrews 10:12-14, has been offered as an explanation of why there are no Christian priests in the New Testament period."[15]

Under Jesus' New Covenant every believer has the privilege of praying to the Father through the Son. That is why we are told that all Christians are part of a holy priesthood:

But you are a chosen generation, a royal priesthood, a holy nation, His own special people, that you may proclaim the praises of Him who called you out of darkness into His marvelous light. -- 1 Peter 2:9

"And have made us kings and priests to our God;
And we shall reign on the earth." – Revelation 5:10

There is one more important consideration about a priesthood in the church. It is normal for those who depend on priests to call them "Father." This is not right either. Jesus said,

> *Do not call anyone on earth your father; for One is your Father, He who is in heaven.* – Matthew 23:9

Infant baptism

In the 3rd Century some church leaders started baptizing little children:

> "And they shall baptize the little children first. And if they can answer for themselves, let them answer. But if they cannot, let their parents answer or someone from their family."[16]

There is no example in the Bible of an infant being baptized. Baptism was meant to be the sign of one's acceptance of Christ—a picture of being buried with Christ and raised again to newness of life (Acts 2:38, 41; Romans 6:1-14).

Infant baptism was undoubtedly done as a preventative measure in case a child might die before he had the opportunity to know Christ. However, King David was surely right when he assumed that God would receive an infant in heaven. When his own newborn boy died, he said,

> *But now he is dead, wherefore should I fast? Can I bring him back again? I shall go to him, but he shall not return to me.* -- 2 Samuel 12

Theologians often speak of an "age of accountability," This is not a biblical expression, but it is based on God's attributes. It is akin to Abraham's question, "Shall not the Judge of all the earth do right?" – Genesis 18:25

The biggest problem with infant baptism is that the child doesn't choose to believe, but he might assume that he is in a right relationship with God just because he was baptized, even if he never accepts Christ as his own personal Savior.

Later (in 418) infant baptism was normalized by the Council of Carthage.[17]

There are a few other important changes that the church experienced just before the beginning of the Middle Ages. From the time of the conversion of Emperor Constantine in 312 until the fall of the Western Roman Empire in 476 several new developments took clerics further away from the practices of the New Testament Church.

It also should be remembered that during this time--and indeed during every epoch of church history--there was always a remnant who were not led astray by false teaching. Defenders of the faith in every generation reminded the hierarchy what the Bible taught, and often warned of the perils of adopting non-biblical beliefs and practices.

However, slowly but surely, the church became ever more encumbered with false ideas.

Compromise with the World

In the letter to the previous church–Pergamum–the influence of other religions and cultures was beginning to be a problem. Jesus warned this next church–Thyatira–that this worldliness had gained a serious foothold. It began, as we explained above (see Chapter 2, verses 14 and 15), when Constantine became a Christian (AD 312) and made Christianity legal (AD 313). Then the floodgates of church membership were opened to a multitude of people who didn't really understand the Gospel, and brought aspects of their own pagan religions and immoral practices into the mix. John had warned of this very thing:

> *Do not love the world or the things in the world. If anyone loves the world, the love of the Father is not in him. For all that is in the world—the lust of the flesh, the lust of the eyes, and the pride of life—is not of the Father but is of the world. And the world is passing away, and the lust of it; but he who does the will of God abides forever. – 1 John 2:15-17*

Salvation by Works

The Gospel is clear that salvation from sin is based only on the sacrificial death of Christ in our place (John 3:16; Romans 5:6-11), and the acceptance of that fact by an individual (John 1:12; Romans 10:9-10). It is a free gift from God ("by grace, through faith") and is definitely "not of works" (Ephesians 2:8-9; Titus 3:5), although it should result in a life of good deeds (Romans 3:19-24; Ephesians 2:10; Titus 3:8). Perhaps this "Amazing Grace" was misunderstood by the new converts of this era because they were basically ignorant of the content of God's Word. Many people in our own biblically illiterate generation make the same mistake. They live like the world does, since they are saved "by grace."

Whatever the reason, many in the church began to teach a religion of good works. The apostle Paul actually had to deal with this same problem hundreds of years earlier. When he wrote to the believers in Galatia, he said,

> *I marvel that you are turning away so soon from Him who called you in the grace of Christ, to a different gospel, which is not another; but there are some who trouble you and want to pervert the gospel of Christ. But even if we, or an angel from heaven, preach any other gospel to you than what we have preached to you, let him be accursed.* – Galatians 1:6-8

And Paul clarified that they could never pay for their sins by their good works:

> *Knowing that a man is not justified by the works of the law but by faith in Jesus Christ, even we have believed in Christ Jesus, that we might be justified by faith in Christ and not by the works of the law; for by the works of the law no flesh shall be justified.* – Galatians 2:16

Those who teach salvation by works cannot offer any assurance that a person who knows the Lord will have eternal life. Here is a modern explanation by a Catholic apologist:

"Scripture teaches that one's final salvation depends on the state of the soul at death. As Jesus himself tells us, "He who endures to the end will be saved" (Matt. 24:13; cf. 25:31–46). One who dies in the state of friendship with God (the state of grace) will go to heaven. The one who dies in a state of enmity and rebellion against God (the state of mortal sin) will go to hell."[18]

The Bible teaches us to examine ourselves to see if we are really true believers (1 Corinthians 11:27-28). And it warns those who are just going through the motions that they will be rejected because Jesus says, "I never knew you" (Matthew 7:21-23). However, those who are born-again by receiving Christ as their personal Savior and Lord (John 3:3; Revelation 3:20) receive eternal life. How could salvation be eternal if it could be taken away?

> *And this is the testimony: that God has given us eternal life, and this life is in His Son. He who has the Son has life; he who does not have the Son of God does not have life. These things I have written to you who believe in the name of the Son of God, that you may know that you have eternal life, and that you may continue to believe in the name of the Son of God. – 1 John 5:11-13*

As we have already seen, at the end of each of these letters to the Seven Churches there is a promise for those who overcome to the end. According to 1 John 5:4-5, every true believer will be an overcomer.

The Eucharist – Continual Sacrifice / Christ on the Cross

The one thing that Jesus taught His disciples to do on a regular basis was to commemorate His death for them by a simple ceremony of eating of bread, symbolizing the sacrifice of His body, and drinking of the fruit of the vine, as a reminder that His blood was shed for them (Matthew 26:26-27; Mark 14:22-23; Luke 22:18-20; 1 Corinthians 11: 22-25). This was done at the Last Supper, which was actually a Passover meal. Jesus' death on the Cross became "our Passover" sacrifice (1 Corinthians 5:7). It was called "communion" in 1 Corinthians 10:15-17; "The Lord's Supper" in 1 Corinthians 11:17-22; and "Love Feast" in Jude 1:12.

From the beginning of the church, true believers have been faithful to observe this central practice because it is the much-needed reminder that the core of our belief system is that Jesus died for our sins (Romans 5:6-9; 1 Corinthians 15:3-4). Thankfully, even today, this is the great common denominator of the church from one end of the globe to the other. Though there are countless differences in the way people conduct their worship services, they all include this "communion" in their practices on a regular basis.

In the 2nd Century some theologians began to call it "The Eucharist." This expression was taken from the Greek word *eucharistia*, meaning "thankfulness" or "gratitude." This grew out of the fact that Jesus gave thanks for the bread and the cup at the Last Supper (Matthew 26:27; Luke 22:19). And, in view of Jesus' sacrifice for us, the writer of Hebrews wrote:

> *Therefore by Him let us continually offer the sacrifice of praise to God, that is, the fruit of our lips, giving thanks to His name.* – Hebrews 13:15 (Read Hebrews 13:10-16)

The Lord's Supper therefore became known as a "sacrifice of praise" in response to Jesus' own surrender of His life. The idea gradually crept in that the purpose of communion was to actually sacrifice Christ over and over. This was probably the result of the many "converts" to Christianity whose former pagan worship involved sacrifices. Church leaders should have resisted this change because of the passages we quoted earlier about Jesus' finished work:

> *Not that He should offer Himself often, as the high priest enters the Most Holy Place every year with blood of another--He then would have had to suffer often since the foundation of the world; but now, once at the end of the ages, He has appeared to put away sin by the sacrifice of Himself.* – Hebrews 9:25-26

> *For by one offering He has perfected forever those who are being sanctified.* – Hebrews 10:14

This was the beginning of a major change in thinking about the death of Christ that would eventually become one of the reasons for the Protestant Reformation. It also explains the origin of The Crucifix, a cross with the image of Christ still on it.

The Cross was always a vital symbol to Christians, but during the first three centuries, while they were being persecuted for their beliefs, they were cautious as to how and where they would use this sacred symbol. Once Christianity became legal, the Cross was used to adorn their churches but it was an empty Cross since the Savior had been raised from the dead!

According to the Catholic Encyclopedia, the Crucifix emerged much later:

> But from the 6th Century onward we find many images—not allegorical, but historical and realistic of the crucified Saviour.[19]

Integration of Church and State

In AD 380 Emperor Theodosius I issued an edict that made Catholic Christianity the state religion of the Roman Empire. This is when the church began to be called "The Catholic Church." The word "catholic" means "universal," and was often used in the writings of early scholars, just as modern teachers use it to refer to the "universal church," meaning the whole body of Christ. This universal church is comprised of true believers from every denomination.

As we pointed out in the previous section, the Message to the church at Pergamum, it was shortly after this that Damascus, the Bishop of Rome, assumed the old pagan title "Pontifex Maximus" (see Chapter 2, verse 15).

Christianity was delivered from its earlier persecution by the favor of the Roman Empire, but it was weakened morally by the blending of its pure Christian doctrine with pagan cultures.

Augustine's *The City of God*, written about a century later, made the case that that the *City of Man* and the *City of God* have both been instituted by God. The City of Man, secular government, might seem ungodly, but it has been placed on Earth for the protection of the City of God.

According to *The History of the Decline and Fall of the Roman Empire*, written by English historian Edward Gibbon, this alliance of church and state was part of the cause of the decline of Rome as well.

Celibacy of the Clergy

Another development during this period of time was the normalization of celibacy for the clergy. According to the New Testament it was permissible to take this position (Matthew 19:12; 1 Corinthians 7:1-7), but not required, or even considered the norm (1 Corinthians 9:5; 1 Timothy 3:1-7; Titus 1:6).

In AD 385 Siricius, Bishop of Rome, decreed that priests should stop cohabitating with their wives. He wrote, "We have indeed discovered that many priests and deacons of Christ brought children into the world, either through union with their wives or through shameful intercourse. And they used as an excuse the fact that in the Old Testament—as we can read—priests and ministers were permitted to beget children."[20]

This rule became a universal mandate in AD 1139 at the Second Lateran Council. Considering all of the immorality this unscriptural regulation has caused, including several grievous pedophilia scandals in our own generation, it causes one to wonder where such ideas originate. The apostle Paul anticipated these extreme demands when he wrote:

> *Now the Spirit expressly says that in latter times some will depart from the faith, giving heed to deceiving spirits and doctrines of demons, speaking lies in hypocrisy, having their own conscience seared with a hot iron, forbidding to marry, and commanding to abstain from foods which God created to be received with thanksgiving by those who believe and know the truth.* – 1 Timothy 4:1-3

Veneration of Mary

It is no wonder that Christians hold Mary, the mother of Jesus, in the highest of regard. The Bible tells us that she was a most virtuous person who was "blessed among women" (Luke 1:28). She loved the Lord and depended on Him to save her (Luke 1:46-47), was receptive to the Angel Gabriel, and obedient to his message (Luke 2:26-38), remained a virgin while bearing the Son of God (Isaiah 7:14; Luke 1:27, 35-37), literally followed Jesus during much of His ministry (John 2:1-5, 12; Matthew 12:46-47), and stayed with Him during His crucifixion (John 19:25-27).

As a pastor, I have often taught about Mary's virtues. She was a godly woman, matchless mother, and wonderful example of Christian virtue. She was a sterling example of what a Christian woman and mother should be. It is proper for us to honor her and to seek to emulate her virtues.

However, some leaders in the church began to make a serious mistake by beginning to venerate her and ascribe to her positions and attributes that are completely non-biblical. This attitude apparently began in the late 4th Century with the teachings of St. Ambrose and St. Jerome. In those days there was general agreement among Christians that Mary and the martyrs (including the apostles) were saints. Soon after the year 400, bishops began to determine who should be called a saint, and by about 1100, the pope had become the only one who could make this decision.

Actually, according to the Bible, all true believers in Christ are saints in the sense of the basic meaning of the Greek word used (*hagiois*--"holy, sanctified, or set apart"). This can be seen especially in Paul's greetings in the epistles he wrote. Even when addressing the Corinthians, who had severe problems with unity, discipline, and even behavior at the Lord's Supper, he wrote:

> *To the church of God which is at Corinth, to **those who are sanctified in Christ Jesus, called to be saints**, with all who in every place call on the name of Jesus Christ our Lord, both theirs and ours:*--1 Corinthians 1:2

In AD 431, at the Third Ecumenical Council, also known as the Council of Ephesus, the primary issue was the nature of Christ, and it was affirmed that He was both God and man. The discussion moved to His mother Mary and the question whether or not that made her the "Mother of God." It was decided that this was a proper title for her. Thus they assigned to her the Greek word *theotokos*–"God-bearer."

Churches began to be dedicated to Mary during the fifth and sixth centuries. In a popular poem in the 7th Century she was called the "Queen of Heaven" (*Regina Coeli* in Latin). At this point a serious alarm sounds to

Bible scholars because Jeremiah the prophet wrote that the queen of heaven was an evil idolatrous figure:

> *Do you not see what they do in the cities of Judah and in the streets of Jerusalem? The children gather wood, the fathers kindle the fire, and the women knead dough, to make cakes for the **queen of heaven**; and they pour out drink offerings to other gods, that they may provoke Me to anger.* – Jeremiah 7:17-18

> *Then all the men who knew that their wives had burned incense to other gods, with all the women who stood by, a great multitude, and all the people who dwelt in the land of Egypt, in Pathros, answered Jeremiah, saying: "As for the word that you have spoken to us in the name of the LORD, we will not listen to you! But we will certainly do whatever has gone out of our own mouth, to burn incense to the **queen of heaven** and pour out drink offerings to her, as we have done, we and our fathers, our kings and our princes, in the cities of Judah and in the streets of Jerusalem. For then we had plenty of food, were well-off, and saw no trouble. But since we stopped burning incense to the **queen of heaven** and pouring out drink offerings to her, we have lacked everything and have been consumed by the sword and by famine."* – Jeremiah 44:15-18

It is most likely that Jeremiah was referring to the idolatrous Sumerian goddess Asherah. Earlier in our commentary we mentioned Semiramis, from the time of Nimrod, whose story was transplanted from culture to culture as mother-goddess. In these different settings she was known by various names. She was also called the "Queen of Heaven." This is a most-unfortunate name for the mother of Our Lord Jesus.

The seeds of false teaching had been sown in the centuries between Constantine and the fall of the Western Roman Empire. Greater errors would take root in the church during the Middle Ages. Jesus had warned the Thyatirans that their "Jezebel" was leading them into immorality and idolatry. The activities of the church during the next Millennium would fulfill these sobering prophecies.

More non-biblical teaching would emerge about Mary in the future. Statues and icons of her and other saints would be destroyed by the Eastern branch of the church (AD 726-842). The "Hail Mary" prayer would become a popular ritual (AD 1050). The doctrine of the perpetual virginity of Mary would be accepted (12th Century). Ritual use of the Rosary would become prevalent (AD 1659). Officials would teach the doctrine of the "Immaculate Conception" (AD 1854)--that she was born without sin and preserved that way, and the doctrine of the "Assumption of Mary" (1950) – that she ascended into heaven like Jesus did. Many church leaders would teach that Mary was a "Mediatrix" and even a "Co-Redemptrix."

"Pontifex Maximus" and the Papacy

We have already discussed these digressions from biblical truth in the notes about the church at Pergamum (see Chapter 2, verse 15), but to put them in chronological order, we need to recall two of the most important developments of all: the assumption of the old Babylonian office of "Pontifex Maximus" (meaning "greatest high priest") by Damascus I, the Bishop of Rome in AD 382, and the beginning of the use of "Pope" in AD 445 to designate the Bishop of Rome as the official head of the church.

Pontifex Maximus is a Latin title, but it was used to describe the succession of pagan priests from Babylon, where all false religion began after the Flood of Noah's time, to Pergamum, where Satan's throne was, and to Julius Caesar and the Roman Emperors who would follow him. During the reign of Gratian (AD 375-383) the title was discarded by the Emperor, who considered it no longer appropriate. However, it was accepted about AD 382 by Damascus I, and passed on to all future Bishops of Rome (later called Popes). This opened the door for sorcery, idolatry, and all the other perversions of paganism.

Then, in AD 445 Emperor Valentinian III issued a decree applying the description "Pope" ("Papa") to the office of the Bishop of Rome. Leo I therefore became the first official Pope of the church. Catholics consider all the Bishops of Rome to have been Popes, going all the way back to Peter, but there are several problems with this claim.

First, there is no biblical or convincing extra-biblical evidence that Peter even visited Rome, much less became Bishop there.

Secondly, Peter did not consider himself head of the church. However, it is true that he was the natural leader of the apostles, and as such was given the "keys of the kingdom," which turned out to be the privilege of preaching the Gospel and being present when the Holy Spirit was first given to believers in Jerusalem, to those in Judea and Samaria, and to the Gentiles (Matthew 16:19: Acts 1:8; Acts 2:14-41; Acts 8:14-17, 25; Acts 10:1-46).

Catholics believe that what Jesus told Peter after his "Great Confession" is a prediction that Peter would be the foundation of the church:

> *He said to them, "But who do you say that I am?"*
> *Simon Peter answered and said, "You are the Christ, the Son of the living God."*
> *Jesus answered and said to him, "Blessed are you, Simon Bar-Jonah, for flesh and blood has not revealed this to you, but My Father who is in heaven. And I also say to you that you are Peter, and on this rock I will build My church, and the gates of Hades shall not prevail against it.* – Matthew 16:15-18

Jesus said "You are Peter." "Peter" (masculine Greek *petros*) was the word for a stone, or rock. Jesus had given him that name when he first called him to be His disciple (John 1:41-42). But the word for the rock upon which Jesus would build His church was a different word (feminine Greek *petra*) meaning a "fixed rock, ledge or shelf of rock." This is the description of a firm foundation. Peter explained his own understanding of this concept in his first epistle:

> *Coming to Him as to a living stone, rejected indeed by men, but chosen by God and precious, you also, as living stones, are being built up a spiritual house, a holy priesthood, to offer up spiritual sacrifices acceptable to God through Jesus Christ. Therefore it is also contained in the Scripture,*
> *"Behold, I lay in Zion*
> *A chief cornerstone, elect, precious,*
> *And he who believes on Him will by no means be put to shame."*– 1 Peter 2:4-6

According to Peter, Jesus is the chief cornerstone, the foundation upon which the church is built, and all of us, including Peter, are "living stones" as part of the spiritual building. Note also that he designates all believers as part of a "holy priesthood."

Paul agreed with Peter's interpretation about the rock, and he clearly taught that Jesus was the head of the church:

> *For no other foundation can anyone lay than that which is laid, which is Jesus Christ.* – 1 Corinthians 3:11

> *For the husband is head of the wife, as also Christ is head of the church; and He is the Savior of the body.* – Ephesians 5:23 also: Ephesians 4:15; Colossians 2:19

Thirdly, Peter taught Christian leaders not to "lord it over" other believers. They should be faithful shepherds, but Jesus is the Chief Shepherd:

> *The elders who are among you I exhort, I who am a fellow elder and a witness of the sufferings of Christ, and also a partaker of the glory that will be revealed: Shepherd the flock of God which is among you, serving as overseers, not by compulsion but willingly, not for dishonest gain but eagerly; nor as being lords over those entrusted to you, but being examples to the flock; and when the Chief Shepherd appears, you will receive the crown of glory that does not fade away.* – 1 Peter 5:1-4

And finally, the concept of "Papa," like the earlier mistake of calling priests "father," is precluded by Jesus' warning not to call mere men "father" because we have one Father, who is in heaven (Matthew 23:9).

Major Changes in the Church during the Middle Ages

At this point we will begin a brief list of major developments in the church from the fall of the Western Roman Empire in AD 476 to the Protestant Reformation in AD 1517. Please notice as we proceed, what we plainly said before, that we should not be against Catholics, but we should oppose false doctrine--whatever is contrary to the teaching of the Bible--wherever it emerges.

During these years there were many devout leaders, teachers, and disciples of the Lord. Like the church at Thyatira, they were often known for their good works. But this long stretch of history--more than a thousand years--was a time of many problems for the church, and too many negative developments in their leadership, theology and practice.

The Mass / Sacrifice of the Mass

The terminology for the Lord's Supper changed from time to time. As we explained above, it was called the Eucharist ("thanksgiving") from about the 2nd Century, and the idea began to grow that communion was not just a remembrance of Jesus's sacrificial death but that it was actually a reenactment of His sacrifice each time it is observed. We also documented that this concept is contrary to the Bible's teaching about the finished work of Christ (Hebrews 9:25-26; Hebrews 10:14).

According to the Catholic Encyclopedia, the word *Mass* (*missa*) first established itself as the general designation for the Eucharistic Sacrifice in the West after the time of Pope Gregory the Great (d. 604), the early Church having used the expression the "breaking of bread."[21]

The Latin word *missa* means "dismissal." After prayers and the Sacrifice of Christ, the priest says *"Ite, missa est,"* thus dismissing the worshippers. Images of Christ on the cross became popular during the early days of observing the Mass. However, the belief in "transubstantiation"--that the priests were given the power to literally change the elements into the body and blood of Christ--was declared much later, at the Fourth Lateran Council in AD 1215.[22]

The Rise of Islam

Another major issue to develop during this time was the birth of Muhammad in AD 570 and the rise of Islam, starting about AD 610. This new religion was a mixture of Old and New Testament history and teaching with the already existing worship of Allah, the local Moon god in the Arabian Peninsula. Islam emerged as a third major monotheistic religion, declaring Allah the one true god, and trying to equate him to Jehovah. This was never believable since the God of the Bible gave His only begotten son to save mankind (John 3:16), while Muslims emphatically denied that Allah had a son. Allah was not seen as a loving god who had any sort of personal relationship with his followers.

People were seldom drawn to the new religion because of its teaching, which was harsh and dependent on good works. Nevertheless, Islam did grow rapidly because it used warfare to conquer Jerusalem, most of the Middle East and North Africa in a short period of time (AD 633-642). In AD 711 the Islamic tide invaded Spain and began to conquer other parts of Europe.

As we continue to consider the many unfortunate changes in the church during the Middle Ages we realize that we have been "stuck" on Revelation 2:20 for quite a while, and still have lots more to say about this. As we mentioned at the beginning of this letter, the message to Thyatira was the longest of the seven epistles. Jesus' words were appropriate for them, but it was also a prophetic message for the Middle Ages of the church. This era lasted more than 1000 years, and deserves our careful attention.

Use of Images in Worship

It was natural that artists would depict Bible characters in paintings and other forms of art, but with the passage of time people began to venerate some of these images by bowing to them or kissing them. For some people this might have been a carry-over from their former pagan practices that involved idolatry. For others it was just a way of showing respect to the memory of Jesus, Mary, or other biblical heroes.

In the Eastern portion of the church (Byzantine), which would eventually split off from the Western portion (Roman), intense campaigns were conducted by religious and governmental authorities from AD 726 to 842 to stop the use of images because they considered the practice idolatrous. This period was called the "Byzantine Iconoclasm" (meaning "icon-breaking") because numerous statues and other works of art were destroyed.

During this same time the Western (Roman) Church defended the practice at the Council of Nicaea II in AD 787. They pointed to the fact that the Bible prescribed sculptured cherubim to decorate the Ark of the Covenant (Deuteronomy 25:19) and the walls of the future millennial Temple (Ezekiel 41:18-21). They concluded that,

> "As the sacred and life-giving cross is everywhere set up as a symbol, so also should the images of Jesus Christ, the Virgin Mary, the holy angels, as well as those of the saints and other pious and holy men be embodied in the manufacture of sacred vessels, tapestries, vestments, etc., and exhibited on the walls of churches, in the homes, and in all conspicuous places, by the roadside and everywhere, to be revered by all who might see them. For the more they are contemplated, the more they move to fervent memory of their prototypes. Therefore, it is proper to accord to them a fervent and reverent adoration, not, however, the veritable worship which, according to our faith, belongs to the Divine Being alone."[23]

They therefore claimed that this practice is not idolatry, However it is at least confusing to those who have come from any idolatrous belief system. Unless congregants are taught how to differentiate between appreciating these images and actually worshipping them, they might violate the warning of the Second Commandment:

> *"You shall not make for yourself a carved image—any likeness of anything that is in heaven above, or that is in the earth beneath, or that is in the water under the earth; you* **shall not bow down to them nor serve them.** *For I, the* LORD *your God, am a jealous God, visiting the iniquity of the fathers upon the children to the third and fourth generations of those who hate Me, but showing mercy to thousands, to those who love Me and keep My commandments. –* Exodus 20:4-6

> *"You shall not make* **idols** *for yourselves;*
> *neither a carved image nor a sacred pillar shall you rear up for yourselves;*
> *nor shall you set up an engraved stone in your land,* **to bow down to it***;*
> *for I am the* LORD *your God.*

You shall keep My Sabbaths and reverence My sanctuary:
I am the LORD. – Leviticus 26:1-2

Little children, keep yourselves from idols. Amen. – 1 John 5:21

The Holy Roman Empire

After the fall of the Western Roman Empire in 476, Europe was ruled by various invaders such as the Visigoths, Vandals, Angles, Saxons, Franks, etc.

On Christmas day in AD 800 Charlemagne ("Charles the Great"), who had been King of the Franks, then King of Italy, was crowned as the first Emperor over part of the old domain. His coronation was held in Old St. Peter's Basilica, and it carried with it the endorsement of the Catholic Church. He restored the unity of most of Europe. He was also a great champion of the church. The official name "Holy Roman Empire" was not adopted until 1254. The beginning of this new Empire brought a unification of church and state that still persists in European thinking, and which has been the cause of many problems. The apostle Paul would not have condoned this development. He warned:

> *Do not be unequally yoked together with unbelievers. For what fellowship has righteousness with lawlessness? And what communion has light with darkness? And what accord has Christ with Belial? Or what part has a believer with an unbeliever? And what agreement has the temple of God with idols? For you are the temple of the living God. As God has said:*
> *"I will dwell in them and walk among them.*
> *I will be their God, and they shall be My people."*
> *Therefore "Come out from among them*
> *And be separate, says the Lord." –* 1 Corinthians 6:14-17

Sainthood/ Prayer through the Saints

In the 900's the church began the process called "canonization" to identify saints. It was explained earlier (in our discussion of the veneration of Mary) that the Bible calls all true believers saints. After the first three centuries of the church the martyrs were officially declared saints by public acclaim. Later this process was formalized by the bishops and finally given over to the Vatican.

Church members were encouraged to ask these saints to pray on their behalf. Catholic theologians will say that it is no different to ask a departed believer to pray for them than it is to ask a Christian friend here on Earth to do the same.

There are no examples in the Bible of asking the dead to pray for us. On the contrary, Paul instructed Timothy,

For there is one God, and one mediator between God and men, the man Christ Jesus. – 1 Timothy 2:5

Also Deuteronomy 18:10-11 prohibits communication with the dead:

There shall not be found among you anyone who makes his son or his daughter pass through the fire, or one who practices witchcraft, or a soothsayer, or one who interprets omens, or a sorcerer, or one who conjures spells, or a medium, or a spiritist, or one who calls up the dead.

Another related issue is a vision of the future in Revelation 5:8:

Now when He had taken the scroll, the four living creatures and the twenty-four elders fell down before the Lamb, each having a harp, and golden bowls full of incense, which are the prayers of the saints.

We will explore this verse more when we get to Chapter 5, but for now, just notice that this symbolic offering is an act of praise on behalf of all the believers. They are "saints" in the biblical meaning of the word, not in the later concept of canonized saints.

The Dark Age

The Catholic Church experienced the low-ebb of its integrity and morality between the years of AD 904, with the installation of Pope Sergius

III, to 964, the death of Pope John XII. This period of time is called the "Dark Age" (Latin: *saeculum obscurum*), and it is also often called the "Pornocracy." A corrupt Roman aristocratic family, the Theophylacti, exerted their evil influence over a number of Popes during these years.

The Catholic Encyclopedia admits the degeneration of this era:

> 'The spiritual and moral debasement in the Italian Peninsula was shocking, even in Rome. The names of Theodora and Marozia recall an unutterably sad chapter of church history. The disorder in the capital of Christendom was only a symptom of the conditions throughout Italy.'[24]

The "unutterable" fact, about this phase is what historian Edward Gibbon called "the influence of two sister prostitutes, Marozia and Theodora." These members of the Theophylacti family misused their wealth and beauty to corrupt the government and the church. Marozia's illegitimate son, a grandson, a great grandson, and two great-great grandsons all became Popes.[25]

Of the last Pope in this Dark Age, John XII, the Catholic Encyclopedia says,

> "The temporal and spiritual authority in Rome were thus again united in one person—a coarse, immoral man, whose life was such that the Lateran [Papal residence] was spoken of as a brothel, and the moral corruption in Rome became the subject of general odium."[26]

The lesson to be learned here is that, if the highest spiritual office in the world can be corrupted morally, it is no wonder that its theology can also degenerate over time.

Split with the Eastern Orthodox Church

In AD 1054, after generations of differences of opinion about various matters, the Eastern branch of the church split off from the rest.

The new denomination was called the Eastern Orthodox Church. Subdivisions of this church were called the "Greek Orthodox Church," the "Russian Orthodox Church," etc.

It is good to remember that there were other branches of the church, some dating back to the Apostolic period. Some of these are the Coptic, the Syriac, the Armenian, the Ethiopian, and the Assyrian Church of the East.

Reasons given for the split were the claims by the Roman Pope of supremacy over the whole church and a theological disagreement about the wording in the Nicene Creed that says the Holy Spirit proceeds from both the Father and the Son. The Eastern Orthodox believed the Spirit only proceeds from the Father, and therefore omitted the words "and the Son" from their version of the creed.[27] The Roman Church disagreed with the veneration of icons.

The Eastern Church doubted that the bread used for the Eucharist needed to be unleavened.[28]

Some historians feel that the East was also upset by Charlemagne's assumption of control over the West. The moral scandals in the West were probably also factors in the separation.

At a certain point, high officials on both sides of the schism excommunicated leaders from the other side.

At the end of these Middle Ages, we will see another great split--the Protestant Reformation. At that point we will discuss the vast number of denominations that we now have in the world.

Infallibility

In AD 1075 a document called *Dictatus Papae* ("Dictated by the Pope") was issued by Pope Gregory VII with a list of 27 powers claimed by the Pope. Some of them were startling in their scope. One of these (# 12) was "That it may be permitted to him to depose emperors."[29]

Another one that we would like to consider here was (#22) "That the Roman church has never erred; nor will it err to all eternity, the Scripture bearing witness."[30]

Taken at face value, anyone can see that this statement is not true. Pope John Paul II made more than 100 apologies[31] for the manifold and

145

sometimes horrendous mistakes made by the Catholic Church during its long history. Some of these mistakes were: Killing innocent victims during the Inquisition, Muslims killed by the Crusaders, involvement in the African slave trade, burning reformers at the stake, injustices to women, and silence during the Holocaust.

Since that time the church's infallibility has been more narrowly limited to teaching about faith and morals. There are said to be two sources of this inerrancy. The first is the decrees of church councils. The second is the case where the Pope speaks "ex cathedra" (Latin for "from the chair," meaning by virtue of his supreme Apostolic authority).

Church councils were employed by the 1st Century Church. Here is an example from the Book of Acts:

> *With them they sent the following letter:*
> **The apostles and elders**, *your brothers,*
> *To the Gentile believers in Antioch, Syria and Cilicia: Greetings.*
> *We have heard that some went out from us without our authorization and disturbed you, troubling your minds by what they said. So* **we all agreed** *to choose some men and send them to you with our dear friends Barnabas and Paul— men who have risked their lives for the name of our Lord Jesus Christ. Therefore we are sending Judas and Silas to confirm by word of mouth what we are writing.* **It seemed good to the Holy Spirit and to us** *not to burden you with anything beyond the following requirements: You are to abstain from food sacrificed to idols, from blood, from the meat of strangled animals and from sexual immorality. You will do well to avoid these things.*
> *Farewell.* – Acts 15: 23-29

When needed, the Early Church brought together godly leaders who discussed issues and depended on the Holy Spirit to give them unanimity in their decisions. Resolutions made in this way were most likely to be correct and to stand the test of time. But there is no indication that they considered their decisions infallible or unchangeable. They did not view them as inspired like the Scriptures.

During the next few centuries a number of church councils were convened to verify the teaching that was considered correct (or "orthodox"). By the 300's Athanasius, Bishop of Alexandria, gave additional weight to Council decisions. He said,

"The word of the Lord pronounced by the ecumenical synod of Nicaea stands for ever."[32]

Papal infallibility was assumed, at least from this time (AD1075 -- *Dictatus Papae)* and it was confirmed in 1870 by Vatican I – the 20th General Council, where it was declared as a divinely revealed dogma:

"The Roman Pontiff, when he speaks ex cathedra — that is, when in the exercise of his office as pastor and teacher of all Christians he defines, by virtue of his supreme Apostolic authority, a doctrine of faith or morals to be held by the whole Church — is, by reason of the Divine assistance promised to him in blessed Peter, possessed of that infallibility with which the Divine Redeemer wished His Church to be endowed in defining doctrines of faith and morals; and consequently that such definitions of the Roman Pontiff are irreformable of their own nature (*ex sese*) and not by reason of the Church's consent."[33]

Recent Catholic information about this concept explains that infallibility is not the same as inspiration–the literal "word of God." Nor is it the same thing as revelation–the supernatural unveiling by God of truth that was previously unknown.[34]

The issue of infallibility is a major issue in what constitutes Catholic belief. Doctrines and practices like praying to the saints, devotion to Mary, the meaning of the Mass, church sacraments, confession and penance, purgatory, indulgences, and others that divided the church at the Reformation, could be "proved" by the findings of councils and the proclamations of Popes. No longer could the sterling test of "What does the Bible say?" keep the church from accepting Jezebel's false teaching and idolatrous rituals.

Indulgences

In AD 1095 Pope Urban II called for a Crusade to take back the Holy Land from the Muslims. One of the great incentives he offered for those who would be willing to risk their lives in that conflict was the offer of indulgences. The word comes from a Latin word for "kindness." The concept grew out of the practice of confessing sins to the priest. He could pronounce that the guilt for a mortal sin (one that would have sent the sinner to hell) was removed, and with it the eternal punishment that would have been due. He would then assign penance–a temporal punishment that was required to be fulfilled during his lifetime. (Later when the concept of purgatory was defined, these temporal punishments could also be fulfilled there.) These might include restitution, prayers and alms, and whatever else the priest felt was appropriate.

Indulgences would free the penitent person from having to pay some, or all, of the aspects of his temporal punishment. By offering indulgences to potential soldiers of the Crusade, those who wished to respond would feel the freedom to risk their lives for the cause even though they had not yet worked off their punishments.

Sometime later indulgences were also offered to those who were unable to join the Crusades but were willing to offer cash contributions to the effort.[35]

Later still, at the Fourth Lateran Council in AD 1215, some abuses of indulgences were addressed. The council also extended them to those who helped with the Inquisition. (That's another horror story we will explore later.)

> "Catholics who have girded themselves with the cross for the extermination of the heretics, shall enjoy the indulgences and privileges granted to those who go in defense of the Holy Land."[36]

During the rest of the Middle Ages indulgences were difficult to control and there were reports of false documents that offered extreme rewards in exchange for purchasing them.[37]

The indulgence issue was seen as a huge moral problem by John Huss, who was a Bohemian priest in the early 1400's. He said that the

Czech people were being exploited by the pope's indulgences, and appealed to the Bible as the ultimate authority to support his reform efforts. He was tried as a heretic and was found guilty.:

> He refused one last chance to recant at the stake, where he prayed, "Lord Jesus, it is for thee that I patiently endure this cruel death. I pray thee to have mercy on my enemies." He was heard reciting the Psalms as the flames engulfed him.[38]

Indulgences in Martin Luther's time were being sold to build St. Peter's Basilica in Rome. He saw the practice as the purchase and sale of salvation. When we study the letter to the church of Sardis we will see that this was apparently the tipping point that led Luther and others to break with the Catholic Church in AD 1517.

The Crusades

The history of the church during the next several centuries revolved around a series of holy wars, known as the Crusades. The major crusades, from AD 1096 to 1291 were a response to the Muslim conquests, and especially to their occupation of Jerusalem, persecution of Christian pilgrims, and destruction of Christian holy sites. The papacy was strong at that time, after a period of reforms, and it convinced European governments to send their knights and all who would volunteer to fight to regain Jerusalem. The name "crusade" was derived from the red cloth *crux* (Latin for "cross") given to the volunteers by the Pope or one of his representatives.

Of the first eight or nine major crusades, only the first was successful in capturing Jerusalem, and that victory was short-lived. There is no general agreement by historians and theologians that the Crusades were either morally good or bad, or more importantly, whether or not they were the will of God. In fairness, the editor of Christianity Today wrote:

> But the crusaders were real Christians. They deplored their sins. They longed for forgiveness. They loved fellow Christians in the East. They yearned to do something noble and lasting for their

Lord. They prayed and fasted before battles and praised God after victories. Their devotion and courage make ours look juvenile.[39]

On the "good" side of the question, it did seem right to most Christians to deliver Jerusalem from the Muslims, and to stop their rapid conquest of Christian territories. There was also extensive Old Testament precedent for defending oneself and for fighting against evil powers if directed by God. On the last evening with His disciples, Jesus did tell them to purchase a sword (Luke 22:36), however, it wasn't His will for Peter to use the sword when Jesus was surrendering Himself for His sacrificial death (Luke 22:49-51; John 18:10-11).

On the "bad" side of the crusade issue, nothing Jesus taught could validate the use of force to establish the Kingdom of Heaven. He said, if His kingdom was of this world, then His servants would fight (John 18:36). But His kingdom will not be established on Earth until He returns as King of Kings, and when that happens He will do all the necessary fighting (Revelation 19:11-16; 20:1-6).

Some might doubt that God was directing the crusades since only the first one was successful, and the victory only lasted for a short time. On the other hand, it can be argued that they stemmed the tide of Islamic conquests, which otherwise might have overrun all of Europe.

There were great mistakes made during the crusades, and unholy actions that have been used to discredit Christianity. Some examples of this were the unnecessary killing of Muslim civilians, the slaughter of Jews in many places, and the growth of a culture of literally hundreds of "holy wars" for some 700 years.

The Knights Templar grew out of the Crusades. They were originally a brave and skillful asset to the wars, but with the passing of time, they developed the prototype of the modern banking system and became what some have called the "first multinational corporation." Their secret initiations made them suspect to church and government powers. In 1312 they were disbanded after many of their members were accused, perhaps falsely, of secrecy, apostasy, heresy, and many other charges, but since torture was used to extract their confessions, it has always been unknown whether or not the charges were true. Freemasonry adopted the titles, symbols and rituals of the Knights Templar in the 18th Century.

On the other hand, the Crusades helped St. Thomas Aquinas develop the "Just War" theory in his *Summa Theologica* to answer the question of when it is right to respond defensively.

The Inquisition

Now we must consider the Inquisition–a series of religious trials that were conducted over the course of hundreds of years to determine the guilt or innocence of people suspected to be heretics. Heretics are people whose beliefs differ from approved teaching of the church. The word "heretic" comes from the Greek *hairesis* ("faction" "sect," "division"). It is found in various forms in the New Testament 139 times. Here are two examples:

> *But there were also false prophets among the people, even as there will be false teachers among you, who will secretly bring in destructive heresies, even denying the Lord who bought them, and bring on themselves swift destruction.* – 2 Peter 2:1

> *Reject a divisive man [heretic] after the first and second admonition, knowing that such a person is warped and sinning, being self-condemned.* – Titus 3:10-11

In fact, even from the time of the Apostolic Church, heresies had been identified and dealt with, but the punishment was simply excommunication from the church, certainly not imprisonment or death (Matthew 13:24-30; Matthew 18:15-17; 1 Corinthians 51-8; Galatians 1:6-9; 1 Timothy 1:20; Titus 3:10;). When the Samaritans rebuffed the disciples, they asked Jesus,

> *"Lord, do You want us to command fire to come down from heaven and consume them, just as Elijah did?"*
> *But He turned and rebuked them, and said, "You do not know what manner of spirit you are of. For the Son of Man did not come to destroy men's lives but to save them."And they went to another village.* – Luke 9:54-56

As the church/state system progressed, there was no acceptable way for people to disagree with the teaching of the church. Some of the suspected heretics held strange, unbiblical ideas, but others, like the Reformers, were trying to be more biblical in their teaching. In either case the dissidents were questioned, tried, and, if found guilty according to the interpretations of the church at that time, punished. The church would pass judgment, but if the accused did not repent, the state would administer the temporal punishment. This was usually burning at the stake.

The Council of Toulouse in 1229 established a special ecclesiastical court called the Inquisition (from the Latin *inquisitio*, meaning "inquiry"). There had been such trials, going back to 1163 or earlier, against the Albigenses (also-called Cathari, from the Greek *katharos*, "pure"). The Albigenses believed in dualism, the concept that the good power created the invisible and spiritual universe, while the evil power created the material world. Those found guilty were burned at the stake.

The extent of torture and executions increased greatly during the Spanish Inquisition beginning in 1481 and lasting until 1834. Confessions were extracted by the use of torture. There were many methods for this, but three of the most frequently used were (1) suspending the suspect with a series of lifts and drops that would often dislocate their arms and legs; (2) pouring water into their mouths to give the impression of drowning, and (3) stretching them on mechanical racks.[40]

In our commentary on the next church (Sardis), we will see that the Catholic Church also persecuted the Reformers with this system. However, the Reformers made the same terrible mistake by persecuting Catholics and members of later church factions, like the Anabaptists. We will consider this later when we study Revelation 3:1-2.

How many were killed? Estimates vary widely depending on the perspective of the "historians" who tell the story. Some Catholic writers say the death toll was only in the hundreds, while avowed anti-Catholics claim that millions were put to death.

In balance, we recommend the thoughts of Chris Armstrong, managing editor of Christian History Magazine in his 2008 article about "Christian Terrorism:"

Christians have far more often suffered than perpetrated terror.

This does not excuse those who in the past have named Christ's name but broken God's Fifth Commandment. But it does put the lie to the skeptic's image of a church characterized throughout its history by brutal oppression and violence.[41]

We will consider two more unfortunate developments in the Church of the Middle Ages.

Restriction of the Laity from Reading the Bible

At the Counsel of Toulouse in AD 1229, the same one we cited above that established the Inquisition, a new church law was adopted that greatly limited the privilege of the laity to read even the official Latin version of the Bible, and declared it strictly forbidden to read any translation of the Bible into other languages. Here is the text of the law:

> Canon 14. We prohibit also that the laity should be permitted to have the books of the Old or New Testament; unless anyone from motive of devotion should wish to have the Psalter or the Breviary for divine offices or the hours of the blessed Virgin; but we most strictly forbid their having any translation of these books.[42]

Remember the earlier notes about the "Nicolaitans" (Greek for "to conquer the people") in Chapter 2, verse 6 (church at Ephesus) and Chapter 2, verse 15 (church at Pergamum). The hierarchy of the church had adopted layer after layer of unbiblical ideas, but since most of the people did not know what the Bible taught, they would tend to go along with the false teaching, especially when they had now accepted the belief in the infallibility of papal decrees and church councils.

This meant that many of the people who were persecuted as "heretics," and were put to death, were people whose ideas were more biblical than the official position of the Catholic Church. But if the general populace couldn't read the Bible for themselves, how would they know this was happening?

Jesus said that man should not live by bread alone, but by every word that proceeds from God (Matthew 4:4). Paul told Timothy,

Be diligent to present yourself approved to God, a worker who does not need to be ashamed, rightly dividing the word of truth. – 2 Timothy 2:15

And,

All Scripture is given by inspiration of God, and is profitable for doctrine, for reproof, for correction, for instruction in righteousness, that the man of God may be complete, thoroughly equipped for every good work. – 2 Timothy 3:16

The New Testament Scriptures were the Gospels, Acts, and the Letters to the churches. They were all meant to be read in their entirety to every Christian. That was one of the first things we noticed about this last book of the Bible–that it promised a blessing to all who read it, and even to those who heard it being read by someone else (Revelation 1:3).

John Wycliffe was one early reformer who defied this church law that prohibited common people from reading the Bible. He was an English theologian and professor at Oxford. He and a group of other scholars translated the Bible into English. It was known as the Wycliffe Bible. He died in 1384, but the Council of Constance declared him a heretic in 1415. It was decreed that his books were to be burned. His remains were dug up, burned, and the ashes were cast into the River Swift.

Purgatory

One of the great differences between Catholic and Protestant theology is the belief in purgatory–a place between heaven and hell where the temporal penance for sins committed during one's lifetime could be discharged. This doctrine stated that after this penance the purified believer could go on to his or her heavenly reward.

There were hints of belief in Purgatory from about AD 1200, but the formal dogma was established in AD 1254 by the First Council of Lyon, confirmed by the Council of Florence in AD 1435-1438, and again at the Council of Trent in AD 1545-1547, after the Reformation.

The church based this belief in Purgatory on a passage from 2 Maccabees 12:42-46, where it was written that it is "a holy and wholesome thought to pray for the dead, that they may be loosed from sins." This book is considered apocryphal by Protestants, and not included in their Bible. The story of the rich man and Lazarus was also cited in support of this concept (Luke 16:19-26), along with the teaching about the Bema Seat judgment (1 Corinthians 3:11-15). However, these passages actually show that once a person has died his condition cannot be changed. Hebrews 9:27 says, "It is appointed for men to die once, but after this the judgment."

This concept of purgatory led to the practice of "prayers for the dead." It also opened the way for the abusive campaign by the church of selling indulgences, whereby the wealthy could presumably pay for the sins of departed loved ones so that they could be released from purgatory. We will take another look at this in the commentary on the next church (Sardis), which represents the period of the Reformation. The selling of indulgences was the primary issue in Martin Luther's "95 Theses" that began the Protestant Reformation.

Critique

And I gave her time to repent of her sexual immorality, and she did not repent. Indeed I will cast her into a sickbed, and those who commit adultery with her into great tribulation, unless they repent of their deeds. I will kill her children with death, and all the churches shall know that I am He who searches the minds and hearts. And I will give to each one of you according to your works. – Revelation 2:21-23

After this lengthy overview of one thousand years of church history, we need to return our attention to the 1st Century Church at Thyatira, where the Lord Jesus gave a stern warning to Jezebel, the evil false teacher there. *"And I gave her time to repent of her sexual immorality, and she did not repent."* The good news is that our God always gives an opportunity to repent (see notes on Chapter 2, verse 5). He does not desire for anyone to perish, but prefers that all should come to repentance (2 Peter 3:9). That is why He always sent prophets to warn people in time to turn from the judgment they deserve. Those who have rejected God's mercy will never be able to blame Him for their plight. In this Book of Revelation the apostle John was the prophet, and his warning was delivered via this written message.

Jezebel's greatest sin was sexual immorality. As we pointed out above, this is a translation of the Greek word *porneia*, which is also rendered as "fornication." We get our word pornography from this same term. It is different from the Greek word for adultery (*moicheuo*), which is used in the next verse. Adultery is unfaithfulness to one's marriage partner. Porneia is the much broader concept of sexual perversion.

This is why Jesus said divorce would not be permitted except in the case of fornication (Matthew 19:9). He didn't use the word "adultery." Adultery is terrible. I always advise couples who are planning to get married that one simple act of adultery will almost always ruin a marriage. However, fornication is even more damaging. If a person's mate is addicted to evil sexual desires like child molestation, homosexuality, pornography, or repeated adultery, Jesus granted that it was not right to be united to such a person.

Jesus therefore pronounced judgment on Jezebel. ***"Indeed I will cast her into a sickbed, and those who commit adultery with her into great tribulation, unless they repent of their deeds."*** The Greek word for bed could also mean a couch used for carrying a sick person. This is the image of the immoral false teacher, afflicted with the diseases that accompany her immorality, both literally and figuratively. False teachers are spiritually ill even if they do not know it.

One of the most shocking stories in the Bible is about the death of Queen Jezebel. Elijah was told to prophesy that the wicked King Ahab would die a violent death and the dogs would lick his blood (1 Kings 21:19). But his queen Jezebel, who was even worse than him, would have a grotesque end:

And concerning Jezebel the LORD also spoke, saying, 'The dogs shall eat Jezebel by the wall of Jezreel. – 1 Kings 21:23

2 Kings 9:30-37 tells the story of her death. She was killed by one of her enemies, and before she could be given a burial her body was eaten by dogs, just as Elijah had predicted.

Those who follow a false teacher will also have to go through "great tribulation." This was true for the church at Thyatira and it was also true for the church during the Middle Ages. And beyond that, it will be true for Christians during the end-times. It is significant that these words are used together in Matthew 24:21, where Jesus talked about that great future period of trials in the end-times:

> *For then there will be great tribulation, such as has not been since the beginning of the world until this time, no, nor ever shall be.* – Matthew 24:21

The only other time the expression is found is in Revelation 7, where it speaks of the martyrs of the Tribulation period:

> *And I said to him, "Sir, you know." So he said to me, "These are the ones who come out of the great tribulation, and washed their robes and made them white in the blood of the Lamb.* – Revelation 7:14

This future Tribulation coincides with the seven-year covenant between the evil world dictator and Israel foretold in the Book of Daniel (Daniel 9:25-27). We will explore Daniel's prophecy when we start Chapter 6 of Revelation.

Again, there is a ray of hope for the followers of the false teacher. This is a last-minute invitation to repent--to believe the Gospel and be converted. Those who would repent will no longer be considered "her children." Their future will be investigated later, starting with verse 24, which is addressed to the believing remnant.

Next Jesus said, **"I will kill her children with death."** This is an unusual description of the fate of Jezebel's unrepentant followers. It could mean a dramatic or violent death similar to Jezebel's. More likely, it a reference to the "second death" mentioned in Revelation 2:11; 20:6, 14; and 21:8. See the notes on death from Chapter 1, verse 18. We discussed the fact that physical death was separation of the body from the soul and spirit. The body is dead and ceases to function. There is also spiritual death (Ephesians 2:1), which is separation of one's spirit from God. This separation ends when one is born again (John 3:3) and a connection is re-established between a person and His Creator. The last, and worst, separation is called the "second death"--eternal separation from God. A person who dies physically while he is still dead suffers this second death.

When this dreadful judgment takes place, Jesus says, *"and all the churches shall know."* This knowledge will not only affect the church at Thyatira, or only the Church of the Middle Ages, but it will be a warning to all churches throughout history.

What is this valuable lesson about Jesus and those who claim to know Him but do not obey Him? It is this: *"That I am He who searches the minds and hearts."* In verse 19 above, we saw that Jesus did commend this church for their good works, but He warned that their efforts could not save them (See also: Matthew 7:21-23). God sees what each person does. But He also knows that person's thoughts. The word translated "minds" is actually the Greek word for kidneys. In those days people supposed that thoughts originated in the kidneys and emotions came from the heart.

As you probably know, scientists have not understood many things about the human body until more recent times. Aristotle, the most brilliant person of his time, thought that the brain was a radiator to cool the blood! In the early days of our country people thought that illness was caused by bad blood, so they had doctors and barbers let blood out when they were ill. It wasn't until the 1860's that doctors really understood germs. Even now we are trying to grasp the amazing facts of genetics. Obviously, the Creator knew how thoughts were processed by the brain, but until it was time for the human race to gain that knowledge, His revealed Word used images that people would understand (like "kidneys" for minds).

Those who have received Christ personally as their Savior will tend to produce good works (Ephesians 2:8-10; Titus 3:5, 8). However those good deeds will be the fruit of a changed life, not an attempt to purchase salvation.

On the other hand, those who stubbornly try to accumulate credit for their efforts, instead of relying on the substitutionary death of Jesus in their place, will indeed be judged on the basis of their performance. To them Jesus says, *"And I will give to each one of you according to your works."* If they insist on paying their own way into heaven they will fail miserably, but if that is what they want, they will be judged by that standard. In Romans the apostle Paul warns against trusting in good works:

As it is written: "There is none righteous, no, not one;
There is none who understands;
There is none who seeks after God.
They have all turned aside;
They have together become unprofitable;
There is none who does good, no, not one." – Romans 3:10-12

Now we know that whatever the law says, it says to those who are under the law, that every mouth may be stopped, and all the world may become guilty before God. [20] Therefore by the deeds of the law no flesh will be justified in His sight, for by the law is the knowledge of sin. – Romans 3:19-20

For all have sinned and fall short of the glory of God,--Romans 3:23

When we get to Revelation Chapter 20, we will study the "Great White Throne Judgment" of unbelievers. Their recorded works will be brought up as a basis for their judgment:

And I saw the dead, small and great, standing before God, and books were opened. And another book was opened, which is the Book of Life. And the dead were judged according to their works, by the things which were written in the books. – Revelation 20:12

True believers in Christ will already have been judged-- and acquitted--on the basis that their name is in "The Book of Life" (Philippians 4:3; Revelation 3:5; 13:8; 17:8; 20:12, 15; 21:27; 22:19). Since Jesus died for the sins of the whole world (1 John 2:2), all names were apparently written in this book "from the foundation of the world" (Revelation 17:8). True believers' names are not blotted out of this book (Revelation 3:5), but those who do not trust Jesus' substitutionary death will evidentially have their names blotted out (John 3:16-18, 36).

This verse is addressed to those who have rejected the gift of eternal life. The next verse is for those who are true believers.

Counsel

"Now to you I say, and to the rest in Thyatira, as many as do not have this doctrine, who have not known the depths of Satan, as they say, I will put on you no other burden. But hold fast what you have till I come. And he who overcomes, and keeps My works until the end, to him I will give power over the nations—
'He shall rule them with a rod of iron;
They shall be dashed to pieces like the potter's vessels'--
as I also have received from My Father; and I will give him the morning star.
"He who has an ear, let him hear what the Spirit says to the churches." – Revelation 2:24-29

It has taken a long time to highlight the problems of the Middle Ages. This is no surprise because that period of history lasted approximately one thousand years, and the changes in the church were numerous and even cataclysmic! Honestly, we have just scratched the surface of all that happened during that time.

I have been eager to get to this point so that I can say, once again, that I am not against everything that is Catholic. It is only unbiblical teaching and actions that must be opposed, no matter what stream of Christianity they came from. And the sad reality is, every denomination has its problems in these areas. All we can do is to keep going back to the Scriptures to minimize the error that can creep in to any of our churches.

In the following segment, we will notice and celebrate the many godly and faithful leaders and members of the church at Thyatira as well as the heroes of the evolving Catholic Church of the Middle Ages.

At the close of our last installment it was noted that verse 23 applied to the corrupt non-believers, but this next verse begins to offer advice to true believers.

First, Jesus addressed the angel/messenger of the church, who was the pastor there. *Now to you I say.* The pastor evidently opposed the false teaching that had corrupted the church in Thyatira. We don't know what he actually did to minimize the damage caused by their "Jezebel," but since he was the shepherd of the flock, many—perhaps even the majority—were preserved by his vigilance.

And to the rest in Thyatira, as many as do not have this doctrine, who have not known the depths of Satan, as they say. Then Jesus included all the others in the church who had resisted the temptation to believe false teaching. Whether or not they realized it, those fallacies had actually originated with Satan himself! The previous church, Pergamum, had been located where Satan's throne existed, but in this church, and the Church Age that it represents, Satan had found ways to make great inroads through false teaching and immoral activities. We might think that the Devil's ways would be immediately recognized and rejected by Christians. However, in his original form he was known as Lucifer, or "light-bearer" (Isaiah 14:12 ff.). Look at what the apostle Paul had to say about people who brought false teaching to Corinth:

> *For such people are false apostles, deceitful workers, masquerading as apostles of Christ. And no wonder, for Satan himself masquerades as an angel of light. It is not surprising, then, if his servants also masquerade as servants of righteousness. Their end will be what their actions deserve.* – 2 Corinthians 11:14-15

I will put on you no other burden. For the faithful saints at Thyatira Jesus did not have any further instructions. Their work had already been most difficult, standing as they did for the truth against such an adversary.

However, He did ask them to stay strong. *But hold fast what you have.* They would be tempted to give up when they felt that they were losing the spiritual battle. At one point the prophet Elijah complained to God,

> *And he said, "I have been very zealous for the LORD God of hosts; because the children of Israel have forsaken Your covenant, torn down Your altars, and*

killed Your prophets with the sword. I alone am left; and they seek to take my life." – 1 Kings 19:14

To this the Lord explained,

Yet I have reserved seven thousand in Israel, all whose knees have not bowed to Baal, and every mouth that has not kissed him." – 1 Kings 19:18

No matter how difficult it has ever been for the church to be successful during its two-thousand-year history, and no matter how brutally Satan has assaulted it, it has never been destroyed! This is a direct fulfillment of Jesus' powerful prophecy in Matthew 16:18, "I will build My church." Let's analyze that magnificent statement.

"I" Untold numbers of rich and powerful people have built their political or business empires, but none has been as successful as Jesus Christ. That is because of who He is. As we have already shown, He is God the Son, the Creator, our Messiah/ Savior, and returning King of Kings. As God, He is omnipotent, omniscient, and omnipresent.

"Will" Everything He has ever set out to do He has accomplished. There is no limitation of His resources, opportunity, willpower, or any other thing that could hinder His progress. By His words He brought the universe into being (Genesis 1:3, 1:6 etc.; John 1:1-3, 10). By His words He predicted the formation of His church. Satanic opposition is a reality, but He declared, "The gates of hades will not prevail against it" (Matthew 16:18).

"Build" Among the many illustrations of His church, one image is that of a building. He is the foundation of the building, and believers are "living stones" (1 Peter 2:5).

"My" There is naturally a sense of ownership for each member of the church. We proudly refer to it as "our church." But in reality, Jesus is the originator, builder, supervisor, and owner of His church.

"Church" The Greek word for church literally means "called out." It was the normal word for an assembly, like the town council. Spiritually, it is an assembly of born-again believers who were "called out" of the evil world system by Jesus. (See the notes on Chapter 1, verse 20).

Because the church is Christ's own work, there is always a "remnant" of true believers. There are tens of thousands of faithful pastors today who are doing their best to follow the Bible and protect their flocks from false teaching. Their denominations, seminaries, and leaders might be slipping, but they "hold fast" to the truth.

In spite of the problems of the Middle Ages, the Catholic Church had many inspirational leaders. They were not perfect, since Jesus was the only sinless human, but they were faithful, and the Lord enabled them to accomplish much for His church.

This list includes scholars like Augustine and Thomas Aquinas, devotional writers like Thomas a Kempis, inspirational leaders like Francis of Assisi, courageous soldiers, like many of the Crusaders and Joan of Arc, reformers like the Waldensians, John Huss, John Wycliffe, and the numerous witnesses listed in Foxes' Book of Martyrs.

These heroes of the faith were not flawless. But like the 7000 faithful prophets in Elijah's day, for every one whose name has come down to us today as a godly example, there were undoubtedly thousands of others who were faithful to the Lord during the Middle Ages.

Jesus encouraged them to be faithful *"till I come."* He is coming back for believers of the Church Age at the Rapture (See Chapter 1, verse 7; Chapter 3, verses 3 to 11 and Appendix A –Jesus' Own Outline of the Future). Then, at the end of the Tribulation, He will come in glory as "King of Kings" (Revelation 19:11-16). It seems that the Lord has this final return in view here because of what he says in the next two verses. At that time He will give overcomers "power over the nations," an allusion to the privilege they will have of reigning with Him.

As we have been pointing out throughout this series of messages to the Seven Churches, *He who overcomes* is a description of all true believers in Christ (See 1 John 5:3-5 and notes above on Chapter 2, verse 1).

Again, the overcomer is one about whom it can be said that he or she *keeps* My works. This does not describe a method of salvation, but a result of following Christ. Salvation is emphatically not a result of good works, but by grace through faith in the atonement of Jesus Christ

(Ephesians 2:9-10; Also see the notes on Chapter 2, verse 19).

The word for "keeps" is the Greek verb *terero*, which in turn comes from the noun *teros*, *meaning* "a guard." This enforces the concept that every overcomer is a veteran of spiritual warfare. He or she is a victor, because, as John himself had taught,

> *You are of God, little children, and have overcome them, because He who is in you is greater than he who is in the world.* – 1 John 4:4

"My works" introduces two key concepts of Christianity. Jesus said they were "My works" because they were the normal outcome of a right relationship with Him. He said,

> *Let your light so shine before men, that they may see your good works and glorify your Father in heaven.* – Matthew 5:16

> *A good tree cannot bear bad fruit, nor can a bad tree bear good fruit. Every tree that does not bear good fruit is cut down and thrown into the fire. Therefore by their fruits you will know them.* – Matthew 7:18-20

> *A new commandment I give to you, that you love one another; as I have loved you, that you also love one another. By this all will know that you are My disciples, if you have love for one another."* – 1 John 13:34-35

> *"If you love Me, keep My commandments."* – John 14:15

(See the notes on good works in Chapter 2, verse 2.)

Jesus called them "My works," also because He actually takes up residence in the lives of true believers, and does through them the things He wants to accomplish. He promised to be with His disciples always, even to the end of the age (Matthew 28:20). He encourages people to invite Him into their lives (Revelation 3:20). The apostle Paul understood this amazing concept. After praying repeatedly for the Lord to remove some "thorn in the flesh," he said,

Concerning this thing I pleaded with the Lord three times that it might depart from me. And He said to me, "My grace is sufficient for you, for My strength is made perfect in weakness." Therefore most gladly I will rather boast in my infirmities, that the power of Christ may rest upon me. Therefore I take pleasure in infirmities, in reproaches, in needs, in persecutions, in distresses, for Christ's sake. For when I am weak, then I am strong.– 2 Corinthians 12:8-10

In some of His other writings Paul also referred to the amazing work of Christ within him:

I can do all things through Christ who strengthens me.– Philippians 4:13

I have been crucified with Christ; it is no longer I who live, but Christ lives in me; and the life which I now live in the flesh I live by faith in the Son of God, who loved me and gave Himself for me. – Galatians 2:20

The expression ***until the end*** is sobering. If one is a true believer, He should be faithful to the end of his life. The spiritual battle continues as long as we live in a sin-corrupted world, but knowing Christ and serving Him makes it a wonderful life, full of meaning!

Consider the martyrs of the past, or even of our current generation. Most of them could have been spared their torture and death by recanting-- giving up their belief in Christ. But that personal bond with Him, and the promise of eternal life, were more valuable to them than physical existence.

One of the most inspiring lessons I learned from some of the great "Promise Keepers" speakers during the big rallies of the 1990's was the concept of "finishing well." In our generation amazing grace has been the emphasis, and rightly so. But for some, this fosters a concept known as **"easy-believism."** This is the false idea that, since we are saved by grace, we can live the same unholy way that the world does. However, living an unchanged life casts doubt on whether or not a person is really born again (John 3:3):

Therefore, if anyone is in Christ, he is a new creation; old things have passed away; behold, all things have become new. – 2 Corinthians 2:14

Paul weighed in on this question in the book of Romans:

What shall we say then? Shall we continue in sin that grace may abound? Certainly not! How shall we who died to sin live any longer in it? Or do you not know that as many of us as were baptized into Christ Jesus were baptized into His death? Therefore we were buried with Him through baptism into death, that just as Christ was raised from the dead by the glory of the Father, even so we also should walk in newness of life. – Romans 6:1-4

In another place he wrote,

Examine yourselves as to whether you are in the faith. Test yourselves. – 2 Corinthians 13:5.

Back to the concept of finishing well, I have known many people who seemed to have grown so rapidly at first, but who gradually drifted away. Some of them were even in the ministry, but at some point they just turned and walked off. This is not the same thing as a true believer falling into sin and then repenting. The Bible is full of examples of fallen believers coming back to the Lord. God always wants a sinner to return. But for some people, it is apparently just a decision not to believe after all. I have to think that those who make that decision learned all they needed to know about God's great love and offer of salvation, but for some illogical reason, decided not to believe it. People like that are doomed because they have already rejected the truth that could have saved them. What more could they learn that would turn them back again? (Hebrews 6:4-6)

By contrast, the tireless apostle Paul expressed his desire to keep on serving the Lord as long as he would live:

But none of these things move me; nor do I count my life dear to myself, so that I may finish my race with joy, and the ministry which I received from the Lord Jesus, to testify to the gospel of the grace of God. – Acts 20:4

Jesus then revealed the reward that these overcomers would experience. He said, ***to him I will give power over the nations.*** In Revelation 20 we will fully consider the reign of Christ on Earth for 1000 years before the final judgment and the creation of a New Heaven and New Earth. All true Christians from the Church Age will return with Jesus (Revelation 19:11-14). The martyrs of the Tribulation Period will be raised (Revelation 20:4), and the Old Testament saints will resurrected (Daniel 12:1-3). All of these groups are part of the "first resurrection," and they will reign with Christ (Revelation 20:6).

The promise to overcomers is authority over the nations. This stands in contrast to the unholy alliance between the church and various governments during the Middle Ages. God was not pleased with papal influence over the nations, but He will be pleased to allow His righteous followers to rule and reign with Christ when He returns as King of Kings.

He shall rule them with a rod of iron; They shall be dashed to pieces like the potter's vessels'—as I also have received from My Father.

This is a quotation from Psalm 2:7-9, where God the Father promises to give all the nations of the Earth to His Son. In that future kingdom peace and prosperity will be maintained by the sure and swift judgment of lawbreakers. Jesus will reign and those He has redeemed will assist Him. In that sense it can be said of them that they also rule with a rod of iron.

And I will give him the morning star. One further reward for the overcomers is this interesting promise. In the last chapter of The New Testament (Revelation 22:16) Jesus calls Himself the morning star. This description is usually applied to the planet Venus when it shines brightly just before sunrise. It is the precursor of an even brighter light, the sun itself. In the last chapter of The Old Testament, in the context of the final judgments, it is prophesied that Messiah (Jesus) will appear as the Sun of Righteousness. This refers to His Glorious Return to dispel the darkness of The Tribulation.

But to you who fear My name
The Sun of Righteousness shall arise

With healing in His wings;
And you shall go out
And grow fat like stall-fed calves. – Malachi 4:2

Ray Stedman notices a relationship here between the Rapture of the church and Christ's Second Coming to set up the Millennial Kingdom.

> So what Jesus is saying to the faithful believers in the corrupt church at Thyatira is that there will be two stages of the appearance of the Lord Jesus Christ. First He will appear as the morning star, shining brightly before dawn, coming for His own. Then, at a later period, He will appear as the shining sun, coming in all His power and glory, visible to all the world.[43]

This is the first of several hints about the Rapture in the Book of Revelation. We will find more in the messages to the churches at Philadelphia and Laodicea. In Chapter 4, when John is told to "come up here," we will see how the Rapture relates to teaching from the rest of the New Testament.

He who has an ear, let him hear what the Spirit says to the churches. See notes about this expression in Chapter 2, verse 7. Again, the responsibility is on the reader or listener to make use of what has been said.

Revelation Chapter 3

To Sardis 3:1-6 (Reformation Church 1517- Mid 1700's)

"And to the angel of the church in Sardis write,

'These things says He who has the seven Spirits of God and the seven stars: "I know your works, that you have a name that you are alive, but you are dead. Be watchful, and strengthen the things which remain, that are ready to die, for I have not found your works perfect before God. Remember therefore how you have received and heard; hold fast and repent. Therefore if you will not watch, I will come upon you as a thief, and you will not know what hour I will come upon you. You have a few names even in Sardis who have not defiled their garments; and they shall walk with Me in white, for they are worthy. He who overcomes shall be clothed in white garments, and I will not blot out his name from the Book of Life; but I will confess his name before My Father and before His angels.

"He who has an ear, let him hear what the Spirit says to the churches."– Revelation 3:1-6

Next, Jesus addressed the pastor of the fifth church: *And to the angel of the church in Sardis write.*

In the 8th Century BC, Sardis was the capital city of Lydia, a stronghold of western Asia Minor (modern Turkey) between the emerging empires of the Persians and the Greeks. It was located in the Hermus Valley, about 50 miles east of Smyrna.

The Pactolus River flowed through its market place and sparkled with gold dust carried from Mt. Timolus, a source of gold and silver. From 595 BC to 547 BC King Croesus became rich and famous because of the discovery by metallurgists of a way to separate gold from silver, and improve the purity of both. Sardis is known as the place where modern currency was invented. They were able to produce gold coins that had a consistent purity.

Part of the city was built on a rocky spur of Mount Timolus. It was well fortified and easily defended. In fact, historians say that the only times invading armies were able to enter this city were when the unworried citizens were too sure of their safety and too involved with comfortable living to even post a guard at the steep face of the mountain that invaders had to climb.

Ruins of the ancient city have been excavated for tourists to see. One of the most impressive features is the huge bath/ gymnasium. This structure, built soon after the time of John's letter, illustrates the luxurious lifestyle that might have led the citizens to complacency.

During the expansion of the Persian Empire, Sardis was conquered by Cyrus the Great. It became the terminus of the Persian Royal Road which began in Persepolis, the capital of the Empire.

The most impressive building of ancient Sardis was its massive Temple of Artemis (Diana), which was built in the 4th Century BC. It was the fourth largest Ionic temple in the world, measuring 327 feet long and 163 feet wide. It had 78 Ionic columns that were 58 feet high. Some of these are still standing today. As mentioned during the study of Ephesus (see the notes on Chapter 2, verse 1), the worship of this pagan goddess was very immoral.

Sardis is mentioned only in Revelation 1:11 and in this brief letter. It is not found in the list of churches planted by the apostle Paul and his associates in the Book of Acts. However, it is likely that it began with Paul's evangelism in Ephesus and the other cities in Asia. Demetrius, a silversmith who made images of the goddess Diana, complained,

> *Moreover you see and hear that not only at Ephesus, but throughout almost all Asia, this Paul has persuaded and turned away many people, saying that they are not gods which are made with hands. —*

Acts 19:26

In the study of church history, Sardis represents the period of the Reformation, from 1517 until the mid-1700's, when the great revivals and modern missions movement began.

Connection

'These things say He who has the seven Spirits of God and the seven stars:' – Revelation 3:1b

The message begins on a stern note: *These things say.* The importance of what one says depends on the authority of the one who is speaking. A good parent can say things to an errant child that no one else has the right to say. The child might not realize the importance of those words, but if not, he or she is unwise, and heading for trouble.

Jesus reveals Himself to this church as *He who has the seven Spirits of God and the seven stars.* As seen in Chapter 1, verse 4, the expression "Seven Spirits" refers to The Holy Spirit, and the seven stars refer to the pastors of the seven churches (Chapter 1, verses 16 to 20). These images indicate His sovereignty and His right to tell them to repent and change their ways.

Commendation

"I know your works, that you have a name that you are alive"--Revelation 3:1c-d

Just as He said to each of the churches, Jesus reminded them, *I know your works.* Of course He knew what was in their hearts as well (John 2:24-25), but this constant reference to their works illustrates the proverbial concept that "As a man thinks, in his heart, so is he" (Proverbs 23:7). In fact, Jesus taught this same principle:

A good man out of the good treasure of his heart brings forth good; and an evil man out of the evil treasure of his heart brings forth evil. For out of the abundance of the heart his mouth speaks.

"But why do you call Me 'Lord, Lord,' and not do the things which I say? – Luke 6:45-46

In more recent times English Prime Minister Margaret Thatcher expressed this idea with these words:

Watch your thoughts for they become words. Watch your words for they become actions. Watch your actions for they become... habits. Watch your habits, for they become your character. And watch your character, for it becomes your destiny! What we think we become.[44]

(See the notes on "works" in Chapter 2, verse 2 and verse 26.)

Jesus told the members of the Sardis church, **you have a name that you are alive.** Some commentators feel that this is not really a commendation because, even though they gave the appearance of vitality, they no longer had any spiritual enthusiasm.

In earlier days, when they first received the Gospel, they must have been full of life. And perhaps they had still been excited about spiritual things for some time. But, like many churches in our own generation, their reputation rested on previous accomplishments—perhaps great Bible teaching, community outreach, and missionary zeal. Those days were past, but they were still known for their earlier activities.

Complaint

"But you are dead." – Revelation 3:1e

Unfortunately, in spite of their good reputation, Jesus had to say, **"But you are dead."** Earlier it was shown that death means "separation." (See the notes on Chapter 1, verse 18.) Spiritual death is separation of man's spirit from God. That is the condition of those who have not yet received

Christ as Savior. They are dead– separated from God because of their sins (Ephesians 2:1). In a church like this one at Sardis, people might still be attending services and perpetuating the boring rituals, but they don't experience the presence of the Lord Jesus and the fullness of the Holy Spirit. What they do on Sunday does not have a great impact on how they live the rest of the week.

Jesus said that the church at Sardis was dead! A "dead" church is no great surprise. There are plenty of them in our time, just as there have always been. These are churches where the evangelistic fire has gone out; where there are few new believers with their catalytic enthusiasm; where there is little sincere hunger to learn God's Word. A dead church might still have a full schedule of meetings, but no intense love for one another, no life-changing appeal for young people, and a shortage of workers and funds for children's ministries. It might be active in caring for social needs and conducting charities for the poor, but stagnant in its concern for revival and taking the Gospel to the lost.

Historical Fulfillment (Reformation Period)

At this point we turn our attention to the next period of church history. It began with good intentions, sincere study of God's Word, and amazing courage on the part of a few leaders to stand against the errors that had crept into the Catholic Church. This was the period of the Reformation.

There had been attempts at reforming the church by others like John Hus, John Wycliffe, and the Waldensians. Dissatisfaction with the Catholic Church was high.

For Martin Luther, who was a German monk, a Catholic priest, and a professor of theology, the fact that the church was selling indulgences was the last straw on the load of theological problems and unfortunate practices the church had adopted during the Middle Ages. Many of these issues were explained in the notes on the previous church–Thyatira.

The Reformation began in 1517, when Martin Luther posted his list of grievances, known as the "95 Theses," on the door of the All Saints' Church in Wittenberg, Germany. He didn't want to start a new denomination. He had hoped that his suggestions would bring about internal change in the church. However, his ideas were rejected by the hierarchy of the Catholic Church.

What was Good about the Reformation?

As we saw above, Jesus told the church at Sardis, *"You have a name that you are alive."* In the big picture of church history, this was also true of the Reformation period. They had a reputation that they were very motivated and active.

Bible Translations and Printed Bibles

One of the most important developments that led to the Reformation was the availability of printed Bibles. Johannes Gutenberg invented the printing press in 1450, and published The Latin Vulgate version of the Bible in 1456. This made it possible for sincere Bible scholars to read the whole Bible themselves.

Another Bible that is said to have inspired Martin Luther was Desiderius Erasmus' Greek New Testament, published in 1516. The ability to study the New Testament in the original language has been a key to careful Bible study ever since that time.

Once the Reformation began, the availability of Bibles in the languages of the common man became very important. Martin Luther provided a German version of the New Testament in 1522. William Tyndale published the first English New Testament in 1526. By 1611 the authorized King James Bible was made available to all in the English-speaking world.

Rejection of Obvious False Teaching and Practices

To Luther and the multitudes of people who followed him, the worst practice of the church was the sale of indulgences. An indulgence was forgiveness of sins from the pope for some special sacrifice by the sinner. The practice originated in 1095 at the call for participants in the Crusades. They were granted by Pope Urban II to knights who would risk their lives for the cause of recapturing Jerusalem and to people who could help finance the cause.[45]

The later doctrine of Purgatory opened the way for the widespread sale of indulgences. As mentioned before, there were sporadic teachings about Purgatory from about AD 1200, but in AD 1254 the concept was established formally by the First Council of Lyon. By Luther's time the practice of selling indulgences had become intolerable. Pope Leo X, who needed funds to complete the building of St. Peter's Basilica in Rome, authorized certain groups to market indulgences. These franchises were highly motivated because the vendors were allowed to keep about half of the proceeds. One authorized seller was Albert of Brandenburg:

[He] advertised that his indulgences (issued by the pope) came with a complete remission of sins, allowing escape from *all* of the pains of purgatory. Moreover, Albert claimed, purchasers of indulgences could use them to free a loved one already dead from the pains of purgatory that he or she might presently be experiencing.[46]

One of Brandenburg's vendors, John Tetzel, made matters even worse. He went from town to town with a procession that included local dignitaries, a cross bearing the papal arms, and the papal bull of indulgence carried on a velvet cushion. In each place he delivered a sermon that promised forgiveness to those who would buy an indulgence. Furthermore, he said, one ought to purchase an indulgence for his friends and relatives who were burning in the flames of purgatory. He created a jingle to help people decide. It was: "As soon as the coin in the coffer rings, the soul from purgatory springs."[47]

Luther and other reformers adopted many theological changes in order to return to the teaching of the Bible. Some of these issues were the priesthood (1 Peter 2:9; Revelation 5:10; Matthew 23:9), the meaning of the Mass (Hebrews 9:24-28; Hebrews 10:10-14), and the veneration of Mary and saints (Exodus 20:4-5).

The next year Ulrich Zwingli began the Swiss Reformation in Zurich. He embraced most of Luther's reforms and abandoned certain Roman Catholic teachings, such as clerical celibacy (1 Corinthians 9:5) and papal infallibility (Galatians 1:8). Church historians identified some 15 points of agreement between the two Reformation camps, and one serious difference. The Swiss disagreed with Luther's concept that the elements of the Lord's Supper retained their original nature (bread and wine) while also changing substance to become the body and blood of Christ. He called this concept "consubstantiation." (The Catholic Church viewed it as "transubstantiation," meaning that it no longer was bread and wine, but only the body and blood of Christ.) Zwingli insisted that the elements did not change, but were just symbolic of Christ's body and blood. Luther would not overlook this difference, so the two reformation movements proceeded separately. Luther's followers became the Lutherans. The followers of Zwingli and theologian John Calvin became the Presbyterians, the Dutch Reformed Church, and other branches of Calvinism in Europe.

During this transition Luther published *The Christian Nobility of the German Nation*, in which he taught the doctrine of the Priesthood of all believers and denied the authority of the Pope to interpret the Bible or confirm interpretation of it. The Catholic Church declared him a heretic in 1521 and formally excommunicated him.

Just a few years later, in 1525, another variation of the Reform movement had begun. This group, known as "Anabaptists," believed that the original Reformation didn't go far enough in the process of returning to biblical roots. They insisted that only adults should be baptized into the Christian faith. The Catholic Church had taught that babies should be baptized in order that, in case they die in infancy, they would go to heaven. These "Anabaptists" accepted the Bible's teaching that baptism was a person's public confession of faith in Christ, and therefore, could not be done by infants (Matthew 28:19-20; Acts 2:38-41; Romans 6:3-11). They considered it harmful to continue with the practice of infant baptism because many people would count on their baptism for salvation instead of developing a personal relationship with Christ.

Anabaptists gradually adopted several other tenets that they felt were more biblical than those of the earlier reformers. Here are some of these reforms and passages they often used in support of them: not taking oaths (Matthew 5:33-37), pacifism (Matthew 5:38-42), and separation of civil government from the church: meaning that believers must not fill any office or hold any rank under government (John 18:36; Romans 13:1-7).

The Mennonites and The Amish are descendants of this Anabaptist movement.

Some of the other major denominations that came out of the Reformation era are the Puritans, the Quakers and the Baptists.

Return to the Bible as the Only Infallible Source of Truth.

One of the primary tenants of Protestantism was expressed by the Latin words, *"Sola Scriptura,"* which means "Only Scripture," or "Scripture alone." Every aspect of our belief must be supported by biblical principles. Anything that disagrees with the Bible is to be rejected. The pronouncements of church leaders would no longer be sufficient to establish doctrine. It would have to be based on the Bible.

In 1536 John Calvin published first edition of *Institutes of the Christian Religion* in which he sought to employ this principle of the preeminence of Scripture.

Return to Faith instead of Works for Salvation

Two other corollaries of *Sola Scriptura* also defined the Protestant Reformation. *"Sola Fide"* (Faith alone) is the expression of the truth that no one is saved by good works, but only by faith. *"Sola Gratia"* (Grace alone) relates the fact that we do not deserve the gift of salvation, but it is given because of God's grace (undeserved favor) (Ephesians 2:8-10).

Courage and Conviction

Another good thing that should be remembered about the Reformation is that the leaders of this movement, and even the followers, were people of great bravery and strong beliefs. We owe an incredible debt of gratitude to those who had the knowledge and the strength of character to stand up to the hierarchy of the corrupt church as well as the kings and other civil authorities who were unduly influenced by the church.

Let us keep these good facets of the Reformation in mind as we explore the other side of the issue: Jesus' stinging rebuke: *But you are dead.*

"I know your works, that you have a name that you are alive, but you are dead."--Revelation 3:1:c-e

What was Wrong with the Reformation?

Now we must ask why Jesus gave this church the most stinging of all His rebukes, *but you are dead.* Many commentators describe this period of history as a time of "dead orthodoxy." The reformers were heroic in causing multitudes of Christians to return to their biblical roots and to embrace the simplicity of justification "by grace through faith." Salvation was accomplished solely by the death of Christ on the Cross. It was "not of works." But in the process, they failed to deal with many other theological errors in the church. This is somewhat understandable, since there was just too much to address all at once. Nevertheless, we need to consider some of these serious problems that were ignored.

Baptism of Infants/ Limited Evangelism

One of the corruptions of the Middle Ages was the teaching that infants should be baptized. As we mentioned above, this was seen as an effective method of keeping new members of families in the church. However, it gave false assurance to children who grew up, thinking that they were in compliance with God's will, even though they had never personally accepted Christ as their Lord and Savior.

The "Anabaptists," believed that the Reformation had not gone far enough toward restoring biblical teaching in several areas. One of the most important matters that still needed to be resolved was the question of when a person should be baptized. As discussed above, the Bible indicates that only adults should be baptized since it was a sign to the world of their belief in Christ.

Because the first wave of the Reformation failed to deal with this issue, there was a tendency to ignore the question of whether or not a person had actually received Christ as Savior. Belief in infant baptism had a stifling effect on evangelism.

To be fair, the reformers did clarify the biblical teaching about the sacrificial death of Christ and how His death became the basis of our salvation. So, the majority of converts to Protestantism probably did know enough to confess Christ and be born again. It should also be conceded that there have been some great evangelists among Lutherans and Presbyterians, who are descendants of the original reformers and still practice infant baptism today. One of the most notable in our generation was D. James Kennedy, the late pastor of Coral Ridge Presbyterian Church in Florida, and author of the "Evangelism Explosion" method of personal soul-winning.

On a personal note, my closest pastoral associate during the years of my first pastorate in East Los Angeles was a Lutheran who helped to bring evangelistic meetings to our area.

On the other hand, today's mainline denominations, including the Anglicans (Episcopalians) Lutherans and Presbyterians, are generally not as interested in evangelism as the newer branches of Christianity, like the Pentecostals and the Calvary Chapel movement.

Church /State Alliance

Another problem with the early Reformation was the continuation of the old corrupt model of the union of church and state, sometimes with the church making the major decisions and sometimes the state establishing the rules. This was all that they had experienced for many generations. Like infant baptism and other issues that would eventually become part of a second wave of reform, they didn't have the time to examine everything at once and make all the necessary changes to return to the simple truth of Scripture.

Luther was opposed to the church/state alliance in principle, but was not able to enforce it. An article in the Encyclopedia Britannica explained:

> Luther expressed, at least in theory, a most radical view of the separation of civil and religious realms through his doctrine of "the

two kingdoms." He could reduce his teaching virtually to an aphorism: God's Gospel ruled in the churchly realm and his law ruled in the civil society. To rule the church by the law or the civil realm by the Gospel would bring legalism to the sphere of grace and sentimentalism into the orbit of justice, thus dethroning God and enthroning Satan. In practice, however, the Lutheran Reformation worked to keep its ties to the civil order and was the established religion wherever it predominated in Germany and Scandinavia.[48]

In the light of the persecution they faced from the Catholic Church, it must have seemed necessary to many of the reformers to solicit the support of the civil authorities and to accept their protection.

Lutheranism became the state religion of Germany. Zwingli's Swiss Reformed Church was favored by the government of Switzerland. The Anglican Church was completely entangled with the government of its native country, England, because King Henry VIII caused the split from the Catholic Church. He wanted an annulment of his marriage to Catherine of Aragon so he could marry Anne Boyeln. His request was denied by Pope Clement VII, so he severed relations with the Catholic Church and took the position of Supreme Head of the Church of England.

While we are on the subject of the unholy alliance of church and civil government, we need to explore a terribly misunderstood concept in our generation. It is the expression "separation of church and state" that is now being used to deny the great spiritual heritage of our American nation and of our Founding Fathers.

As we have just seen, the *"union* of church and state" is a bad thing. But so is the modern concept of the *"separation* of church and state!"

Most of the original settlers of the United States were opposed to the European pattern of the merger of church and state. That union limited the religious freedom of many of the most devout Christians in Europe. The Puritans, Anabaptists, Baptists, Quakers, and other persecuted groups migrated to America in order to experience freedom of worship.

Those pioneers, and almost all of the Founding Fathers of our Republic, included references to God, prayers and quotations from the Bible in their charters, their speeches, their Declaration of Independence, their monuments, their courthouses, their legislative halls, and their schools! Only a person who is willfully ignorant can read the accounts of our early history and deny that this is true.

But in our generation, people who no longer want what our forefathers desired have taken a remark from one of Thomas Jefferson's letters ("separation of church and state") out of context, in order to mischaracterize the First Amendment of our Constitution. That amendment says that Congress shall not *establish* any religion. That is a prohibition against the union of church and state, and virtually all early Americans agreed with that principle; just as we all do today! It was a safeguard against the mistakes that were made in Europe. The amendment does not use the words, "separation of church and state." It does, however, guarantee freedom of religion and freedom of speech. Those are the very freedoms that resulted in the nearly endless biblical quotations in the literature and monuments of our capital, in prayers in Congress, in the posting of the Ten Commandments in the Supreme Court, in the mandating of Bibles for the Indians and in Judeo-Christian principles in the public school curriculum.

Today, people who do not believe the Bible are using the "separation of church and state" notion to corrupt the courts, strip morality from our schools, and redefine timeless institutions like marriage and family.

Persecution of Anabaptists and Other Reformers

This period of numerous differences in theology and alliances with various governments led to the emergence of many new denominations. This, in turn, resulted in persecutions and religious wars.

It could be expected that the Catholic Church would persecute reformers. It had been continuously engaged in various forms of the inquisition for nearly 300 years before the Reformation began. However, it comes as a surprise to most Christians today to learn that there was also widespread cruel persecution by the original reformers against the various denominations that emerged after them, especially the Anabaptists.

There were, to be sure, some heretical groups that emerged during the Reformation era, and some radical groups that were dangerous to society, such as the followers of Jan Mattijs who took over the Dutch city of Münster by force. However, most of the Anabaptists were pacifists, and none of their reforms are considered heretical by the Christians of today. Nevertheless, the Anabaptists were hunted down by the governments that were controlled by the other reformers. They were arrested, and put to death, often without any trial. Some were drowned, others burned at the stake, buried alive, or beheaded.

The exact number of Anabaptist martyrs is not known, but conservative estimates set the number at more than 4000.[49]

The Encyclopedia Britannica states, "Most of the early Anabaptist leaders died in prison or were executed."[50]

One popular book, The Martyr's Mirror, used woodcut illustrations to dramatize some of the hundreds of stories about the martyrdom of these early Anabaptists. One of the accounts is about Dirk Willems of Holland who was re-baptized and allowed others to be re-baptized in his home:

> Concerning his apprehension, it is stated by trustworthy persons, that when he fled he was hotly pursued by a thief-catcher, and as there had been some frost, said Dirk Willems ran before over the ice, getting across with considerable peril. The thief-catcher following him broke through, when Dirk Willems, perceiving that the former was in danger of his life, quickly returned and aided him in getting out, and thus saved his life. The thief-catcher wanted to let him go, but the burgomaster, very sternly called to him to consider his oath, and thus he was again seized by the thief-catcher, and, at said place, after severe imprisonment ... put to death at a lingering fire.[51]

In this overview of what was wrong with the Reformation, we will see two other important issues: their erroneous eschatology (teaching about the end time) and the rise of an unbelievably powerful counter-reformation led by the Jesuits.

Misunderstanding of the Future

One of the worst mistakes of the Reformers was the failure of most of them to correct the erroneous interpretation of Bible prophecies that had developed during the Middle Ages about Israel, the Second Coming of Christ and the other aspects of the future that were given by the Old Testament prophets, the Lord Jesus Himself, the apostles, and the Book of Revelation.

As we mentioned above, the best guiding principle of the Reformation was expressed by the concept called *Sola Scriptura*, meaning "only Scripture," or "by Scripture alone." This was understood to mean that the Bible is the only inspired—and therefore the most authoritative--source of truth. There is value in exposition (explanation) of the Word, as is done in preaching, and in the writing of theological books, commentaries, and devotional literature, but all of these are subordinate to, and are to be corrected by, the written Word of God.

Jesus, the "living Word" (John 1:1, 14), declared Himself to be "the way, the truth, and the life," (John 14:5), but even this great fact is revealed by the "written Word," The Bible:

Sanctify them by Your truth. Your word is truth. – John 17:17

Heaven and earth will pass away, but My words will by no means pass away. – Matthew 24:35

The Reformers meant well, but there were just so many misunderstandings about the plain teaching of the Bible that it was virtually impossible to correct everything at once. Therefore eschatology (the study of "last things"–from the Greek word *eschatos*) was not revised, and was made even more confusing during the Reformation period.

Near the beginning of this commentary (Chapter 1, verse 10) we discussed various ways that people have interpreted Bible prophecy through the years.

The main question about the prophecies of the Bible is whether or not they will be fulfilled literally. This is especially true about the many places in the New Testament where we are told that Jesus is returning and that His coming could take place at any time.

The Early Church interpreted these passages literally, and lived in the anticipation of Christ's any-moment return. Knowing this had a purifying and motivating effect on believers. They wanted to be living holy lives when Jesus would return. And, if He might return at any time, there was always an urgency to share the Gospel with those who had not yet received Him as Savior and Lord:

> *Therefore, since all these things will be dissolved, what manner of persons ought you to be in holy conduct and godliness, looking for and hastening the coming of the day of God. . .* – 2 Peter 3:11-12a.

The other kind of interpretation is the allegorical method. An allegory is a story that is meant to teach a moral lesson. Of course the Bible does contain allegories and many other kinds of symbolic language, but the literal approach to interpretation accepts the idea that once the figure of speech is understood; there is a literal fulfillment for any prophetic utterance. This allegorical approach does not look for a future historical event, but is satisfied with the idea that the story teaches a general moral principle. From this point of view, the promises to Israel might be mistakenly transferred to the church, and the numerous Bible promises of a glorious messianic kingdom and a literal thousand-year reign of Christ can be wrongly interpreted as a gradual transformation of the culture from a pagan civilization to a Christian kingdom.

Now we need to look at the predominant beliefs about the future over the course of history.

- Early Church Eschatology

The first three of the churches in this prophecy would all be part of the Early Church. They were: Ephesus (Apostolic), Smyrna (Persecution), and Pergamum (Compromise). These churches took the simple, biblical "futurist" method of interpretation, which resulted in a "premillennial" view of eschatology. These are pretty technical expressions, so let us break these terms down a little bit.

The "futurist" interpretation accepts what the Bible says about future events literally.

The "premillennial" eschatology was built on this literal futurist approach. It was the belief that Jesus will return to Earth to reign for a thousand years. The Early Christians expected that, at any time, Christ might "catch up" His church at the Rapture (John 14:1-3; 1 Corinthians 15:50-58; 1 Thessalonians 4:13-18; Revelation 4:1). Then, after the Tribulation period (Jeremiah 30:1-7; Daniel 11:20-45; Ezekiel Chapters 38 and 39; Matthew 24:9-28; Revelation Chapters 6 through 19), they believed that Jesus will return to establish the Messianic Kingdom that Isaiah and most of the Old Testament prophets promised extensively in the Old Testament. According to this Book of Revelation, the Kingdom will be a thousand-year reign of righteousness over a peaceful and prosperous world (Matthew 24:29-32; Revelation 20:1-8). After the millennium there will be a judgment of non-believers (Revelation 20:11-15). This will be followed by the creation of a New Heaven and New Earth (Revelation Chapters 21 and 22).

- Catholic Eschatology

The Catholic Church is defined by the fourth church of this prophecy: Thyatira (Middle Ages). The leaders of the church felt that they were establishing the Kingdom of Heaven. They employed the historicist (allegorical) method of interpretation, believing that the events in their generations were gradually fulfilling the prophecies.

Since the theologians of the Middle Ages thought that they were building the kingdom they didn't feel a need for a literal thousand-year reign of Christ in the future. Using the allegorical method of interpretation, they taught that the Old Testament prophecies of a messianic millennium referred to the kingdom they were creating themselves, that would last forever. They believed that Jesus would come back to reign once they had finished preparing for His return. And from their point of view, Israel had been replaced by the church, so they did not look for literal fulfillments of the Old Testament promises. Therefore their eschatology (teaching about "last things" or the end time) was "amillennial."

- Reformation Eschatology

The Reformation is represented by Sardis, the fifth church of this prophecy. As we noted above, it failed to live up to its own standard of "Scripture only," and continued to hold the amillennial view of the future which they thought would result in a godly church/state union to which Christ could eventually return as King.

John Calvin did introduce a variation to the eschatology the Reformers had inherited from the Catholic Church. He called it "Covenant Theology." This viewpoint considers all of history as the development of three overarching theological covenants--the covenants of redemption, of works, and of grace. In their system, the covenants include the return of Christ, resurrection of the dead, and the Great White Throne Judgment, but no literal 1000 year Millennium.

It was common for the Reformers to consider the Catholic Church, with its church/state alliances, the evil last world empire of the Book of Revelation, and to claim that the Pope was the Antichrist.

A completely new view of the future was invented during the Reformation period by the Jesuits, a new Catholic order that we will explore next. It was called Preterism (from the Latin *praeter—meaning "past."*) Versions of this theory relate most, or even all, of the Book of Revelation to the events of the 1st Century, revolving around the destruction of Jerusalem in AD 70 and/or the persecutions of the Roman Empire. It was presented as an alternative to the growing belief that the Pope was Antichrist. Preterism was later adopted by some Protestants.

- Later Developments in Eschatology

When we study the next church in Revelation 3 we will see that there was a strong return to the literal interpretation of prophecy, resulting in a renewed interest in the Rapture of the church and the development of end time events. It was also a boon to evangelism and the missionary movement.

The Counter-Reformation

Another important reason the Reformation period might be considered "dead" was the success of the Catholic Counter-Reformation and the failure of the new Protestants to walk in the fullness of the Holy Spirit.

Rise of the Jesuits

Most Christians have heard of the Jesuits but don't know much about them. This is especially interesting in the light of the fact that they are now the largest order in the Catholic Church, and Pope Francis, who was recently enthroned as Pope, is the first Jesuit ever to become Pope.

Their story began with the dramatic life of Ignatius of Loyola (1491 to 1556), an aristocratic young man who became a Spanish knight, but was seriously wounded in the Battle of Pamplona in 1521 when he was struck by a cannonball. The injury left him partially disabled, but during his long recovery he devoted himself to serve God with a zeal that was equal to his former military discipline. He had spiritual visions and developed an intense devotional life, from which he conceived and published "Spiritual Exercises" that would eventually be required of all who would follow him.

Ignatius travelled to the Holy Land, and some believe he received secret information about the practices of the Knights Templar, which had been disbanded in 1312.[52]

He studied theology during the early days of the Spanish Inquisition and the Protestant Reformation. He became a priest, and then, with a few disciplined followers, including Francis Xavier, who would become a missionary the to the far East, formed the "Society of Jesus" in 1539. This organization was recognized by Pope Paul III in 1540 as a new Catholic order. Their purpose was to "do battle in the Lord God's service under the banner of the Cross."[53] They pledged absolute loyalty to the Pope. One of Loyola's most famous quotations is:

That we may be altogether of the same mind and in conformity with the Church herself, if she shall have defined anything to be black which appears to our eyes to be white, we ought in like manner to pronounce it to be black.[54]

Loyola was appointed the first Superior General, with dictatorial powers over the members of the order. In this role he was to be honored, like the Pope, as the representative of Christ. This equality with the Pope led to the unofficial title of "The Black Pope."

Loyola and his followers were extremely devout and disciplined. With Xavier's influence, the order became a formidable force for missionary expansion.

With the passing of time the Catholic Church began to depend on the vitality of this new order to help suppress the spread of the Reformation.

The emphasis of the Reformation was to return to the Bible, and to allow common people to read and study it in their own languages. This raised serious questions about all of the un-biblical concepts that had been adopted by the church during the thousand-plus years of the Middle Ages.

The Society of Jesus, which began to be called "Jesuits," sought to supplement biblical knowledge with other kinds of information. They became the champions of science and education. Their members, who were actually monks, were encouraged to wear normal clothing and assume positions in all areas of influence. In essence, they became agents for the Catholic Church to discredit Protestant beliefs and bring people back into the fold of the Catholic Church.

The statue of Ignatius of Loyola in St. Peter's Basilica in Rome portrays him stepping on the neck of a Protestant (presumably Martin Luther).

Loyola died in 1556 but his successors kept building on his foundational concepts.

By the 1700's Jesuits were viewed as foreign agents in some countries (as were other missionary groups). They were banned in France and Spain, and then, in 1773, Pope Clement XIV dissolved the order. They were restored however in 1814.[55]

They have now grown from a small band of dedicated soldiers to the largest men's single religious order of priests and brothers in the Catholic Church with approximately 18,000 members world-wide. Critics claim that they are constantly infiltrating governments, businesses, the arts, and especially education.

There are now 28 Jesuit colleges and universities in the United States and some 189 Jesuit institutions of higher learning worldwide![56] Their students are not generally trained to accept the Bible literally, which would advance the Protestant agenda, but to trust also in humanism, psychology, and philosophy.

More will be seen about the influence of the Jesuits in the historical portions of Church of Philadelphia in Revelation 3.

The Council of Trent

If the Jesuits were the agents of the Counter Reformation, the Council of Trent was the visible, spectacular, and formal declaration of war against Protestants. It was a series of meetings over a period of 18 years in various venues. It began in 1545 and concluded in 1563.

The Council reconfirmed all of the beliefs and practices that were questioned by the Protestant Reformation, and pronounced anathemas (eternal damnations) upon anyone who believed the things the Reformers taught, which are basically the same things that evangelicals believe and teach today![57]

Some of the key concepts of Catholicism that were reaffirmed by the Council of Trent were:

> Works-based salvation through the sacraments and confession. Man participates in his own salvation. There was no mention of assurance of salvation--one could die with an unconfessed mortal sin.
> Indulgences
> Purgatory
> Sacrifice of the Mass
> Transubstantiation
> Veneration of Saints/ Images
> Prayers for the dead[58]

The result of this Council was great persecution of Reformers and the prolonging of the Inquisitions. Whole groups of dissenters, such as the Huguenots and Waldensians were massacred. Religious wars continued for decades in France, the Netherlands and Spain. The "Thirty-Years War" (1618--1648) involved fighting between Catholics and Protestants throughout all of Europe, and is considered the continent's most devastating war.

Need for the Fullness of the Holy Spirit

As we saw at the beginning of this verse, Jesus described Himself as *He who has the seven Spirits of God and the seven stars."* This expression was first given in Chapter 1, verse 4. It was a reference to the Holy Spirit. We have already seen that the number seven is used repeatedly in Revelation to signify completeness and inclusiveness ("seven churches," "seven stars," etc.). John MacArthur suggests that it might also be a reference to an Old Testament description of the Holy Spirit:

> *The Spirit of the LORD shall rest upon Him,*
> *The Spirit of wisdom and understanding,*
> *The Spirit of counsel and might,*
> *The Spirit of knowledge and of the fear of the LORD.* -- Isaiah 11:1-2

MacArthur comments, "The Spirit of the Lord is described as the Spirit of wisdom and understanding, counsel, strength, knowledge and fear, adding those six to the title Spirit of the Lord gives you the seven-fold Spirit, that would be the Holy Spirit described in the fullness of His operation."[59]

This gives us an insight about the biggest problem of all for the Reformation Church. In spite of their diligent study and their courageous actions, they often failed to realize that victory in spiritual warfare depends on the power of the Holy Spirit. Spiritual life and vitality does not come from merely knowing the truth, but from the power of the Holy Spirit literally living within us and controlling our thoughts and actions (John 14:15-27; 16;5-15; Galatians 5:16-26; Ephesians 5:18-21; 6:10-18).

The apostles and other early church leaders depended completely on the Holy Spirit. It has been noted by many commentators that the Book of Acts is really a record of The Acts of the Holy Spirit. By the time of the Reformation the church was no longer steeped in the details of God's Word. We have no doubt that the Reformation was the work of the Holy Spirit, or that godly Christians during this period were often led by the Spirit. However, there was little emphasis on the work of the Holy Spirit. Unfortunately this was another error that was carried over into the Reformation Church—a dependence on self-effort instead of dependence on the Third Person of the Trinity.

When we study the next church—Philadelphia—we will see that later reformation groups like the Pietists, the Moravians, and the Methodists, were characterized by much greater reliance on the power of the Holy Spirit. This is the way it will be in the future kingdom predicted by Zechariah:

> *"This is: the word of the LORD to Zerubbabel:*
> *'Not by might nor by power, but by My Spirit,"*
> *Says the LORD of hosts.* – Zechariah 4:6

Critique

Be watchful, and strengthen the things which remain, that are ready to die, for I have not found your works perfect before God. – Revelation 3:2

We come now to Our Lord's critique of the church at Sardis. First He said, *"Be watchful."* The Greek word translated "watchful" is *gregoreo*. It means "stay awake; watch; be awake, vigilant." Jesus used this word in His great Olivet Discourse. When His disciples asked when He was going to return to Earth, He said,

> *Watch therefore, for you do not know what hour your Lord is coming.* – Matthew 24:42

In the same sermon, after giving the parable of the five wise and five foolish virgins, He warned,

"Watch therefore, for you know neither the day nor the hour in which the Son of Man is coming." – Matthew 25:13

It is also interesting that in the next chapter, when Jesus went into the Garden of Gethsemane to pray, he took Peter, James and John with Him,

Then He said to them, "My soul is exceedingly sorrowful, even to death. Stay here and watch with Me." – Matthew 26:38

This brings up the wonderful concept of Revival. When the church (or even an individual) is in spiritual decline, or complacency, it is like falling into a stupor or a deep sleep. But like a call to "get up" in the morning, it is possible for the comatose believer to be restored to His "first love" for Christ (see notes on Chapter 2, verse 4).

There is so much need for revival in our day. Thankfully, there are many signs that God is at work, hopefully planning to send a great in-gathering of young people who have been raised in secular homes and subjected to an anti-Christian education and an immoral culture.

The spiritual atmosphere today reminds me of some of the disappointing trends in the 1960's, when I first began to pastor a church in East Los Angeles. They were the days of hippies, psychedelic drugs, free-love, and riots. I wrote a little book just for our congregation. It was called *Reveille: Arise and Conquer.* Reveille is the bugle call used to awaken the troops to prepare for battle. We were seeing signs of revival around us: massive Billy Graham crusades, the birth of Campus Crusade for Christ, and the early days of the Jesus People Movement. We mobilized into small groups to study, pray, and be a part of what The Lord was doing in our needy world.

Jesus continued His instruction for those who would be willing to be revived: **and strengthen the things which remain, that are ready to die.** The things that remain were the good things about the Reformation: The return to God's Word; the rejection of non-Biblical ideas; the amazing zeal and courage that infused the church. However, as good as those things were, unless the church in Smyrna would be revived, even those gains would be lost.

There is something encouraging about our Lord's warning for His church to wake up. Even if the majority of Christians at Sardis were in a spiritual coma, and were not walking in the Holy Spirit, this situation could evidently be reversed. Jesus' call to revival implies strongly that they should have, and more importantly, that they could have, an awakening!

To God's glory, the Reformation Period of history, which the church of Sardis prefigured, also had its revivals. The Anabaptist movement and all the martyrs of the period from various branches of the Reformation bear witness to revivals, big and small, during those years.

In our own times, C.S. Lewis, John Stott and others from "old-line reformation churches" were examples of renewed thinking and teaching. The charismatic Catholic movement was also an encouraging development.

Then Jesus said, *for I have not found your works perfect before God.* The word for "found" in the original Greek is *heurisko, meaning* 'to discover." From this word we derive "Eureka,"–"I found it!"–popularized during the gold-rush days in California.

The Lord is looking for the hidden gold in our lives. Good works are not enough. Deeds can't save, but they are the inevitable result of a changed life (Ephesians 2:8-10), walking in the Spirit. We noted earlier that the lack of this this was the greatest failure of the Reformation age.

The word for 'perfect" is the Greek pleroo, which means to be full, complete. This should not be thought of as sinless perfection, but of a generally godly and productive life.

Recently we participated in the memorial service for a close personal friend and long-term missionary to Brazil with Youth for Christ. Paul Overholt, in his eighties, was still organizing teams to go there to improve the YFC camp even more! He was seriously ill and weakened, but he still hoped to go there again the next summer. Paul was responsible for the salvation of many thousands of Brazilian young people. He was so venerated there that, when I saw him in action and noted the reverence Brazilian Christians had for him, I started calling him "The Pope of Brazil." Was he perfect? He would be the first to say "no!" But his deeds proceeded from a life of personal commitment to Jesus Christ and a dependence on the filling of the Holy Spirit.

Counsel

Remember therefore how you have received and heard; hold fast and repent. Therefore if you will not watch, I will come upon you as a thief, and you will not know what hour I will come upon you. You have a few names even in Sardis who have not defiled their garments; and they shall walk with Me in white, for they are worthy. He who overcomes shall be clothed in white garments, and I will not blot out his name from the Book of Life; but I will confess his name before My Father and before His angels.

"He who has an ear, let him hear what the Spirit says to the churches."--Revelation 3:3-6

Jesus told the believers at Sardis, ***Remember therefore!*** There are times in the lives of most Christians when they realize that they no longer care as deeply about spiritual things as they once did. They have slowly drifted away from the excitement of being a new creation in Christ (2 Corinthians 5:17). They have forgotten some of the vital truths that were so life-changing at the time. To the church at Ephesus Jesus said they had lost their "first love" (See notes on Chapter 2, verse 4).

What did the Lord suggest that they remember? It should include ***how you have received and heard.*** How indeed had the church at Sardis first received the Gospel? It was by the sacrificial missionary service of the apostle Paul or one of his students. The Good News was delivered to them at considerable effort and risk by people who cared more about the spiritual condition of strangers than they cared about their own comfort. They had to boldly proclaim the truth in the face of persecution and hardship (Acts 13:50; 2 Timothy 2:1-7).

By the time this Revelation was read to the church at Smyrna, they would have heard the reading of the Gospels and Paul's letters (2 Peter 3:15-16). (See the notes on Chapter 1, verse 3, about the blessing promised to those who could not read, but who would listen to the words of the book.) These had all been circulated to the churches before Revelation was written.

They would also have heard the testimonies of the missionaries who visited their city, and the stories of faithful believers in the early years of their history as a church.

If they would just remember these wonderful truths, their hearts would surely be softened. The same is true for us. If we would allow ourselves to recall the circumstances that led to our acceptance of Jesus Christ as Savior; remember how we felt when we made that decision; remember the joys of Bible study and Christian fellowship; and remember the other events that shaped our early Christian life, we would undoubtedly desire to regain that blessed state of mind.

Every Christian should have vivid memories of his or her Christian journey. It is a good idea to record the key events of one's spiritual life. The best time to write it down in a journal (or diary) is as soon as possible after a major event, such as accepting Christ, being baptized, leading a friend to Christ, etc. Unfortunately, most people fail to do this at the proper time. The good news is that our wonderful God-given minds will help us remember much of the detail if we will sit down and think about it. We can write what we remember (maybe using a computer, so it can be expanded later), and most of us will begin to recall more of the story later. We can then add the additional information to what we have already begun. This testimony, or story of our spiritual lives, will help us remember what we have "received and heard."

Hold fast and repent, were two action points that Jesus recommended to several of these churches in Asia. To hold fast means to "keep." Some things should be kept as long as we live. That is why we save photographs, love letters, and keepsakes passed down to us. In this context, Jesus was telling the members at Sardis to treasure and guard the things they had received and heard. There is a tendency in every generation, and we certainly see it in our days, to jettison too much of the past so that we will be considered fresh and relevant. We can, and should, change our methodology in order to relate to our changing culture, but we dare not lose the vital and timeless truth taught in God's Word! The motto of the Youth for Christ organization puts it succinctly: "Geared to the times, anchored to the Rock."

And, as we have already seen in the messages to Ephesus and Pergamum, Jesus calls worldly believers to repent! (See the notes on Chapter 2, verses 5 and 16.) True repentance includes honest confession of sin, and a change of heart that is sincere enough to bring about a change of behavior as well.

Fortunately we have the Holy Spirit to guide us in our journey. Being "filled with the Holy Spirit" (Ephesians 5:18; also called "walking in the Spirit" Galatians 5:16) is a choice that every Christian must make on a daily basis. The failure to yield to God's control causes us to drift away from the blessings and victories that the Lord has in mind for us. Remember that we discovered above, in the history of the Reformation Age (See the notes on Chapter 3, verse 1), that failure to be controlled by the Holy Spirit was the big mistake that many of the reformers made, and because of it, even though they had a reputation of being alive, in the Lord's eyes they were "dead."

Therefore if you will not watch...

As in the previous verse, the Greek word for "watch" is *gregoreo*, meaning "to be awake." This is a return to the concept of revival, or "awakening." The believers at Sardis had been advised to allow God to revive them. Now Jesus cautions that if they will still not be roused from their spiritual slumber, He will visit them in their comatose state like a thief.

I will come upon you as a thief, and you will not know what hour I will come upon you.

The primary application of this warning is the danger that, if the members of the church at Sardis do not repent and experience a revival, Jesus will remove their church completely. This is similar to the notice that He had given the church at Ephesus when He said,

> *Remember therefore from where you have fallen; repent and do the first works, or else I will come to you quickly and remove your lampstand from its place— unless you repent. – Revelation 2:5*

Unfortunately, The Lord has had to remove a great number of dead churches down through the centuries. This is reminiscent of the story of Ichabod in the Old Testament:

Now his daughter-in-law, Phinehas's wife, was with child, due to be delivered; and when she heard the news that the ark of God was captured, and that her father-in-law and her husband were dead, she bowed herself and gave birth, for her labor pains came upon her. And about the time of her death the women who stood by her said to her, "Do not fear, for you have borne a son." But she did not answer, nor did she regard it. Then she named the child Ichabod, saying, "The glory has departed from Israel!" because the ark of God had been captured and because of her father-in-law and her husband. – 1 Samuel 4:19-21

A church might still exist for some time after the congregation has lost its spiritual vitality, but unless the people allow the Lord to awaken them, He will write "Ichabod–The Glory has departed," over them.

During His earthly life, Jesus used the imagery of a thief in another way. He described the plight of those who will claim to be believers, but will not truly know Him when He appears at His Glorious Return (at the end of the Tribulation). The return of The Lord Jesus is a major theme in the Book of Revelation, so we will review His teaching briefly here:

"Immediately after the tribulation of those days the sun will be darkened, and the moon will not give its light; the stars will fall from heaven, and the powers of the heavens will be shaken. Then the sign of the Son of Man will appear in heaven, and then all the tribes of the earth will mourn, and they will see the Son of Man coming on the clouds of heaven with power and great glory. And He will send His angels with a great sound of a trumpet, and they will gather together His elect from the four winds, from one end of heaven to the other.

"Now learn this parable from the fig tree: When its branch has already become tender and puts forth leaves, you know that summer is near. So you also, when you see all these things, know that it is near—at the doors! Assuredly, I say to you, this generation will by no means pass away till all these things take place. Heaven and earth will pass away, but My words will by no means pass away.

*"But of that day and hour no one knows, not even the angels of heaven, but My Father only. But as the days of Noah were, so also will the coming of the Son of Man be. For as in the days before the flood, they were eating and drinking, marrying and giving in marriage, until the day that Noah entered the ark, and did not know until the flood came and took them all away, so also will the coming of the Son of Man be. Then two men will be in the field: one will be taken and the other left. Two women will be grinding at the mill: one will be taken and the other left. Watch therefore, for you do not know what hour your Lord is coming. But know this, that if the master of the house had known what hour **the thief would come**, he would have watched and not allowed his house to be broken into. Therefore you also be ready, for the Son of Man is coming at an hour you do not expect.* – Matthew 24:29-44; (See also Luke 12:37-40; Revelation 16:15-16; and Peter's commentary on the same matter in 2 Peter 3:10-13).

The apostle Paul used the imagery of the thief to describe the sudden and unexpected event of the Rapture of the church (before the Tribulation).

> *But I do not want you to be ignorant, brethren, concerning those who have fallen asleep, lest you sorrow as others who have no hope. For if we believe that Jesus died and rose again, even so God will bring with Him those who sleep in Jesus.*
>
> *For this we say to you by the word of the Lord, that we who are alive and remain until the coming of the Lord will by no means precede those who are asleep. For the Lord Himself will descend from heaven with a shout, with the voice of an archangel, and with the trumpet of God. And the dead in Christ will rise first. Then we who are alive and remain shall be caught up together with them in the clouds to meet the Lord in the air. And thus we shall always be with the Lord. Therefore comfort one another with these words.*
>
> *But concerning the times and the seasons, brethren, you have no need that I should write to you. For you yourselves know perfectly that the day of the Lord so comes as **a thief in the night**. For when they say, "Peace and safety!" then sudden destruction comes upon them, as labor pains upon a pregnant woman. And they shall not escape. But you, brethren, are not in*

darkness, so that this Day should overtake you as a thief. You are all sons of light and sons of the day. We are not of the night nor of darkness. Therefore let us not sleep, as others do, but let us watch and be sober. For those who sleep, sleep at night, and those who get drunk are drunk at night. But let us who are of the day be sober, putting on the breastplate of faith and love, and as a helmet the hope of salvation. For God did not appoint us to wrath, but to obtain salvation through our Lord Jesus Christ, who died for us, that whether we wake or sleep, we should live together with Him.

Therefore comfort each other and edify one another, just as you also are doing. – 1 Thessalonians 4:13 - 5:11

There are many significant differences between the Rapture and the Glorious Return of Christ. We will consider these in detail when we study the message to the church at Philadelphia in verses 10 and 11 of this third chapter of Revelation.

The first part of this counsel from the Lord Jesus to the church at Sardis was a strong warning ("hold fast," "repent," "I will come on you as a thief…"). However, the rest of the message is most positive. It reminds us of the central thesis of the story that John had recorded at an earlier time in his Gospel account:

"For God did not send His Son into the world to condemn the world, but that the world through Him might be saved." – John 3:17

Jesus said, ***"You have a few*** names even in Sardis who have not defiled their garments." Unfortunately, there were not many outstanding Christians left there, but at least, there were a few! As we have mentioned before, there is always a remnant of true believers, even in the worst of times (See the notes on Chapter 2, verses 24-25). The apostle Paul mentioned this fact:

I say then, has God cast away His people? Certainly not! For I also am an Israelite, of the seed of Abraham, of the tribe of Benjamin. God has not cast away His people whom He foreknew. Or do you not know what the Scripture says of Elijah, how he pleads with God against Israel, saying, "LORD, they have killed Your prophets and torn down Your altars, and I alone am left, and they seek my life"? But what does the divine response say to him? "I have reserved for Myself seven thousand men who have not bowed the knee to Baal." Even so then, at this present time there is a remnant according to the election of grace. – Romans 11:1-5

It is interesting that Jesus said there are a few **"names"** who had kept the faith. Some versions of the Bible translate this word as "people," and that is an acceptable translation in this context. But the choice of the word "names" emphasizes the fact that the Lord knows the personal identity of each of those godly believers. We discussed this before in Chapter 2, verse 13, where Jesus mentioned "Antipas, My faithful martyr." Antipas is not mentioned anywhere else in the Bible, but Jesus knew him by name and loved him!

Jesus said that this remnant had **not defiled their garments**. The Greek word for "defiled" is *molyno*, which means "to pollute, stain, contaminate, or defile [by sin]." The concept of stained garments was very familiar to the people of Sardis because garment-dying was one of their major industries. A garment was made more beautiful and valuable by dying it with purple or other regal colors. On the other hand, people everywhere know that it is a disappointment, or even a disgrace to stain their best clothes with an unwanted substance. Two of the many ways a person can be "defiled" by sin are illicit sex and idol worship (Revelation 14:4; 1 Corinthians 8:7). The worst stain for one who claims to be a follower of Christ is unfaithfulness to Him and His Word.

Jesus promised that members of this faithful remnant **will walk with Me** in white. Walking with the Lord Jesus is a picture of the ultimate phase of redemption: going to be where He is. Most people refer to this as "heaven," but there is much to learn about heaven and hell and other places of temporary dwelling after this life has been spent. These important theological aspects will be studied in later commentaries.

There is a folk-story of a boy who heard his elders trying to sort out biblical teaching about Paradise, Heaven, the Third Heaven, and the New Heaven and New Earth. He just listened until one of them turned to him and asked him where he thought heaven was. He ended the discussion by his simple answer, "Wherever Jesus is, that must be heaven."

In the light of these key passages of Scripture, the boy's answer was pretty good:

> [Paul] *So we are always confident, knowing that while we are at home in the body we are absent from the Lord. For we walk by faith, not by sight. We are confident, yes, well pleased rather to be absent from the body and to be present with the Lord.*– 2 Corinthians 5:6-8

> [Jesus] *And if I go and prepare a place for you, I will come again and receive you to Myself; that where I am, there you may be also.* – John 14:3

> [Paul] *For the Lord Himself will descend from heaven with a shout, with the voice of an archangel, and with the trumpet of God. And the dead in Christ will rise first. Then we who are alive and remain shall be caught up together with them in the clouds to meet the Lord in the air. And thus we shall always be with the Lord.* – 1 Thessalonians 4:16-17

When Jesus said believers will walk with Him **in white, for they are worthy.** He was referring to the imputation of His own righteousness to those who were sinners, and therefore unrighteous (Romans 3:21-26; 4:3, 6, 22-25; 6:1-23).

This divine cleansing was described in various places in the Old Testament:

> *Wash me thoroughly from my iniquity,*
> *And cleanse me from my sin…*
> *Purge me with hyssop, and I shall be clean;*
> *Wash me, and I shall be whiter than snow.* – Psalm 51:2, 7

> *"Come now, and let us reason together," Says the LORD,*
> *"Though your sins are like scarlet,*
> *They shall be as white as snow;*
> *Though they are red like crimson,*
> *They shall be as wool.* – Isaiah 1:18

Later in Revelation we will also see this symbolism of white robes for those whose sins have been washed away by faith in Jesus Christ (Revelation 7:9, 14; 19:14).

A popular Christian song by the Newsboys expresses what happens when our sins were taken by Jesus and His righteousness was imputed to us.

Doctor's coming, looking grim
"Do you have a favorite hymn?"
Check your balance through the years
All accounts are in arrears
Guilt is bitter, grace is sweet
Park it here on the mercy seat

When we don't get what we deserve
That's a real good thing, a real good thing
When we get what we don't deserve
That's a real good thing, a real good thing.

He who overcomes shall be clothed in white garments. This is a re-statement of the vital truth we just explored above about the forgiveness of our sin. For a discussion about the fact that every true Christian is an overcomer, see the notes on Chapter 2, verse 1. Also, see the notes on Chapter 3, verse 26, where it is specified that an overcomer is one who remains true to Christ to the end!

And I will not blot out his name from the Book of Life. In chapter 2, verse 23 we considered what it meant for sinners to be judged according to their works. In contrast, true believers will be forgiven because their names are written in the Book of Life. We need to repeat a summary of our findings here because this is the primary passage for the expression, "Book of Life."

When we get to Revelation Chapter 20, we will study the "Great White Throne Judgment" of unbelievers. Their recorded works will be brought up as a basis for their judgment:

And I saw the dead, small and great, standing before God, and books were opened. And another book was opened, which is the Book of Life. And the dead were judged according to their works, by the things which were written in the books. – Revelation 20:12

True believers in Christ will already have been judged--and acquitted- on the basis that their name is in "The Book of Life" (Philippians 4:3; Revelation 3:5; 13:8; 17:8; 20:12, 15; 21:27; 22:19). Since Jesus died for the sins of the whole world (1 John 2:2), All names were apparently written in this book "from the foundation of the world" (Revelation 17:8). True believers' names are not blotted out of this book (Revelation 3:5), but those who do not trust Jesus' substitutionary death will evidentially have their names blotted out (John 3:16-18, 36).

But I will confess his name before My Father and before His angels. John had undoubtedly heard these words of Jesus when He told his disciples,

"Therefore whoever confesses Me before men, him I will also confess before My Father who is in heaven. But whoever denies Me before men, him I will also deny before My Father who is in heaven. – John 10:32-33

He who has an ear, let him hear what the Spirit says to the churches. Once again, the Lord reminds the readers (and listeners) that this message is from God by His Holy Spirit (See notes on Chapter 2, verse 7).

To Philadelphia   3:7-13   (Missionary Church   Mid-1700's – 1900's)

"And to the angel of the church in Philadelphia write,
'These things says He who is holy, He who is true, "He
who has the key of David, He who opens and no one shuts,
and shuts and no one opens": "I know your works. See, I have
set before you an open door, and no one can shut it; for you
have a little strength, have kept My word, and have not
denied My name. Indeed I will make those of the synagogue of
Satan, who say they are Jews and are not, but lie—indeed I
will make them come and worship before your feet, and to
know that I have loved you. Because you have kept My
command to persevere, I also will keep you from the hour of
trial which shall come upon the whole world, to test those
who dwell on the earth. Behold, I am coming quickly! Hold
fast what you have, that no one may take your crown. He who
overcomes, I will make him a pillar in the temple of My God,
and he shall go out no more. I will write on him the name of
My God and the name of the city of My God, the New
Jerusalem, which comes down out of heaven from My God.
And I will write on him My new name.
"He who has an ear, let him hear what the Spirit says
to the churches."'" – Revelation 3:7-13

Connection

And to the angel of the church in Philadelphia write... The
city of Philadelphia was founded during the 2nd Century BC by either King
Eumenes II of Pergamum or his brother, King Attalus II. Eumenes gave
his brother the title "Philadelphus" (meaning "brotherly love," or "lover of
a brother"). He called him that because there was a time when Attalus could
have stolen Eumenes' throne, but he would not do so because of his loyalty
to his brother.

The new city was called Philadelphia in honor of Attalus. It was intended from the beginning to be a center of Greek culture and language. As such, it would be an outpost for the spread of Hellenism to Phrygia and Lydia.

Philadelphia was built on a hill some 800 feet above the fertile Hermus Valley, and was situated about 30 miles southeast of Sardis. By the time this letter was written, the city was strategically located as a stop on the "Imperial Post Road." This was one of the famous Roman roads; the wide stone-paved long-distance highways from Rome to the edges of its empire. This segment passed through Troas and the harbor at Smyrna on the way to the East. Like the "Pony Express" of early American history, it was travelled by official messengers, and facilitated commerce.

The origin of the community of Christians in Philadelphia is not described in the Bible, but it was probably evangelized while Paul was in Ephesus for three years (Acts Chapters Nineteen and Twenty--See the notes on Chapter 2, verse. 1).

The only references to Philadelphia in the Bible are found in the Book of Revelation (1:11 and 3:7). However, Ignatius of Antioch, the church father and pupil of St. John, recorded information about it and sent an epistle to the believers there.[60]

As we will discover, the church at Philadelphia was the best of the seven churches. Its very name is a reminder that the essence of Christian community is love for one another. After the Last Supper, on the night before He was crucified, Jesus told His disciples,

> *A new commandment I give unto you, That ye love one another; as I have loved you, that ye also love one another. By this shall all men know that ye are my disciples, if ye have love one to another.* – John 13:34-35 (See also: John 15:12, 17; Romans 12:10; 13:8; Galatians 5:13; Ephesians 4:2; 1 Thessalonians 3:12; 4:9; Hebrews 10:24; 1 Peter 1:22; 3:8; 1 John 3:11, 23; 4:7, 11-12; 2 John 1:5)

These things says He who is holy... The author of this letter, the Lord Jesus Christ, gives some of His credentials at this point, as He did with all of the other churches. In the previous letters He applied images from the shocking revelation of Himself in Chapter 1 to the various churches. But for the last two letters He introduces other vital information about who He is.

Holiness is one of the major themes of Scripture. The word "holy" comes from the Greek word *hagios*, which means "venerated, sanctified (set apart)". It particularly designates separation from sin. Surprisingly, it comes from the root word *hagos*, which means "an awful thing." The concept is that it is terrifying to envision just how opposite God is from anything that is evil. Thus we understand the many places in God's Word where we are told to fear the Lord:

> *"And now, Israel, what does the Lord your God require of you, but to fear the Lord your God, to walk in all His ways and to love Him, to serve the Lord your God with all your heart and with all your soul."*--Deuteronomy 10:12

> *The fear of the Lord is the beginning of knowledge, But fools despise wisdom and instruction.* – Proverbs 1:7

Isaiah and Ezekiel were both awe-stricken when they had visions about the holiness of God (Isaiah 6:1-7; Ezekiel 1). The apostle Paul had a similar experience when he beheld an image of the risen Christ (Acts 9:1-9).

The word "holy" is used 27 times in the Book of Revelation, and this is the first of those instances. We will discover that it is often used of things or beings other than God, such as holy angels, and the holy city. In fact, it is repeatedly used of true believers. "Saints" are holy ones, those who are sanctified or set apart to God. When we get to Revelation 5:8 we will consider the first of 14 places where this same word is translated "saints."

This image of believers being "set apart, sanctified, holy" is closely related to what we studied in Sardis, where Jesus said there were a few who had not defiled their garments and they will walk with Him in white robes (Chapter 3, verse 4). Their white robes were symbolic of the fact that their sins were forgiven and God had imputed to them the righteousness of Christ. The apostle Paul addressed all believers as "saints," even in his letter to the unspiritual Corinthians (1 Corinthians 1:2; cf. 3:1).

Saints are not perfect and yet we are told to be holy:

But as He who called you is holy, you also be holy in all your conduct, because it is written, "Be holy, for I am holy." – 1 Peter 1:15-16

Theologians explain that there is a difference between our *standing* and our *state*. In our redeemed standing before God, we are declared righteous because of what Christ has done for us (Romans 6:6; 1 Corinthians 6:11; Ephesians 2:6; Colossians 1:12-13), but in our current state, we still struggle with the temptation to sin (Romans 7:13-25; Philippians 3:12; 1 John 1:8-10), and sometimes we fail. That is why we are taught to regularly confess our sins, and consciously allow ourselves to be filled anew, or controlled, by the Holy Spirit (1 John 1:9; Ephesians 5:18).

Jesus also described Himself as, **He who is true.** The intrinsically holy Son of God is truth personified. We get a glimpse of Jesus' concept of truth from His trial before Pontius Pilate, the Roman governor:

> *Pilate therefore said to Him, "Are You a king then?"*
>
> *Jesus answered, "You say rightly that I am a king. For this cause I was born, and for this cause I have come into the world, that I should bear witness to the truth. Everyone who is of the truth hears My voice."*
>
> *Pilate said to Him, "What is truth?" And when he had said this, he went out again to the Jews, and said to them, "I find no fault in Him at all.*
> – John 18:37-38

Pilate was influenced by the philosophers of the day, especially the more famous ones from the Greek era. Philosophers were most concerned with what is true, but in a period of moral decline it was fashionable to dismiss the demands of morality by asking the rhetorical question, "What is truth?" For many people of the 1st Century--and indeed, too many from our own generation--that question would end the conversation.

Jesus had already taught His disciples that He was "the way, the truth, and the life," and most amazingly, "No one comes to the Father except by me." (John 14:6) This, of course, is completely contrary to the notion that all religions are equal. That error has been present in some form for our entire generation. When I was young I heard people say, "It doesn't matter what you believe as long as you are sincere." However, it has become much worse in recent years with people parroting the illogical statement that, "Everything is relative," denying that there is any absolute truth. (See the notes on the new definition of "toleration," in Chapter 2, verse 20). On judgment day, everyone will realize that there is absolute truth, and that it is centered in Jesus Christ.

The New Testament makes it very clear that Jesus was a "son of David" (Matthew 1:1; 9:27; 21:9, etc.), meaning that He was of the family or lineage of David (Matthew 1:17; Luke 1:27; John 7:42; Romans 1:3; Revelation 5:5; 22:16), but here He makes the additional claim that He is:

He who has the key of David.

What would the key of David unlock? Since God had promised that David's throne would be eternal (2 Samuel 7:13; Isaiah 9:7; Luke 1:32), David himself will be king in Israel in the Millennial Kingdom (Jeremiah 30:9; Ezekiel 37:24-25) under Jesus, the "King of Kings (Revelation 19:11-16). It appears that this key is the right to determine who may enter into that kingdom. This is consistent with what we just mentioned–that Jesus was the only way for people to reach the Heavenly Father. In his Gospel, John had described it this way, showing that Jesus opened a way to the Father, but individuals would need to "receive Him" in order to become God's children:

> *He was in the world, and the world was made through Him, and the world did not know Him. He came to His own, and His own did not receive Him. But as many as received Him, to them He gave the right to become children of God, to those who believe in His name:* --John 1:11-12

He who opens and no one shuts, and shuts and no one opens.
As mentioned before, Philadelphia was established as a center of Hellenistic culture in order to export that way of life to the adjoining regions of Lydia and Phrygia. The church there had an even higher purpose—that of exporting the Gospel. It had evidently not been "closed" or kept from accomplishing its purpose up to this time.

The Lord Jesus had plans to use the city as a beacon of truth to those around it, and history tells us that once it became a Christian community, it held out against the advances of Islam for centuries, and was the last city of Asia Minor to surrender to the Ottoman conquerors.

The door of Philadelphia's Christian testimony was finally closed in AD 1390, but with the Lord's permission. This should give us comfort in the Lord's plan for His church in a day like ours, when Christians are being driven out of their ancient homelands in the Middle East by radical Islamists. God had often allowed His people to be scattered, in Bible times, and in all of history, so that He might open new areas of evangelism.

Commendation

"I know your works. See, I have set before you an open door, and no one can shut it; for you have a little strength, have kept My word, and have not denied My name. Indeed I will make those of the synagogue of Satan, who say they are Jews and are not, but lie—indeed I will make them come and worship before your feet, and to know that I have loved you. -- Revelation 3:8-9

With the exact words that Jesus had spoken to each of the other churches, He told the Philadelphians, *I know your works.* Again, we cannot possibly earn our way into heaven by our good woks, but having a right relationship with Christ just naturally results in a life of good deeds (Ephesians 2:8-10; Titus 3:5,8. See the notes on "works" in Chapter 2, verse 2 and verse 26).

As He continued His commendation, the Lord gave them more promises than any other church. There is no criticism in this letter. The only other assembly that received no criticism was Smyrna, the persecuted church.

See, I have set before you an open door, and no one can shut it.

In the previous verse Jesus described himself as the one who opens and closes doors. No one else can close what He has opened or open what He has closed.

Jesus' omnipotence makes this situation possible. He is the all-powerful Son of God, the Creator (John 1:1-3, 14; Colossians 1:15-17; Hebrews 1:1-3), whose earthly life overflowed with miraculous events. He cleansed lepers with a word, gave sight to the blind, and even raised the dead. He calmed the storms, walked on water, and turned water into wine. And most amazingly, after He had submitted Himself to death for us, He was resurrected from the dead, and after more than a month, He ascended into heaven!

This promise speaks loudly about Jesus' divine direction in the lives of His followers. For this group of faithful believers, and indeed, for those in every place, He arranges just the right set of circumstances to bring about His good plan for their lives and ministries.

In our individual lives, and in our corporate lives, as members of His church, there are countless ways that the eye of faith can see His power and providence. For the church at Philadelphia, there were at least three ways that Jesus opened doors:

1- Salvation
2- Opportunity/missions
3- Deliverance from wrath by the Rapture

1 - Salvation

Jesus told His disciples,

"Most assuredly, I say to you, I am the door of the sheep. All who ever came before Me are thieves and robbers, but the sheep did not hear them. I am the door. If anyone enters by Me, he will be saved, and will go in and out and find pasture. – John 10:7-9

He is the door. In this most important sense, He provides an entrance into eternal life and adoption into the family of God (John 1:12; John 3:16; Ephesians 1:5). Yet, in another sense, He stands at the door and knocks (we will consider this in Revelation 3:20).

The fact that He has no criticism of this group, nor any call to repentance, shows that they were well aware of the simple Gospel of salvation, and that most of them had already committed their lives to Him.

2 - Opportunity/Missions

The Philadelphians would already be familiar with the idea that their city was a door, or an opening, to the adjoining regions for the purpose of exporting Greek culture to others. They could easily imagine that their thriving church would be responsible to proclaim an even greater way of life: Christianity. Through their obedience to the Great Commission, untold numbers of others in Asia Minor and beyond would hear the life-changing Gospel and respond to it by believing in Jesus!

Jesus' will, expressed in the Great Commission, is to spread the Gospel.

> *"But you shall receive power when the Holy Spirit has come upon you; and you shall be witnesses to Me in Jerusalem, and in all Judea and Samaria, and to the end of the earth."* – Acts 1:8 (See also: Matthew 28:18-20; Mark 16:15-16; Luke 24:46-49; John 20:21-22)

As mentioned before, Philadelphia was on a highly-maintained segment of the Roman Roads. This was a boon to evangelism because it made it so much easier for Christians to travel to places far and wide in the vast Roman Empire. Missionaries like Paul and Silas could move from place to place sharing the Gospel. Christians who needed to travel for business or other reasons would take their beliefs with them to share wherever they stopped on the highway. Visitors from other, sometimes far-away, places would visit Philadelphia on their journey. Christians there could provide hospitality, and offer them the most valuable gift: the story of Jesus.

If the Philadelphians could be encouraged to spread the Word because of their privileged position on the Roman Road, how much more should we, in our time and place, make use of the broad roads of our life-style to take the Gospel to others all over the world, and to share God's message with those who have come to our area for work or study. Not only do we have freeways and highways in the skies for jetliners, but we have radio and television airwaves, cell phone and satellite connections, and the most incredible path for knowledge: the Internet.

The "information explosion" of our generation, and the instantaneous connection of our devices to sources of knowledge anywhere on the Earth, were surely envisioned in Daniel's vision hundreds of years before Christ.

"But you, Daniel, shut up the words, and seal the book until the time of the end; many shall run to and fro, and knowledge shall increase." – Daniel 12:4

We are blessed to live at such a time as this, and even though modern technology can be used for evil as well as for good, every Christian has the opportunity of sharing his or her faith and influencing others for good through the many social networks that exist, such as Facebook, Twitter, and others.

After we have seen the application of this section to the original church at Philadelphia we will contemplate how this church was the prototype of the great missionary movements of the 18th to 20th Centuries.

3 - Deliverance from Wrath

Another vital way that Jesus opens a door for this church era is the Rapture of the church! We will soon consider the Lord's counsel to the recipients of this letter and His promise to deliver them from the Tribulation Period (Chapter 3, verses 10-13) when He returns to "catch up" believers of the Church Age.

"For you have a little strength." As Jesus continued His commendation of the Philadelphia church, He noted that they had some strength. This was not a criticism. He was not calling them weak. It is like the little encouragements a good coach gives to a young athlete when he shows improvement. "Great job, Bud! Keep up the good work!" The believers in Philadelphia didn't have all of the advantages that some Christians had in a major city, or in a place where the apostle Paul had spent months or years, like Ephesus,

In Christian theology, the knowledge that one has limited strength is an important prerequisite to "letting go, and letting God" take control of the details of our life. It is like Paul's "thorn in the flesh." He did not enjoy his weaknesses, but because of them, Christ's strength was released in his life:

And lest I should be exalted above measure by the abundance of the revelations, a thorn in the flesh was given to me, a messenger of Satan to buffet me, lest I be

exalted above measure. Concerning this thing I pleaded with the Lord three times that it might depart from me. And He said to me, "My grace is sufficient for you, for My strength is made perfect in weakness." Therefore most gladly I will rather boast in my infirmities, that the power of Christ may rest upon me. Therefore I take pleasure in infirmities, in reproaches, in needs, in persecutions, in distresses, for Christ's sake. For when I am weak, then I am strong. – 2 Corinthians 12:7-10

Another commendable fact about this church was that they **have kept My word and have not denied My name.** There is a definite correlation between keeping God's Word and not becoming a failure. Keeping God's Word involves knowing and declaring the "whole counsel of God" (Acts 20:27). In too many churches there is limited exposure to the incredible wealth of "the whole Bible." Topical messages have their place, but the mainstay of instruction for God's people should be expository preaching of whole books of the Bible.

Following the recent death of Chuck Smith, the founder of Calvary Chapel and the "Jesus People" movement, a nearly endless number of people, including hundreds of pastors, called his radio station to honor his faithful service to the Lord. Many of them especially mentioned his example of teaching verse-by-verse through whole books of the Bible.

The other thing the Philadelphia believers surely must have done in order to keep Jesus' word was to remember and observe His commandments (John 14:15-25; 15:10). James explained the importance of not only knowing, but of doing God's will:

But be doers of the word, and not hearers only, deceiving yourselves. For if anyone is a hearer of the word and not a doer, he is like a man observing his natural face in a mirror; for he observes himself, goes away, and immediately forgets what kind of man he was. But he who looks into the perfect law of liberty and continues in it, and is not a forgetful hearer but a doer of the work, this one will be blessed in what he does.– James 1:22-25

Jesus said that the people who antagonized the Philadelphia Church were from the **synagogue of Satan.** This was surely not what the false Jews called themselves, but it was how the Lord saw them.

Jewish places of worship were called synagogues. The word *synagoges* means "bringing together," or "assembling." It is, therefore, very similar to *ekklesia*, "church," which means "assembly." Jesus undoubtedly chose this name for His followers (Matthew 16:18) because it was a familiar relationship, but with a slightly different application. The church would be an organism in which each person has a role to fulfill (1 Corinthians 12:12-27; Romans 12:3-8; Ephesians 4:1-16).

Those agitators *Say they are Jews.* The same description of these opponents of the Gospel was used in Revelation 2:9 in reference to troublemakers in Smyrna. In that passage they were said to be guilty of blasphemy (Greek *blasphemia*, meaning "slander," or "speech injurious to another's good name"). As noted before, this often meant saying false things about God Himself, but it could also mean spreading lies about other humans.

These enemies might actually have believed they were true Jews because of their heritage, their conversion to Judaism, or actual membership in a synagogue.

In the early days of evangelizing the Gentiles, Paul had confronted Peter about the problem of legalism:

> But when I saw that they were not straightforward about the truth of the gospel, I said to Peter before them all, "If you, being a Jew, live in the manner of Gentiles and not as the Jews, why do you compel Gentiles to live as Jews? -- Galatians 2:4.

The Greek word translated "to live as Jews" is the only occurrence in the Bible of *Ioudaizo*. Many commentators have used the expression "Judaizers" to describe the misguided attempt by those who would impose the law and customs of the Jews on Gentiles.

Ignatius of Antioch, who wrote a letter, *"To the Philadelphians,"* a few decades later, mentioned Judaizing of Gentiles there.[61]

Fortunately Peter and the other leaders in Jerusalem decided that circumcision, and a myriad of other Jewish rules, did not need to be observed by Christian Gentiles, except, "to abstain from things polluted by idols, *from* sexual immorality, *from* things strangled, and *from* blood."–Acts 15:20 (Read the entire chapter for the context).

Jews who had rejected their Messiah were therefore clinging to a false religion. The same situation will prevail during the Tribulation Period, when so-called churches will depart from what the Bible teaches. True believers during that time will not be associated with such apostate organizations.

Paul had written:

For you are all sons of God through faith in Christ Jesus. For as many of you as were baptized into Christ have put on Christ. There is neither Jew nor Greek, there is neither slave nor free, there is neither male nor female; for you are all one in Christ Jesus. And if you are Christ's, then you are Abraham's seed, and heirs according to the promise. – Galatians 3:26-29

In Romans he explained that Jewish people who reject Jesus as their Messiah are temporarily blinded:

What then? Israel has not obtained what it seeks; but the elect have obtained it, and the rest were blinded. Just as it is written:
"God has given them a spirit of stupor,
Eyes that they should not see
And ears that they should not hear,
To this very day."
And David says:
"Let their table become a snare and a trap,
A stumbling block and a recompense to them.
Let their eyes be darkened, so that they do not see,
And bow down their back always." – Romans 11:7-10

And yet, Paul was very forceful in his insistence that Israel still has a future, as predicted in the Old Testament (Romans 11:11-36). This will be explained more fully in our future studies in Revelation.

Indeed I will make them come and worship before your feet, and to know that I have loved you. This promise to the Philadelphians should not be taken as any sort of anti-Semitic sentiment. Jesus was Jewish, and He had been their Creator and their Messiah, whether or not they had accepted Him as such. Nearly all of the first church members were Jewish.

Even Paul, the Apostle to the Gentiles was Jewish, and he was passionately devoted to their well-being (Romans 10).

However, those Jewish people who reject their Messiah will not experience the salvation God provided for them, and for all humanity, by the death of His Son.

If anything, believers who were oppressed by these Judaizers should love them. Jesus had taught His followers to love their enemies (Matthew 5:44). Furthermore, they should not try to take revenge on others:

"Vengeance is Mine, I will repay," says the Lord. – Romans 12:19. (See verses 17-21)

When the Lord does, bring judgment, finally and reluctantly, on these enemies of the Gospel, they will be compelled to worship, not the Philadelphian Christians, but the Lord Himself:

That at the name of Jesus every knee should bow, of things in heaven, and things in earth, and things under the earth;
And that every tongue should confess that Jesus Christ is Lord, to the glory of God the Father. – Philippians 2:10-11

The Judaizers will worship at the feet of the Philadelphians only in the sense that the true Believers will evidently be there also, and will witness the event.

Recall the encouraging words that Jesus had given to this missionary church:

"I know your works. See, I have set before you an open door, and no one can shut it; for you have a little strength, have kept My word, and have not denied My name.– Revelation 3:8

We have already studied this verse, but we need to take another look at Jesus' amazing promise, *"I have set before you an open door."* Christianity is all about missions in every age. Those who knew and believed God's Word have always understood the imperative of fulfilling the Great Commission. Jesus said:

> *Go therefore and make disciples of all the nations, baptizing them in the name of the Father and of the Son and of the Holy Spirit,* – Matthew 28:19 (See also Acts 1:8; Mark 16:15-16; Luke 24:46-49; John 20:21-22)

The saga of the spread of Christianity is demonstrably the largest enterprise in the history of humanity. Countless books have been written on the subject. This brief summary will only begin to demonstrate the breath-taking spread of the Gospel from the time of Christ to the present.

Missionary Activity during the Seven Periods of Church History

Remember that there have been churches in every generation that were similar to one of the Seven Churches in Revelation 2 and 3. This has especially been true of the church in Philadelphia. There have always been congregations in each age that could identify with the Philadelphia church because of its missions emphasis.

Therefore missionary activity can be identified in each period of time. We will present a very brief summary of how evangelism was conducted during the historical periods of the first five churches, and then we will consider the sixth period of church history as "The Age of Missions."

Here is a simple chart listing the various periods of church history and the kind of "open door" for missionary progress age enjoyed.

Missionary Activity
During the Seven Periods of Church History

32-100–Apostolic Church	Open Door of Evangelism
100-312–Persecuted Church	Open Door of Testimony
312-476–Compromised Church	Open Door of Influence
476-1517–Middle Ages of the Church	Open Door of Privilege
1517-Mid-1700's –Reformation Church	Open Door of Restoration
Mid-1700's-1900's –Missionary Church	Open Door of Revival
1900's-Present –Worldly Church	Open Door of Escape

Ephesus--The Apostolic Church – Revelation 2:1-7
<u>Open Door of Evangelism</u>

Shortly after the resurrection and ascension of the Lord Jesus, the Holy Spirit was sent to empower the disciples on the day of Pentecost (Acts 2). There were Jewish converts in Jerusalem to celebrate the festival, and those who witnessed this great event also heard the "the wonderful works of God" proclaimed in their own native languages by uneducated followers of Christ. Then Peter preached the Gospel and more than 3000 people decided to believe in Christ and were all baptized! They then returned to their home countries all over the Mediterranean world, where they undoubtedly told others about Jesus.

The whole Book of Acts documents the incredible spread of the message that Jesus was the Savior who had come to die for the sins of the world. It contains numerous stories of missionary work, such as Philip's mass evangelism to the Samaritans (Acts 8:4-8), and his personal evangelism with the Ethiopian Eunuch (Acts 8:39).

Acts also records the divine appointment the Lord had for Peter that led to sharing the Gospel with Cornelius, who was a Gentile (Acts 10). This evidently fulfilled Jesus' promise to Peter that he would have the keys to the Kingdom (Matthew 16:19). He officiated over the giving of the Gospel first to Jerusalem (Acts 2:38-41), then to Judea and Samaria (Acts 8:14-17), and finally, to the Gentiles (Acts 10:44-46).

Christians were persecuted and scattered from Jerusalem so that they could take their new belief to other cities far and wide:

At that time a great persecution arose against the church which was at Jerusalem; and they were all scattered throughout the regions of Judea and Samaria, except the apostles. And devout men carried Stephen to his burial, and made great lamentation over him. . . Therefore those who were scattered went everywhere preaching the word.--Acts 8:1-4

Just a few years after the death and resurrection of Christ, Paul, the Pharisee that had persecuted the Early Church, was converted by an appearance of Jesus (Acts 9), and he then became the foremost missionary of his time, leading evangelistic teams to Syria, Asia Minor, Macedonia, Greece, the Mediterranean Islands, and Rome. He explained how the Lord had made his incredibly successful work possible:

Furthermore, when I came to Troas to preach Christ's gospel, and a door was opened to me by the Lord. --2 Corinthians 2:12

Within a few more years, the impact of Paul and his associates had been so great that the rulers of Thessalonica complained:

"These who have turned the world upside down have come here too." – Acts 17:8

Meanwhile, the apostles and other great 1st Century leaders of the church travelled to many distant lands to preach the Gospel. According to historians like Hippolytus, Peter preached in many parts of Asia; Thomas went to Persia and India; Bartholomew also went to India; Jude went to Mesopotamia; Andrew went to Greece; Mark went to Egypt, Matthew went to Parthia; and Thaddeus went to Armenia.

Smyrna--The Persecuted Church – Revelation 2:8-11
<u>Open Door of Testimony</u>

During this era of severe persecution (AD 100 to AD 312), missionary work was not accomplished by sending out teams of evangelists, as had been the case in the 1st Century, but by the scattering of believers to remote places.

The courageous martyrs of this period provided an unforgettable proof of the reality of their faith. Their very lives and deaths convinced others who might not have believed without such a powerful illustration. The Greek word for martyr, *marturia*, also means "witness." Those who were willing to die for their belief in Christ were a tremendous testimony to the power of the Gospel (Revelation 2:13; 6:9; 17:6)! As mentioned before, Tertullian, a Church Father of that period of time wrote, "The blood of martyrs is the seed of the church" (See the notes on Chapter 2, verse 9).

In spite of the death of so many Christians during this time, and the lack of "official" missionaries, the Gospel continued to spread. By the time of Constantine it had reached virtually all of the then-known world.

Pergamum--The Compromised Church – Revelation 2:12-17
<u>Open Door of Influence</u>

This, as we have already seen, was the period of the worldly influence on the church caused by Emperor Constantine's adoption of Christianity (AD 312 to AD 476). After seeing the sign of the cross in the sky to predict his victory in a great battle, he became a Christian. Then he issued the Edict of Milan (AD 313), which made all religions acceptable. The good news was that this ended the horrific persecution of Christians. At a later date (AD 380), Christianity was adopted by Emperor Theodosius I as the official religion of the empire.

Multitudes of people began to call themselves Christians even though they didn't fully understand its teachings and still clung to many of their old pagan beliefs and practices.

In a sense, Christianity was spread through conquest during this era even though such an idea was foreign to the teaching of Jesus, the Prince of Peace (Isaiah 9:6, Matthew 5:38-40; John 14:27).

True Christian doctrine was clarified by several church councils during this time. Magnificent church buildings were built, Bible translation was begun, and there were strong theologians, and notable evangelists. Nevertheless, this phase of church history lacked the missionary zeal of the Apostolic Church.

Constantine and his mother, Helena, directed the building of great church buildings in the Holy Land such as the Church of the Holy Sepulcher in Jerusalem and the Church of the Nativity in Bethlehem.

Excellent scholars clarified the history and doctrine that was beginning to be considered official "Christianity." Jerome was commissioned to translate the Gospels, and later the whole Bible into Latin. He did his translation from a grotto in the Church of the Nativity. Visitors to the Holy Land can still see the cave under the church where he did his work. A Bible in the language of the people became a founding principle of missionary activity.

Eusebius, the Bishop of Caesarea wrote "Ecclesiastical History," about the story of the Early Church. Great theologians like John Chrysostom, Archbishop of Constantinople, Cyril, Bishop of Alexandria, and Augustine, Bishop of Hippo, captured the essence of Biblical teaching about the person and the work of Jesus and the nature and progress of the church. During this timeframe several church councils were convened to debate variations of belief about Christ and to determine what had been considered orthodoxy ("straight teaching"), and what should be taught in the future. The Nicene Council in 325 established the belief in the Trinity, and affirmed that Jesus was true God, co-eternal with the Father, and "begotten" from the same "substance," as the Father, therefore not created.

The Council of Chalcedon in 451 declared that Jesus had two natures (Godhead and manhood) in one person; a hypostatic union.

Some who disagreed with the rulings of these councils formed splinter groups, Some of the dissidents from the Nicene Council, called Arians (from Arius, the name of their teacher), were missionaries to the Germanic tribes.

Likewise, those who were unhappy with the Chalcedonian Council, were known as Monophysites ("one nature"). They continued to spread their viewpoint in the Armenian, Syrian, and Egyptian churches. Because their beliefs had been discredited by the church councils, they were persecuted by the larger church, and were pushed out into more remote areas. This resulted in a missionary expansion of some questionable branches of Christianity.

One especially inspiring story of the spread of the Gospel in this era is the story of Aspebet, the sheik of nomadic Arab tribes in the Judean desert.

It comes as a surprise to many in our generation that not all Arabs are Muslims. In truth, there are a great many Arab Christians in the Middle East. Sadly though, recent Islamic uprisings, like the "Arab Spring," have resulted in intense persecution of Christians in Egypt, Lebanon, Syria and various other countries. This trend actually threatens to empty the Middle East of Christians.

Long before Muhammad and the later evolution of Islam, Christianity made great inroads among the Arabs. Even at the "birthday of the church," the Day of Pentecost, there were some Arabs among the crowd of Jewish converts in Jerusalem who saw the miraculous events and heard Peter's message (Acts 2:11).

Over the course of time, many Arab tribes heard the message of Christianity, the new religion, in the various marketplaces of their world. One Bedouin sheik named Aspebet had a son who became paralyzed. Doctors were not able to cure his ailment. One night the boy asked God for a miraculous cure, and promised to become a Christian if his prayer was answered. He then had a dream in which he saw a monk with a long beard.

The monk was identified as Euthyme, who was living by a stream near the road to Jericho.

Aspebet found Euthyme, and the child was healed. Euthyme baptized Aspebet and his son, along with the rest of the tribe. He also renamed the sheik Aspebet-Peter. The sheik considered himself the apostle of his tribe, and brought new members to be baptized. He built a chapel and monastery, and was appointed a bishop in Palestine, over an area not defined by cities or villages, but only of Bedouin camps.[62]

Another example of missionary work during this period from Constantine to the fall of the Western Roman Empire is the familiar story of St. Patrick in Ireland. Patrick was taken captive in his teen years by a wild band of Irish raiders, who took him to Ireland along with thousands of other captives.

Patrick became a believer in Christ while he was in Ireland. After some time he had a dream about how God wanted him to escape. He did leave Ireland, and after some great difficulty, he finally returned to his home in Britain.

As he grew in faith, Patrick felt called by God to return to Ireland as a freelance missionary in AD 432. The Lord blessed his endeavors, and multitudes of people became Christians there, ultimately changing the future of the country.[63]

Thyatira--The Church of the Middle Ages – Revelation 2:18-29
<u>Open Door of Privilege</u>

Even during the frustrating Middle Ages, when the church fell prey to so many problems, the Lord used those who truly knew Him to continue spreading the Gospel. In fact, in spite of the corruption of church doctrine and the unfortunate behavior of many clergymen, this thousand-year-plus stretch of time saw an immense missionary expansion to far-away places.

Furthermore, those who were missionaries at heart didn't always agree with the changing doctrine of the church. It is the same today. Missionaries to distant lands tend to be more faithful to the Bible than they are to traditions that have crept in over the years. They are also more conservative on moral issues than their mother churches are, for example, the Episcopal and Methodist traditions.

The circumstances that made this expansion possible grew out of the favor that the Roman Empire, and later, the Holy Roman Empire showed to the church. Thus, the missionaries of this time enjoyed an "Open Door" of privilege. They had the blessing of the government as well as the financial support of a wealthy ecclesiastical establishment.

Our list of vital missionary activity during the Middle Ages does not tell the full story, but it will hopefully demonstrate the fact that the message of Christianity was taken to ever-farther horizons. It is true that many of the converts of this period might not have known Christ in the personal way prescribed by the Bible, but many others did understand enough about the story of redemption to be true believers.

Interspersed among the missionaries sent out by the Roman Catholic Church, there were individuals, like Patrick, who was mentioned above. He evangelized Ireland without a commission from the church. And there were break-away "denominations" that left the Catholic Church even before the Reformation. The spread of these dissident groups was a type of missionary activity in itself.

Some of these were:

The Nestorian Church--including the Assyrian Apostolic Church in areas now called Iraq, Iran, and Turkey; and the Nestorian Malabar Christians in India.

The Oriental Orthodox Church--including the Coptic Orthodox (mostly in Egypt), the Abyssinian Orthodox, the Armenian Orthodox, the Jacobites/ Syrian Orthodox, and the Jacobite Malabar Christians (mostly in India).

The Eastern Orthodox Church--with its various branches, including the Greek, Russian, and many others.

There are many lists of Christian missionary activities. For simplicity, we have included some from the Wikipedia list, "Timeline of Christian Missions."[64]

Major Missionary Developments during the Middle Ages

496 – Frankish King Clovis I was converted, along with 3000 warriors in Gaul.

508 – Philoxenus of Mabug translated the Bible into Syriac .Bible translation was always a vital part of good missionary work.

509 – Loginus from Nobatia evangelized what is now Sudan.

596 – Augustine and a team of missionaries were sent to Canterbury, in what is now England, and baptized 10,000 people.

635 – Nestorian monks took the Gospel to China. An engraved tablet called the Nestorian Stele was erected in 781 to describe the early history of Christianity in China. After 878 the Christian church was evidently wiped out by the Mongol invasion.

647 – Amadeus, bishop of Maastricht, became a missionary to Frisia (Netherlands).

716 – Boniface took the Gospel to the Germanic tribes.

771 – King Charlemagne decreed that sermons should be given in the language of the people. He also commissioned Bible translations.

828 – First missionaries arrived at the area now known as the Czech Republic.

900 – Missionaries from Bremen-Hamburg reached Norway. By 1015 Olaf II Haroldsson became the country's first king and began its integration into Christian Europe.

965 – In Denmark, King Harold I was converted to Christianity.

966 – King Mieszko I of Poland was converted to Christianity.

1000 – Iceland was declared a Christian nation, and Leif the Lucky introduced the Gospel to Greenland.

1003 – Transylvania received missionaries from Hungary.

1008 – King Olaf of Sweden was baptized by Sigfrid from England.

1015 – Russia was "comprehensively" converted to Orthodox Christianity.

1200 – The Bible had been translated into 22 different languages.

1210 – The Franciscan Order was established.

1216 – The Dominican Order was established.

1253 – Franciscan William of Rubruck began his journey to the Mongols. In 1266 the leader of the Mongols, Khan, asked the Pope to send 100 missionaries, but only two responded, and one of them died on the way. However, Nestorian Christians had evangelized some of the tribes, and when the Mongols conquered northern China in 1271, Christianity was re-introduced to China.[65] In 1368 The Ming Dynasty abolished Christianity in China.

1382 – John Wycliffe translated the Bible into English.

1462 – Johannes Gutenberg began printing the Bible with his movable-type printing process.

1486 – Dominicans sent missionaries to West Africa.

1491 – Franciscan and Dominican priests took the Gospel to the Congo. The king was baptized and a church built at the capital.

1492 – Christopher Columbus discovered America. In 1493 Pope Alexander VI commanded Spain to colonize the New World and sends priests with Columbus on his second journey.

1500 – Franciscans sent missionaries to Brazil.

1508 – Franciscans took the Gospel to Venezuela.

1510 – Dominican missionaries arrived in Haiti.

1514 – Franciscans began their work in California.

Rise of Islam

We must admit that the rise of Islam cut deeply into the gains of the church during this period of time. Islam was spread by military conquest rather than by any superior ideology.

Historian Tom Holland's book, *In the Shadow of the Sword*, explains that Muhammad and his followers built their beliefs on the base of Jewish and Christian theology. Their emerging religion, stoked by revelations that Muhammad received periodically, made them unwelcome in their home (Mecca, or, as some historians think, some place Southeast of the Judean wilderness). They immigrated to Yathrib (Medina), and armed with the belief that immigration and conquest were God's will for them, they began a process of violent conversions that would make them rich and powerful, and eventually affect the whole world.

Holland shows that in the 6th Century the collapsing Roman Empire under Justinian, and the Persians under Khusrow I, practically destroyed each other in a Great War, and the Bubonic Plague wiped out approximately one-third of the population, leaving most of the world in a greatly weakened state.[66]

Arab tribes were not affected by the Great War. And because of their nomadic life-style, they were not weakened by the Plague. A century later, Muhammad and his followers were in a position to sweep through the Arabian Peninsula and then country after country, conquering the struggling populace, and increasing their wealth.

Soon after Muhammad's death in 632, his successors conquered Palestine, Syria, Persian areas now known as Iran and Iraq, Egypt, and other parts of Africa. In 674 they tried to overrun Constantinople, the Capital of the Roman Empire, but were repelled for the time being. They conquered the rest of Northern Africa and then crossed the Straits of Gibraltar to occupy Spain. Muslim Arab traders carried their new religion to various parts of the known world. Colonies of Muslims were established in India, where they gradually grew alongside the Hindu and Buddhist people. The same thing happened in Indonesia. In the 9th and 10th centuries Muslims occupied Crete, Malta and Sicily and were a threat to other colonies around the Mediterranean Sea.

By the end of the 11th Century Islam controlled Asia Minor (Turkey) and most of the coast of the Mediterranean.

From 1096 to 1291 a series of "crusades" were fought between the Holy Roman Empire and the Islamic caliphates. During part of that time (1099-1187) the Christians reoccupied Jerusalem and parts of Palestine, but Saladin the Great took it back, and Islamic forces maintained control until the end of World War I in 1918.

After several earlier attempts, Muslim forces from the Ottoman Empire again occupied Constantinople in 1453.

Sardis--The Reformation Church – Revelation 3:1-6

227

Open Door of Restoration

From the beginning of the Reformation in 1517 to the Mid-1700's there were more than a hundred significant developments in the Christian missionary movement--many of them by the reformers, and many by the Catholic Church. We will simplify this data by grouping some of it together, and by listing only the most influential events.

First, let's look at Reformation Missions. In a sense, the whole Reformation movement was a missionary enterprise to Roman Catholics. Martin Luther did not want to leave the Catholic Church; he just wanted to see a revival by the establishment and a return to faithful interpretation of God's Word.

However, Luther and the other reformers who followed him were persecuted for their beliefs. Those persecuted followers were scattered, and moving to other places, they spread the faith just as the earlier persecuted Christians had done.

Earlier we studied the Anabaptist movement, a continuation of the Reformation, and saw that they were persecuted by the earlier Reformers: the Lutherans and Calvinists (See the notes on Chapter 3, verses 1 and 2). Many of them were driven from their homelands, and they shared the Gospel with others as they moved to new locations.

Because of these hardships, and their emphasis on repairing Christianity, the Reformers were admittedly less involved in sending missionaries as such, but this following list[67] will show that it was in their hearts to continue evangelizing non-Christians.

> 1523 – Martin Luther wrote "May God Bestow On Us His Grace," which has been called the "first missionary hymn of Protestantism."
>
> 1527 – Anabaptists organized a conference in Augsburg, Germany, and sent out missionaries who were killed for their faith. Afterwards, this first Protestant missionary conference was dubbed the "Martyrs' Synod."
>
> 1543 – The Anabaptist Menno Simons left the Netherlands to plant churches in Germany.

1550 – Printed Scriptures had become available in 28 languages.

1555 – John Calvin sent Huguenots to Brazil.

1595 – The Dutch East India Company began sending missionaries to reach nationals in the areas they had colonized.

1643 – 1949 American Indians were evangelized by Lutheran missionary John Campanius, Reformed pastor Johannes Megapolensis, Puritan missionary John Eliot and others. The Society for the Propagation of the Gospel in New England was formed.

1651 – Count Truchess of Wetzhausen asked the theological school at Wittenberg why Lutherans were not sending out missionaries in obedience to the Great Commission.

1656 – The first Quaker missionaries arrived at what is now Boston, Massachusetts.

1661 – Quaker George Fox, founder of the Religious Society of Friends, sent three missionaries to China, but they never arrived there.

1671 – Quaker missionaries arrived in the Carolinas.

1701 – The Society for Promoting Christian Knowledge was organized by Anglicans, and began to send missionaries to America and the West Indies.

1710 --The first modern Bible Society was founded in Germany by Count Canstein.

1714 – In India the New Testament was translated into Tamil.

1714 – The Royal Danish College of Missions was organized in Copenhagen.

1719 – Isaac Watts wrote the missionary hymn, "Jesus Shall Reign Where're the Sun."

1726 – John Wright, Quaker missionary to Native Americans, settled in Pennsylvania.

Now let's consider the missionary endeavors of the Roman Catholic Church during this era of church history.

As noted earlier, two powerful orders in the Catholic Church, the Franciscan and Dominican, had been organized in the 11th Century for the purpose of spreading the influence of Christianity. There were Dominican missionaries from time to time, but the Franciscans were much more active in establishing foreign outposts in the "New World" (Americas). Some of them went with Cortes to Mexico in 1519, and during the following century they established missions in many parts of the Americas settled by the Spanish and French explorers.

> 1529 – Franciscan Peter of Ghent wrote that he and a colleague had baptized 14,000 people in Latin America in one day.
>
> 1532 – Missionaries arrived in Peru with Francisco Pizarro's military expedition.
>
> 1541 – Franciscans began establishing missions in California.

The primary missionary thrust by the Roman Catholics during this period of church history was the work of a *new order, the Jesuits*, which began in 1534 as the "Society of Jesus" and was approved by the Pope in 1540 (See the notes on Revelation Chapter 3, verse 1 about "The Rise of the Jesuits"). One of the later purposes of the Jesuits was to counter the Protestant movement. The co-founders of the movement were Ignatius Loyola and Francis Xavier. Xavier was a tireless missionary, first to the Eastern destinations of India, Goa, and the West Indies. One entire caste of Paravas in India were baptized--perhaps as many as 20,000 people. He was also effective in Indonesia and Japan, where there were eventually more than 100,000 converts.[68]

Unfortunately, Christianity was banned in Japan by the military governor in 1606, and those who did not renounce their faith were gradually extinguished from the nation.

Jesuits also took their message to China, the Philippines, Viet Nam, and Ethiopia.

In 1622 the Catholic Church established the "Sacred Congregation for the Propagation of the Faith" (later renamed "Congregation for the Evangelization of Peoples") to coordinate and direct missionary work.[69]

One of their vital objectives was to spread Catholicism in the Americas. Some of their efforts failed, but one interesting story is the work in "New Spain" of Italian Jesuit Eusebio Kino. He was described by one writer as "the most picturesque missionary pioneer of all North America." He was "an explorer, astronomer, cartographer, mission builder, ranchman, cattle king, and defender of the frontier."[70]

The Jesuits were missionaries also to the countries that had already been Christianized, many of which were being lost to the Reformation movement. As explained earlier in this commentary, in the notes for Revelation 3:1-2, great numbers of them were employed in positions of science and education, working to discredit Protestantism and bring people back to the Catholic Church. They were actually banned in France and Spain but were restored in 1814.

Philadelphia – The Missionary Church – Revelation 3:7-13
<u>Open Door of Revival</u>

We have just gone through a review of missionary activity in each of the previous periods of church history, but we come now to the sixth major phase, represented by the Philadelphia Church. This is the great "Age of Modern Missions" (Middle 1700's to the middle 1900's). The name "Philadelphia" is especially appropriate for this wonderful era, because, as we saw at the beginning of this letter (see Chapter 3, verse 7), the name means "brotherly love." The highest motive for the outpouring of missionary activity during this time was love for the lost! God-given love motivates believers to evangelize others (Romans 5:5).

In terms of the number of people reached with the Gospel, this is certainly the most exciting period of history, and we have had the unbelievable privilege of living while a significant portion of this missionary movement was still unfolding! On the other hand, we are now seeing the gradual encroachment of that final dark period on the Church Age, causing a time of drifting away from the truth. We will study this in the next section, the letter to the church at Laodicea.

Historical Fulfillment (Missionary Age)

What we can write in these few pages is only a beginning of the wealth of wonderful knowledge that exists about missions. There are encyclopedias of missions, and a separate discipline called "Missiology" with schools, colleges and seminaries dedicated to this topic. I have just included some of the history that stands out to me in the hope that you will devote much more time and effort to learning about the Great Commission (Matthew 28:18-20; Mark 16:15-16; Luke 24:46-49; John 20:21-22; Acts 1:8), its history, and the fact that it is an unfinished task.

This great open door for modern missions was characterized by several major factors: Revivals; Bible translation and publication; courageous missionary pioneers and their stories; unprecedented opportunities; and the formation of effective missionary organizations.

Powerful Revivals and the Emphasis on the Holy Spirit

The "First Great Awakening" started in 1727. It was known as "The Golden Summer" in the Moravian Church in Germany. Count Nikolaus Ludwig Zinzendorf led this renewal of dependence on the Holy Spirit and love for one another. The Moravian's thinking was influenced by Pietism, which had been changing the lives of Lutherans for some 50 years. The Moravians were responsible for the first large-scale Protestant missions effort. Hundreds of missionaries were sent out to various fields of service around the world. In the American colonies the revival was spread in 1734 by the Reformed theologian Jonathan Edwards. He was assisted by George Whitefield in 1737, who came from England to preach. John Wesley also came to America during this time and was greatly influenced by the Moravians.

The Methodist movement started in the Church of England by the ministry of John and Charles Wesley and George Whitefield in the 1730's. It was a further reformation of the Anglican beliefs, emphasizing justification by faith alone and personal holiness produced by the work of the Holy Spirit. The radical message and revival that it produced caused the eventual break from the mother church and the formation of the Methodists and other similar denominations. The movement spread like wildfire throughout the British Empire, the United States and beyond.

The "Second Great Awakening" from circa 1790 to 1840 started about the time that William Carey, "The Father of Modern Missions," wrote a missions manifesto and went to Calcutta as a missionary. In the U.S. Methodist circuit riders, Baptist and Presbyterian camp meetings, and revival meetings like those conducted by Charles Finney all stimulated a renewed commitment to the Lord, openness to control by the Holy Spirit, and great interest in missionary work. In the second half of that century the most famous preachers were C.H. Spurgeon in England and D.L. Moody in the U.S.

The Salvation Army was begun in London in 1865 by William Booth, who had a Methodist background. Its mission field was the "down and out" element of society. It took on a military structure over which Booth was the "General." It ministered by providing soup, soap, and salvation. The Army spread rapidly throughout the world.

In 1906 the Azusa Street Revival in Los Angeles was an extended period of spiritual awakening (until 1915) led by William J. Seymour, an African American preacher, and was characterized by dramatic, and what many considered unorthodox, behaviors, such as speaking in tongues and miraculous healings. Seymour had been profoundly influenced by Charles F. Parham, founder of the Apostolic Faith Movement. Again, the emphasis was on the work of the Holy Spirit, and the revival was therefore called the "Pentecostal Movement." Out of this fervency the Foursquare Church and the Assemblies of God denominations emerged. These groups became great examples of missionary zeal, and are responsible for a high percentage of successful missionary outreach that continues to this time.

Many great evangelists have fanned the flames of revival, both here in the United States, and in key places throughout the world. Fiery preachers like R.A. Torrey and Billy Sunday attracted huge crowds to tent meetings, auditoriums and stadiums.

In the 1960's the so-called "Charismatic Movement" brought similar revivalist elements into mainline churches with mixed results, re-energizing some members, but upsetting others.

Another great revival was a development called "The Jesus People Movement." This outreach to the "hippies" of the 1970's, and other people who were disenchanted by the traditional church, was led by Calvary Chapel of Costa Mesa, California. Under Pastor Chuck Smith. It became a gigantic church with an exciting young Christian culture. It also gave rise to a new "Contemporary Christian" genre of music. Though claiming not to be a denomination, there are now many hundreds of Calvary Chapels around the world. They are known for their strong salvation message and systematic teaching of the Bible. Their missionary method is to start new Calvary Chapel outposts everywhere.

In our own generation we have been blessed with the Billy Graham Crusades and Greg Laurie's Harvest Crusades. In the '90's a men's movement called "Promise Keepers" was able to attract more than a million men to the Washington Mall to pray for revival.

Today we have the earnest hope of one more great revival to reach this generation of young people with the Gospel. Too many of them do not know what the Bible teaches. They don't know what they need to do in order to have a right relationship with Christ. In what he characterized as his last message to the world, Billy Graham, who has spoken to more people about Christ than any other person in history, and who is now 95 years old, just delivered a world-wide challenge calling on people everywhere to renewed hope, based on the Cross--the sacrificial death of Jesus Christ on our behalf.

During this great era of modern missions there were not only revivals and a renewed emphasis on the work of the Holy Spirit, but there were at least four other major factors. In general, the progress of each of these avenues of progress developed concurrently with the others.

This is not an exhaustive list. For every item mentioned, there were many other missionary advances made during this time.

Proliferation of Bible Translation and Printing

Just as the invention of the movable type printing press had a great impact on the Reformation, so the continued improvement of printing technologies and lower costs for books helped make this age of missionary expansion possible. The most effective missionary work required translation of God's Word into the language of the people who needed to hear the Gospel. Once the Bible, or even a small portion of it, had been translated, it was then necessary to provide copies to the people. In many cases missionaries needed to teach them to read also. So Bible translation, printing and education were basic methods of missionary evangelism.

In 1804 the British and Foreign Bible Society was formed to address the problem that most people could not afford a Bible. The

American Bible Society was then launched in 1816. Ten years later it sent the first shipment of Bibles to Mexico. Over the course of time new Bible Societies have been formed in numerous places all over the world.

In 1934 William Cameron Townsend launched the Summer Institute of Linguistics to teach prospective missionaries the best methods to translate the Scriptures. In 1942 he established Wycliffe Bible Translators. This organization has become the preeminent group for making the Bible available to previously unreached people in their own tongue.

An umbrella organization called the United Bible Societies was incorporated in 1946 to be a worldwide association of Bible societies. It has 146 member groups, working in more than 200 countries and territories to translate and distribute the Bible.[71] They report that there are nearly 500 complete Bible translations, and each year more are added. Currently, there are Scriptures available in over 2,550 of the world's estimated 7,100 languages.[72]

Thanks in part to these amazing Bible societies, the Bible is by far the #1 best-seller in history with more than 6 billion copies, while the next book in the list has sold less than 1 billion.[73]

Pioneer Missionaries and Their Biographies

Next to the Bible, the most inspiring thing a Christian can read is a good missionary biography. Missionary work is considered by many, myself included, the greatest of all forms of Christian service. It requires the greatest sacrifices and demonstrates the greatest love of any ministry, but it is also often the most difficult and dangerous task of all. During these years, the Mid-1700's to the 1900's, some of the most powerful books ever printed chronicled the lives and adventures of pioneer missionaries to various places in the world. We recommend that Christians read the stories of as many of these heroes of the faith as they can! There are said to be approximately 80,000 evangelical missionaries serving overseas.[74] Most of them were undoubtedly influenced to devote their lives to such a worthy cause by reading biographies of other missionaries.

Again, we cannot mention all of the outstanding pioneer missionaries, but here are some inspiring examples for your consideration.

Some of them labored for years before their work began to produce converts. Some were killed by the people they came to serve. But in the end, their labor was not in vain (1 Corinthians 15:58). Their biographies illustrate the importance of reaching the lost, the way the Lord calls a person to be a missionary, the importance of faith, prayer, and faithfulness, and the privilege of serving God in this most-special way.

> 1743 – David Brainerd – ministry to North American Indians.
>
> 1793 – William Carey – Calcutta, India. He is known as the father of Modern Missions.
>
> 1812 – Adoniram Judson and Luther Rice – Serampore, India. Judson then went on to Burma.
>
> 1849 – George Müller – Orphans in England
>
> 1854 – Hudson Taylor – China
>
> 1851 – David Livingstone – Africa
>
> 1858 – John G. Paton – New Hebrides
>
> 1876 – Mary Slessor – Nigeria
>
> 1901 – James Chalmers – Papua New Guinea
>
> 1901 – Amy Carmichael – Orphans in India
>
> 1956 – Mission Aviation Fellowship missionaries Jim Elliot, Pete Fleming, Edward McCully, Nate Saint, and Roger Youderian – killed by Huaorani Indians in eastern Ecuador
>
> 1958 – Elisabeth Elliot and Rachel Saint – Ecuador
>
> 1962 – Don Richardson – Papua New Guinea

Unprecedented opportunities for expansion

Like the Roman Roads in the 1st Century, new trade routes made it possible to take the Gospel to distant lands. And technological advances made the effort much more successful.

Colonization – The establishment of distant colonies by Great Britain, Spain, France, Portugal, Netherlands and other countries opened the way for missionary work in all their outposts. In the New World–the Americas–many persecuted Christian groups planted themselves, far from their hostile homeland, and eventually reached out to indigenous groups near their colonies. When revivals stirred the hearts of Christians in Europe, they began to send missionaries to the multitudes who did not know about Christ.

Transportation – Every advance in transportation methodology was an advance for missionary activity. Better roads, explorer' ships, freighters, railroads, and eventually airplanes were all improvements that made sending and maintaining missionaries possible.

Communications and Technology – Every invention made the distance more manageable, or enhanced the work of the missionary. Photography, telegraphs, telephones, electrical devices of all sorts, tape recordings, moving pictures, radio, television and video recording all made the work more effective and also made it easier to promote the work among Christians at home. In more recent years computers have enhanced the work of translation and assisted many other tasks of the missionary. Today, with the Internet and smart phones, the Gospel is virtually available everywhere!

Formation of Effective Missionary Organizations – Nearly every denomination formed its own missions outreach program, but there was also a need for larger missionary institutions and parachurch organizations to do the things that took more extensive cooperation. During this golden age of missions, medical ministries and hospitals were established, schools were maintained, orphanages were built, disaster relief was administered, economic development was implemented, and Bible translation and production was increased. During these two centuries hundreds of highly significant missionary events occurred.[75]

The following list of mission societies and parachurch organizations is not intended to be a complete catalog.

Missionaries and Missions Organizations

1731 –Moravian Church missions began under the leadership of Count Nicolaus Ludwig Zinzendorf. They reached slaves in the Caribbean and the Inuit of Greenland. They also started working with American Indians in 1742.

1735 – John Wesley ministered to Indians in Georgia with the Society for the Propagation of the Gospel in Foreign Parts (SPG), an Anglican institution. Later this organization sent missionaries to many distant places, including Africa's Gold Coast.

1786 – The Society for the Establishment of Missions among the Heathen was begun by Methodist minister Thomas Coke. Their first undertaking was in the British West Indies.

1787 – William Carey, a Particular Baptist in England began to urge the establishment of worldwide missions. In 1792 he wrote a book about this goal and formed the Baptist Missionary Society to begin missionary work in India.

1800 – Many missionary enterprises became active during the next few decades, including the New York Missionary Society, The Massachusetts Baptist Missionary Society, The Netherlands Missionary Society, The British and Foreign Bible Society, the Church Missionary Society, The London Missionary Society, The American Board of Commissioners for Foreign Missions, the Wesleyan Missionary Society, the American Baptist Foreign Missionary, and the Netherlands Bible Society. Missions were planted in various parts of Africa, China, New Zealand, and other countries. Scores of missionaries were dispatched all over the world.

1873 – Regions Beyond Missionary Union was founded in London.

1883 – The first Protestant church in Amazonia (Brazil) was established.

1886 – The Student Volunteer Movement was launched with 100 university and seminary students at Mount Hermon,

Massachusetts. They signed the Princeton Pledge: "I purpose, God willing, to become a foreign missionary."

1890 – The Central American Mission was founded by C.I. Scofield, editor of the Scofield Reference Bible.

1901 – The Oriental Missionary Society was founded by Charles Cowman (his wife was the compiler of the popular devotional book *Streams in the Desert*).

1908 – The Gideons International began distributing Bibles.

1931 – HCJB Radio was begun in South America by World Radio Missionary Fellowship.

1932 – The Assemblies of God opened mission work in Colombia.

1933 – The Navigators was founded by Dawson Trotman.

1935 – "Each one teach one" literacy program was begun in the Philippines by Frank C. Laubach.

1937 – Child Evangelism Fellowship was founded by Jesse Irvin Overholzer.

1939 – Gospel Recordings began.

1944 – Youth for Christ was begun by Torrey Johnson and Billy Graham.

1945 – The Far East Broadcasting Company (FEBC) was founded.

1945 – Mission Aviation Fellowship was formed.

1945 – The Evangelical Foreign Missions Association was formed by denominational mission boards.

1946 – The first Inter-Varsity missionary convention (now called "Urbana") was held.

1950 – World Vision was begun by Bob Pierce.

1950 – The Mennonite Disaster Service, relief agency of Anabaptists, was begun.

1950 – The Billy Graham Evangelistic Association was begun.

1951 – Campus Crusade for Christ (now known as Cru) was founded by Bill and Vonette Bright. In 1996, *USA Today* called Cru the largest evangelical organization in the United States. Today, the organization employs over 25,000 full-time missionaries and has trained 225,000 volunteers around the world.[76]

1952 – Trans World Radio was founded.

1957 – Operation Mobilization was begun by George Verwer.

1962 – Evangelism Explosion was established by D. James Kennedy.

1960 – Youth with a Mission was founded by Loren Cunningham.

1960--The Asia Evangelistic Fellowship (AEF), one of the largest Asian indigenous missionary organizations, was launched in Singapore by G. D. James.

1963--Theological Education by Extension movement was launched in Guatemala by Ralph Winter and James Emery.

1970 – Samaritan's Purse was founded by Bob Pierce. It has been led by Franklin Graham since 1978.

1976 – Habitat for Humanity began work.

1976 – The U.S. Center for World Missions began in Pasadena, California. It was established under the leadership of Ralph Winter. It is one of the ministries of the Frontier Missions Fellowship. It has been described as a missions think tank or "missions Pentagon."

1977 – Trinity Broadcasting Network began as KTBN-TV. Paul and Jan Crouch began broadcasting in Fontana, California and later moved to Orange County, expanding to become the largest Christian broadcasting network in the world.

1978 – Operation Blessing was begun by Pat Robertson.

1978 – The Jesus Film Project released *Jesus*. Since 1981, *Jesus* has been translated into 1,049 languages and shown in 228 nations. It is available in various video formats. The organization states that, with a cumulative audience in excess of 6 billion, *Jesus* is the most-watched film ever produced.[77]

2000 – Multiplication Network Ministries began helping various missions organizations plant thousands of new churches.

For those who would like to have more information and join in prayer for the ongoing work of missions, Patrick Johnstone offers a frequently revised handbook on the subject called *Operation World*.

Perspectives On the World Christian Movement is a thorough course offered by the U.S. Center for World Missions. It traces the history of missions and explores ways every Christian can be involved in the task of reaching the whole world with the Gospel. Each believer can be a "Goer," "Sender," "Mobilizer," or "Welcomer."

Complaint

There is no complaint or warning for this church, but there are many promises, including these: an encouragement that Jesus is "coming soon," and that He will keep them from the hour of trial that is coming on the world.

Critique

Because you have kept My command to persevere, I also will keep you from the hour of trial which shall come upon the whole world, to test those who dwell on the earth. Behold, I am coming quickly! – Revelation 3:10-11b

Because you have kept My command to persevere... The normal word for command is not used here. Instead, it is the Greek expression, *ton logon tes hypomones*--literally "the word of my patient endurance." It reminds us of the words of Hebrews 12, following the great list of heroes of the faith in Chapter 11:

> *Therefore we also, since we are surrounded by so great a cloud of witnesses, let us lay aside every weight, and the sin which so easily ensnares us, and let us run with endurance the race that is set before us, looking unto Jesus, the author and finisher of our faith, who for the joy that was set before Him endured the cross, despising the shame, and has sat down at the right hand of the throne of God.*
> – Hebrews 12:1-2

The Philadelphian Christians were privileged to live in the time and place of a great "open door" of missions, but like all Christians they had their own trials, as noted above with Judaizers who opposed the teaching of grace. In addition, all 1st Century Christians were considered suspect by people of Greek and Roman backgrounds. But they followed Jesus, the "author and finisher" of their faith who was persecuted more severely than they would be.

To these faithful followers Jesus promised, *I also will keep you from the hour of trial which shall come upon the whole world, to test those who dwell on the earth*. This is the promise of the Rapture of the church. As mentioned before, there is a vast difference between the normal (though possibly deadly) trials caused by being a true Christian (2 Timothy 3:12), and this dreaded "hour of trial which shall come on the whole world." This tribulation is still future, and will be a fulfillment of the last "week" (seven years) of Daniel's prophecy. That will be the last of the 70 "weeks" of years of Israel's history (Daniel 9:24-27) leading to the establishment of the Messianic Kingdom. It also corresponds to an intense time of suffering that Jeremiah called "Jacob's trouble:"

> *Alas! For that day is great,*
> *So that none is like it;*
> *And it is the time of Jacob's trouble,*
> *But he shall be saved out of it* – Jeremiah 30:7

As you can see from this promise to the Philadelphians, the Rapture appears to come before the Tribulation. More information will be given about this timing when we begin our study of Chapter 4. At that point we will also consider the difference between the Rapture of the church and Christ's Glorious Return as King of Kings.

The Lord then reinforces this expectation of His return for the church by saying, ***Behold, I am coming quickly!"*** This has been the "blessed hope" (Titus 2:13) of the church in every generation from the 1st Century until now. Those who understood this promise that was given by Jesus Himself to the disciples (John 14:1-6), lived each day of their lives in the wondrous expectation that He might return for them quickly–meaning immediately. Living in this way has a powerful influence on maintaining holiness and being faithful to share the Gospel with others as quickly as possible (2 Peter 3:11-12).

It should be noted that not all missionaries hold this "pre-millennial, pre-tribulation" orientation, but those who do so have been highly motivated to hasten the task of reaching the whole world while there is still time. Renewed teaching about the Rapture by theologians at Seminaries like Dallas and Talbot; an excellent study Bible compiled by C.I. Schofield; and popular teaching by evangelists and pastors such as Billy Graham, J. Vernon McGee and Chuck Smith, all contributed to the missionary fervor of this "Last Generation." Books like Hal Lindsey's *The Late Great Planet Earth,* and the all-time best-selling novel series, *Left Behind,* by Tim LaHaye and Jerry Jenkins have continued to inspire evangelism and missions. Internet sites, such as the Blue Letter Bible provide a treasure-trove of Bible scholarship and commentary for those who see "the signs of the times" in these days.

Counsel

> *Hold fast what you have, that no one may take your crown. He who overcomes, I will make him a pillar in the temple of My God, and he shall go out no more. I will write on him the name of My God and the name of the city of My God, the New Jerusalem, which comes down out of heaven from My God. And I will write on him My new name.*
>
> *"He who has an ear, let him hear what the Spirit says to the churches.'" – Revelation 3:11c-13*

Hold fast what you have, that no one may take your crown... This probably refers to the Crown of Life, which was also promised to the overcomers of the Smyrna church (See Chapter 2, verse 10). Sadly, some people have failed to receive Christ as Savior, and thus receive eternal life because of the influence of another person who misled them. The apostle John described such people in this way:

> *They went out from us, but they were not of us; for if they had been of us, they would have continued with us; but they went out that they might be made manifest, that none of them were of us. – 1 John 2:19*

As in the message to each of the seven churches, *he who overcomes* is a description of a true believer. See the notes on Chapter 2, verse 1 and Chapter 3, verse 26, where an overcomer is defined as one who's faith is strong enough to remains true to Christ to the end.

To the overcomers in this particular church, Jesus added this: *I will make him a pillar in the temple of My God.* Some commentators consider this a reference to a place of safety. There were no Christian temples, or even church buildings at that time, but in that future New Jerusalem there will be a glorious temple, and it will be a most-secure location. To be a pillar there would be the privilege of providing some supporting service in the place where the Lord Himself will dwell.

For the residents of Philadelphia this concept would have had some temporary relevance too. A few decades earlier a massive earthquake struck the area, followed by many major aftershocks for a long time afterwards. The residents of Philadelphia would prefer to spend their nights in the fields for many years rather than trust the weakened buildings of the city. That might have been why the Lord added, *and he shall go out no more.*

As a further picture of adoption and ownership, Jesus said, these believers would receive a three-fold mark of identification. First He said, *I will write on him the name of My God.* Jesus is God the Son, (see Chapter 1, verse 4), but when He refers to God or His God, He is speaking about the Father. This new name, like the changed last name of a bride or an adopted child in our society, is a mark of ownership or adoption, and privilege.

The overcomer will also receive the name of the New Jerusalem: *and the name of the city of My God, the New Jerusalem, which comes down out of heaven from My God.* No one knows yet what that name will be. We will study the amazing New Jerusalem that will descend from outer space in Revelation Chapter 21!

Finally, the privileged new member of God's family will also receive a new name from Jesus. *And I will write on him My new name.* This also shows His eternal love for His followers.

He who has an ear let him hear what the Spirit says to the churches. As in all the previous letters, this closing thought is repeated. See notes about this expression in Chapter 2, verse 7.

To Laodicea 3:14-22 (Apostate Church 1900's- Present)

"And to the angel of the church of the Laodiceans write,

'These things says the Amen, the Faithful and True Witness, the Beginning of the creation of God: "I know your works, that you are neither cold nor hot. I could wish you were cold or hot. So then, because you are lukewarm, and neither cold nor hot, I will vomit you out of My mouth. Because you say, 'I am rich, have become wealthy, and have need of nothing'—and do not know that you are wretched, miserable, poor, blind, and naked— I counsel you to buy from Me gold refined in the fire, that you may be rich; and white garments, that you may be clothed, that the shame of your nakedness may not be revealed; and anoint your eyes with eye salve, that you may see. As many as I love, I rebuke and chasten. Therefore be zealous and repent. Behold, I stand at the door and knock. If anyone hears My voice and opens the door, I will come in to him and dine with him, and he with Me. To him who overcomes I will grant to sit with Me on My throne, as I also overcame and sat down with My Father on His throne.

"He who has an ear, let him hear what the Spirit says to the churches."'" – Revelation 3:14-21

Connection

And to the angel... As in all the earlier messages to the churches, the *angel* of the church is most likely the pastor since the word's basic meaning is "messenger" (see Chapter 1, verses 1, and 20; and Chapter 2, verse 1).

This letter is written to ***the church of the Laodiceans.*** There might have been multiple groups of Christians meeting in various homes and other places in the city of Laodicea, but, true to the pattern seen throughout the New Testament, all of the professing believers in any given city were part of the one church in that city. Laodicea was about 40 miles east of Ephesus. It was closer to Colosse and Hierapolis, and, even though it was apparently not visited by the apostle Paul, it was mentioned several times in his letter to the Colossians (Colossians 2:1; 4:13-16). Paul told the Colossians to share the letter written to them (now known as the New Testament book of Colossians) with the people of Laodicea. He also mentioned a letter to Laodicea that should be shared with the Colossians. There is no known epistle from Paul to the Laodiceans, but some of the early church fathers thought that this was a reference to the letter sent first to the Ephesians. They believed that the Ephesian letter was evidently meant to be an "encyclical": one that was to be circulated to other churches. The oldest known manuscripts omit "to Ephesus." Another reason for this possibility is that the letter to that city, where Paul had spent the most time, three years, did not have the normal personal references he usually included.

The city was originally named Diospolis, then Rhoas, and later Laodicea to honor Laodice, the wife of Antiochus II, king of Syria, who rebuilt it.[78]

It was located in the Lycos Valley in Anatolia, a part of modern Turkey. It was situated on a major trade route and was a center of commerce. It became very prosperous during the "Pax Romana"--the "Roman Peace"--that was established by Augustus and prevailed for nearly three centuries.

This 1st Century city had thousands of Jewish residents, mostly brought by Antiochus the Great from Babylon.[79]

Various commentators on the Book of Revelation usually name three industries that were particularly successful in Laodicea and that were used by Jesus as illustrations in His address to this church (see verses 17 and 18 below). These were the financial trade, a garment industry specializing in black wool, and a great medical school.

Over the centuries repeated earthquakes in the area made it a less desirable place to live. It gradually declined in size and importance but was still occupied in AD 1230. It was destroyed during the invasions of the Turks and Mongols. Today it is just a field of ruins near the village of Eski Hissar in Turkey.

Jesus referred to Himself with three powerful descriptions that were not used at the beginning of the Book of Revelation. Together they validate His shocking negative opinion of the church. Those who understood who He really was would repent and return to a lifestyle of humble discipleship.

First, He said, *"These things says the Amen."* The word "Amen" is an interjection found 9 times in the Book of Revelation and 143 times in the entire New Testament. In fact, it is the very last word of this Book of Revelation--the last word of the entire Bible!

> *The grace of our Lord Jesus Christ be with you all.* **Amen.** – Revelation 22:21

Amen is often translated "truly," or "verily." It is an affirmation of the truthfulness of something that is about to be said, or, if it follows a statement, it signifies agreement with what was already said. Thus, at the end of a prayer or a hymn it carries the sense of agreement. It could be translated "so be it!"

> *Blessed be the LORD forevermore!* **Amen and Amen.** – Psalm 89:52

Here in this message to the Laodiceans, it is used in a unique way. Jesus is "*The* Amen!" He is the very essence of truth. He had taught His disciples,

> *Jesus said to him, "I am the way, the truth, and the life. No one comes to the Father except through Me.* – John 14:6

Continuing this thought, Jesus also told them the second of His self-descriptions. He said He was **the Faithful and True Witness.** A witness is expected to tell the truth. In a court setting he is legally required to do so. There is a severe penalty if he does not. One cannot really imagine God the Son, the Messiah, and our Savior, failing to tell the truth. The

Laodiceans would need to keep this in mind when they would read, or hear, the sad truth about their inadequate faith. They would not dare to contradict His opinion.

In a third self-description, Jesus said that He was **the Beginning of the creation of God.** The Greek word for "beginning" is *arche.* It is the same word used in the opening words of John's Gospel:

> *In the beginning was the Word, and the Word was with God, and the Word was God. He was in the beginning with God. All things were made through Him, and without Him nothing was made that was made.* – John 1:1-3

The apostle Paul affirmed the same great truth:

> *He is the image of the invisible God, the firstborn over all creation. For by Him all things were created that are in heaven and that are on earth, visible and invisible, whether thrones or dominions or principalities or powers. All things were created through Him and for Him. And He is before all things, and in Him all things consist. And He is the head of the body, the church, who is the beginning, the firstborn from the dead, that in all things He may have the preeminence.* – Colossians 1:15-18

And the writer of Hebrews records this (God the Father is speaking):

> *But to the Son He says:*
> *"Your throne, O God, is forever and ever;*
> *A scepter of righteousness is the scepter of Your kingdom.*
> *You have loved righteousness and hated lawlessness;*
> *Therefore God, Your God, has anointed You*
> *With the oil of gladness more than Your companions."*
> *And:*
> *"You, LORD, in the beginning laid the foundation of the earth,*
> *And the heavens are the work of Your hands.* – Hebrews 1:8-10

Orthodox Christianity agrees that the One True God exists eternally in three persons: The Father, The Son, and The Holy Spirit; and that the work of Creation was done primarily by God the Son.

> *Yet for us there is one God, the Father, of whom are all things, and we for Him; and one Lord Jesus Christ, through whom are all things, and through whom we live.* – 1 Corinthians 8:6

In his commentary on this passage, Ray Stedman reminds us that Jesus is not only responsible for the original creation, but also the new creation.[80]

> *Therefore, if anyone is in Christ, he is a new creation; old things have passed away; behold, all things have become new.* – 1 Corinthians 5:17; Also: John 3:3-7; 1 Peter 1:23)

Commendation

No particular commendation is given to this church. We will see that the Lord's complaint is so severe that there is nothing to their credit that is worth mentioning.

However, we will see that there is still an affirmation of God's love for them and an invitation to them to enter into a personal relationship with Christ. There is also a promise to the overcomers from this church. In the light of that encouragement, we should mention that even in this church there is some missionary activity. Remember that in every age there are some churches that represent each of the seven types of churches. Some will be like the Apostolic period, some will be more like the Persecuted Church, or like the Compromised Church, the Church of the Middle Ages, the Reformed Church, or the great Missionary Church. As we have seen, in all of these different periods of time, spreading the Gospel was always accomplished to one degree or another.

Thus, there will still be missionary-minded church groups in this last apostate age. The missionary emphasis of this era will be *An Open Door of Escape* from the hypocrisy of this post-Christian age.

Complaint

"I know your works, that you are neither cold nor hot. I could wish you were cold or hot.—" – Revelation 3:15

At this point, as in His previous letters, Jesus tells them *I know your works.* As always, good works are not a means of salvation because no one's good works are "good enough," (Ephesians 2:8-9; Titus 3:5; Romans 3:9-12, 23), and the wages of sin is spiritual death (Romans 6:23). Salvation is a gracious gift from God for those who place their faith in Jesus. It was purchased for us by His death on the cross (John 3:16; 1 Peter 1:17-21; Romans 5:8-10). Good works are a result of being in a right relationship with Christ (Ephesians 2:10; Titus 3:8).

Jesus described them as *neither cold nor hot.* The sad thing is that the Laodiceans probably thought that they were pretty good Christians. Most of them were not cold-hearted, like atheists or pagans. On the other hand, they weren't "on fire" for the Lord. Most of them were just middle-of-the-road "Christians," in name only--compromising in their own practices and tolerant of other people's beliefs. They did not see the need for separation from the world. They didn't have a hunger for God's Word, or a sincere love for the Lord Jesus.

I could wish you were cold or hot. In his commentary on Revelation, Ray Stedman explained that this hot/cold imagery would make sense to the residents of Laodicea because they obtained their water from a hot spring in Hierapolis, about six miles away. It was carried by an aqueduct, and by the time it reached Laodicea it was no longer hot, but it wasn't cold either. Cold water is refreshing, and hot water is useful in many ways, but the tepid water was not appetizing.[81]

If they were totally indifferent to spiritual things, or even if they were quite hostile to Christianity, there would be more hope for them. They might then realize how wrong they were. But since they were "lukewarm," they thought they were normal.

Jesus warned against this kind of belief:

> *"Not everyone who says to Me, 'Lord, Lord,' shall enter the kingdom of heaven, but he who does the will of My Father in heaven. Many will say to Me in that day, 'Lord, Lord, have we not prophesied in Your name, cast out demons in Your name, and done many wonders in Your name?' And then I will declare to them, 'I never knew you; depart from Me, you who practice lawlessness!'*-- Matthew 7:21-23 (See the discussion of this in Chapter 2, verse 19.)

As a pastor, this was always my greatest concern. Were there people who attended faithfully and went through all the motions of being a good member of the congregation, but who had never really accepted Christ (John 1:12) and been "born again" (John 3:3)? I couldn't bear the thought that any of them would ever have to hear the Lord Jesus say, "I *never* knew you!" That would not mean that they had given up their faith, but that they had never even become God's children in the first place! How dreadful it will be for a person to think he was a Christian when he had never received the gift of eternal life.

Critique

> **So then, because you are lukewarm, and neither cold nor hot, I will vomit you out of My mouth. Because you say, 'I am rich, have become wealthy, and have need of nothing'—and do not know that you are wretched, miserable, poor, blind, and naked**--*Revelation 3:16-17*

What Jesus said next is really shocking. He is loving and patient. Even when He rebuked the Ephesians for having lost their first love for Him, he had something good to say about them. But in this case, He said, **"So then, because you are lukewarm, and neither cold nor hot, I will vomit you out of My mouth."**

That's harsh! But because He loved them so much, He spoke in the way a worried parent would respond to his children's careless attitudes.

Surely this would jolt some of them back to reality, and they would accept the life-saving advice He was going to give them.

The name of their city was significant in the light of this rebuke. Laodicea comes from two Greek words: *laos*, or "people," and *dike*, meaning "judgment," or "legal finding." Thus Laodicea means the judgment or the rule of the people. In a democracy this is a good thing, but in the church it is a big mistake. In the churches that represented earlier phases of church history, we saw that they were infiltrated by Nicolaitans. That name was descriptive of an ecclesiastical hierarchy in the church that "conquered" the people or ruled over them. We saw that this was the beginning of an official priesthood (see Chapter 2, verses 6 and 15).

The church at Laodicea fit this description, "rule of the people," because they had moved beyond what they must have considered the narrow teaching of God's Word, and beyond the controlling wishes of church leaders. The church now had become a social club, designed to enhance the lifestyle of its members. It was, in essence, the "people's church."

They had forgotten, or maybe they didn't even realize, that Jesus said it was *His* church! (Matthew 16:18).

Now, in case any one of those who read or heard this letter was missing the point that they were not living the victorious Christian life, Jesus added this wake-up call: *Because you say, 'I am rich, have become wealthy, and have need of nothing'—and do not know that you are wretched, miserable, poor, blind, and naked.*

By the standards of this material world, most of the Laodiceans were prosperous. The city was a hub of commerce, an industrial center, and the financial core of their part of the world.

Jesus warned that riches could blind a person to their spiritual need:

> *Then Jesus said to His disciples, "Assuredly, I say to you that it is hard for a rich man to enter the kingdom of heaven. And again I say to you, it is easier for a camel to go through the eye of a needle than for a rich man to enter the kingdom of God."*- Matthew 19:23-24

I will never forget one Sunday morning in the first church I pastored when one of our young men ran into my study just before services began, and told me that his parents were attending for the very first time. We had been praying for their salvation, so my first reaction was, "Praise the Lord!" But before I finished saying it I realized that his folks, some of the wealthiest people in our community, would probably not understand why I was using that very text for my message! With grave concern for our new visitors, I delivered the message about how hard it is for a rich person to enter heaven. At the end of the message I gave an invitation to receive Christ, and could hardly believe it when my friend's mother stepped up to make that decision. A few months later his father made the same commitment. Fortunately, they could see their spiritual need in spite of their wealth.

The comfort of "the good life" causes many wealthy people to miss the greater treasure of knowing Christ personally, and gaining eternal life. They don't even realize that from Jesus' point of view they own nothing of spiritual value.

He said that they were "wretched," a Greek word meaning "bearing callouses." This was the very opposite of privileged. He said they were "miserable,"–the opposite of satisfied. They were "poor,"–the opposite of rich. They were "blind,"–the opposite of all-seeing/all-knowing. And they were "naked,"–the opposite of armored/protected.

The good news is that Jesus doesn't leave the Laodiceans in a hopeless state. We will see that, even for them, there is salvation.

Historical Fulfillment (Worldly Church)

At this point we can apply the same verses (Revelation 3:15-17) to the last period of the prophesied Church Age–from the 1900's to the beginning of the Tribulation Period. During these years we have seen a gradual erosion of biblical values and the increase of immorality. More and more, our culture is ignoring God's revealed will, and the church is allowing it to happen by not standing against it. This is a spiritual struggle that has raged from the 1st Century until now. But it is getting worse in our generation for a number of reasons.

Before we list some of those reasons, let us explain why we call this seventh period the "worldly church." Bible teachers often call it the era of the "apostate church." In our own website, Prophecy Central, we have tracked "apostasy" as one of the most significant sub-topics of prophecy. This section features Bible passages that predict a downturn in morality during the end time. It also records many disturbing news stories that show we are living in a time of serious moral decline. Some of these prophecies apply to the "beginning of birth pains" (the generation just before the Tribulation begins) and some apply to the Tribulation Period when things will get even worse (see Appendix A – Jesus' Own Outline of the Future). They all describe the decay of true Christian influence on culture:

And because lawlessness will abound, the love of many will grow cold. – Matthew 24:12

The Spirit clearly says that in later times some will abandon the faith and follow deceiving spirits and things taught by demons. Such teachings come through hypocritical liars, whose consciences have been seared as with a hot iron. – 1 Timothy 4:1-2

But mark this: There will be terrible times in the last days. People will be lovers of themselves, lovers of money, boastful, proud, abusive, disobedient to their parents, ungrateful, unholy, without love, unforgiving, slanderous, without self-control, brutal, not lovers of the good, treacherous, rash, conceited, lovers of pleasure rather than lovers of God— having a form of godliness but denying its power. Have nothing to do with such people. – 2 Timothy 3:1-5

The normal use of the word "apostasy" today refers to those who have defected from their belief system. It implies a serious, permanent decision to leave the faith, and a harsh judgment against them by those who still believe.

However, the members of the church at Laodicea had not formally given up on their Christian orientation; they had just gradually drifted away from a firm belief in what the Bible teaches about Jesus, salvation, and a godly lifestyle. That is why Jesus said," ***I could wish you were cold or hot.*** " If they were cold they wouldn't even have pretended to be

Christians. If they were hot, they would have been committed, "on fire" believers. But, for the most part they were in the middle–just lukewarm–and were not pleasing at all to the Lord.

The Greek word that is translated "apostasy" is *apostasia*, from a verb meaning "to stand apart," or "to depart." The word is used only twice in the Bible. Once it pertains to Moses (Acts 21:21), and the other is most likely a reference to the "departure" at the Rapture (2 Thessalonians 2:3). In its verb form the Greek word is used fifteen times in the New Testament. Dr. Thomas Ice explains:

> Of these fifteen, only three have anything to do with a departure from the faith (Luke 8;13; 1 Tim. 4:1; Heb 3:12). The word is used for departing from iniquity (2 Tim. 2:19), from ungodly men (1 Tim. 6:5), from the temple (Luke 2:27), from the body (2 Cor. 12:8), and from persons (Acts 12:10; Luke 4:13).[82]

So, to return to Jesus' descriptions: if His readers or listeners were cold, they would be apostate, separated completely from Him. If they were hot, they would be faithful and vibrant Christians. But, if they were lukewarm they, would best be described as "worldly." Jesus used this concept in His teaching to His disciples:

> *Do not love the world or the things in the world. If anyone loves the world, the love of the Father is not in him. For all that is in the world—the lust of the flesh, the lust of the eyes, and the pride of life—is not of the Father but is of the world. And the world is passing away, and the lust of it; but he who does the will of God abides forever.* – 1 John 2:14-17

The Bible sometimes refers to "the world "as the Earth and the created universe, but at other times it means the corrupted "cosmos" world system that is temporarily dominated by Satan (Matthew 4:8-10; John 12:31; John 14:30; Ephesians 2:2; 1 John 15:9).

The apostle Paul also warned against being conformed to this evil world system:

I beseech you therefore, brethren, by the mercies of God, that you present your bodies a living sacrifice, holy, acceptable to God, which is your reasonable service. And do not be conformed to this world, but be transformed by the renewing of your mind, that you may prove what is that good and acceptable and perfect will of God. –Romans 12:1-2

Paul had a different way of describing the "lukewarm" Christian. In his letter to the Corinthians he explains a similar division of mankind according to one's spiritual condition. Where our current passage in Revelation describes the three possibilities as "cold, lukewarm, or hot," Paul speaks of people being "natural, carnal, or spiritual." He starts with the two extremes: natural and spiritual, and then describes the unfortunate middle position as carnal.

But the natural man does not receive the things of the Spirit of God, for they are foolishness to him; nor can he know them, because they are spiritually discerned. But he who is spiritual judges all things, yet he himself is rightly judged by no one. For "who has known the mind of the LORD that he may instruct Him?" But we have the mind of Christ.

And I, brethren, could not speak to you as to spiritual people but as to carnal, as to babes in Christ. I fed you with milk and not with solid food; for until now you were not able to receive it, and even now you are still not able; for you are still carnal. For where there are envy, strife, and divisions among you, are you not carnal and behaving like mere men? – 1 Corinthians 2:14-3:3

These three states correspond to the three-fold nature of humanity:

Now may the God of peace Himself sanctify you completely; and may your whole spirit, soul, and body be preserved blameless at the coming of our Lord Jesus Christ. – 1 Thessalonians 5:23

All living creatures on Earth, including plants, have a *body*. A living body normally does certain physical things, like eating, growing, and reproduction. It might do other things, like responding to its environment.

Animal life has another aspect: *soul,* or "personality," which includes the invisible characteristics of intellect, emotion, and will. As you know, plants do not have these (though some plant-lovers might think they do), but animals do have them. Your pets can be smart, loving, and obedient.

Human beings have an additional attribute: a *spirit.* This is the part of man that was created "in the image of God" (Genesis 1:26-28). Jesus said, "God is spirit..." (John 4:24). However, because of sin, humans are spiritually dead (separated from God) until they are born again (made alive spiritually). They are then "spiritual" beings, able to communicate with God (John 3:3 ff.).

> *And you He made alive, who were dead in trespasses and sins, in which you once walked according to the course of this world, according to the prince of the power of the air, the spirit who now works in the sons of disobedience, among whom also we all once conducted ourselves in the lusts of our flesh, fulfilling the desires of the flesh and of the mind, and were by nature children of wrath, just as the others.*
>
> *But God, who is rich in mercy, because of His great love with which He loved us, even when we were dead in trespasses, made us alive together with Christ (by grace you have been saved), and raised us up together, and made us sit together in the heavenly places in Christ Jesus.*--Ephesians 2:1-6

Returning to Paul's explanation: a "natural" person (Greek *psuchikos*--"having a soul) can be intelligent, talented, and even "good" by human standards, but he or she does not know Christ or have the gift of, eternal life (John 1:12; 3:16). Such a person is *controlled by his or her soul.* In the context of our passage in Revelation, Jesus would call such a person spiritually "cold."

On the other hand, a "spiritual" person (Greek *pneumatikos*), is a "new creation in Christ (2 Corinthians 5:17), and is *controlled by his or her spirit,* which, in turn, is directed by the Holy Spirit, as long as he or she submits to His control (Ephesians 5:18; Galatians 5:16). Jesus would call this person spiritually "hot."

But Paul complained that he could not talk with the Corinthian believers as spiritual people. They were not walking in the Spirit. Therefore, they were "carnal" (Greek *sarkikos*–"fleshly") or *controlled by the appetites of the body*. These are the ones Jesus would call "lukewarm."

What is happening in the Christian world today that would be a fulfillment of this prophecy? Is the church of our day really "lukewarm," or "worldly"? Please keep in mind that in every age of the church there were representatives of all seven churches, and at this stage of history there is still a large, dedicated remnant, especially from the missionary era. But if we look at the trends honestly, we must admit that its numbers are declining, and a less-biblical, more theologically-liberal element of the church is growing.

Now we are ready to consider some of the reasons that our present era of history is producing a "worldly" church, and that impaired organization is not stemming the tide of corruption and immorality.

However, as we look at these negative trends, we should also be mindful that there have been some amazing spiritual advances during this time as well. There is always a spiritual war in progress in the church (Ephesians 6:10-20; 1 Peter 5:8-9.). Yet Jesus Himself said that this war will be won ("The gates of Hades will not prevail against it." – Matthew 16:18 – See the notes on Chapter 2, verse 10). The pendulum is always swinging, and there have been many cycles during the past 2000 years where the church lost ground to spiritual attacks, and later experienced revival and returned to the Lord.

As the night gets darker, the light shines brighter. In spite of the worldliness of this age, we are expecting an end time revival!

> *Then He spoke a parable to them that men always ought to pray and not lose heart, saying: "There was in a certain city a judge who did not fear God nor regard man. Now there was a widow in that city; and she came to him, saying, 'Get justice for me from my adversary.' And he would not for a while; but afterward he said within himself, 'Though I do not fear God nor regard man, yet because this widow troubles me I will avenge her, lest by her continual coming she weary me.' "*
>
> *Then the Lord said, "Hear what the unjust judge said. And shall God not avenge His own elect who cry out day and night to Him, though He bears long with them? I tell you that He will avenge them speedily. Nevertheless, **when the Son of Man comes, will He really find faith on***

the earth?"- Luke 18:1-8

The answer is "yes!" When Jesus returns He will find a godly remnant. Evidently the majority of people will not be true believers (The wide vs. the narrow way–Matthew 7:13-14), but there are still multiplied millions of faithful born-again people among the 2.2 billion who call themselves Christians.

The Bible tells us that God does not want any to perish (2 Peter 3:9). For that reason, He always gives opportunity to sinners to repent before allowing judgment to fall on their city or nation. If He could have found 10 righteous He would have spared Sodom (Genesis 18:23-33). In the case of Nineveh (Book of Jonah), there was a great revival when the people realized that they deserved judgment.

Toward the end of the book of Daniel, the prophet recorded a prediction about the end time that he himself did not understand:

> *"But you, Daniel, shut up the words, and seal the book until the time of the end;* **many shall run to and fro, and knowledge shall increase.**" – Daniel 12:4

> *Although I heard, I did not understand. Then I said, "My lord, what shall be the end of these things?"*
> *And he said, "Go your way, Daniel, for the words are closed up and sealed till the time of the end.* – Daniel `12:8-9

It was a prediction of the increase of knowledge, but not necessarily an increase of wisdom. This might have been partially fulfilled by the phenomenal resurgence of knowledge during the Renaissance that started in the 15th Century and continued in the Enlightenment or Age of Reason in the 17th and 18th Centuries. It will help us to take a look at these historical roots, and then we will see an even more striking fulfillment in our own generation during this "Information Age."

Science, Philosophy and Liberal Theology

The Renaissance (French "rebirth") was a period of revived interest in learning and art. It was fueled by the increased exploration of the world with better ships and navigation methods, and by the invention of Gutenberg's movable type printing press, which made it possible to produce inexpensive books.

The Enlightenment or "Age of Reason" followed the Renaissance. Beginning in the 1600's, it elevated science and philosophy, and cast doubt on many existing traditions, including religious beliefs. Brilliant philosophers and scientists like René Descartes, Baruch Spinoza, John Locke, Voltaire, Immanuel Kant, and Sir Isaac Newton published their thoughts during this age. Many of them were especially disdainful of the Catholic Church because of the mistakes that had been made during the former millennium. For instance, the church had condemned the findings of astronomers Nicolaus Copernicus and Galileo Galilei who had demonstrated that the Earth revolves around the Sun. The Reformation also had brought to light many of the theological and practical errors of the church.

Through Benjamin Franklin and Thomas Jefferson, the Enlightenment influenced the writing of the Declaration of Independence in America and the revolution that followed it. During this time Harvard was founded in Massachusetts. It was the first institution of higher learning in the New World, and was established primarily to train clergy.

Coincidentally, but of great importance to church historians, **Christian forces defeated Islamic troops** in Vienna in 1683. This was the last effort by Islamic military forces to impose their rule on Western European or North American nations until the 9/11 attacks in New York and Washington in 2001. However, they maintained their hold on the Arab world and the rest of the Middle East, Indonesia, parts of India now known as Pakistan, and large sections of Eastern Europe. And following their concept of emigration, which has been part of the "DNA" of Islam ever since Muhammad first moved to Medina, they have successfully infiltrated many other countries, including most of Western Europe. Christian evangelization was quenched in all these vital portions of the world. Churches were turned into mosques, and while "Christian countries" offered tolerance to them, most Islamic countries did not allow freedom of religion in return.

Of even greater significance, European skeptics from the Enlightenment began a new field of study called **Biblical Criticism**. Its proponents suggested that biblical texts had human origins rather than supernatural. Richard Simon's controversial *Critical History*, published in 1685, denied that Moses wrote the Pentateuch (the first five books of the Bible). His books were destroyed, but his theory took root among the rationalists of the era.

Biblical Criticism grew in popularity among liberal theologians. In 1701 Yale College was founded by Congregationalists to combat the theological liberalism that had infiltrated Harvard. Princeton was begun in 1746 to educate ministers of the Gospel.

In 1878 German scholar Julius Wellhausen published his *Prolegomena to the History of Israel.* It analyzed the first six books of the Bible and proposed the so-called "documentary hypothesis"–a theory that the Pentateuch was actually written by several authors, and pieces of their writings were put together by later editors or redactors.

Another influential German writer was Albert Schweitzer. In 1906 he wrote *The Quest of the Historical Jesus.* Since then it has been fashionable for "liberal Christians" to imagine their own versions of who Jesus really was–usually a messiah figure who didn't consider Himself to be the Son of God, and who was unfortunately put to death by people who didn't understand Him. To these people Jesus was a great teacher and a worthy example, but not a savior from sin. They downplayed the miraculous elements of the Bible.

Another important development in the second half of the 1800's was the growth of the socio-economic concepts of **Socialism and the emergence of Communism** on the political scene. In 1848 Karl Marx and Friedrich Engels published the Communist Manifesto. The Communist revolutions in Russia (1917), China (1949), and other countries would be a major step backward for Christianity. Atheism became the norm for Communists. Missionaries in these nations were driven out or killed.

In addition to all of these movements that had a negative influence on Christianity, another controversial development in the scientific world shook the faith of many Christians. Charles Darwin published *On the Origin of Species* explaining his **Theory of Evolution** by gradual mutations and natural selection. This notion was rapidly adopted by the European academic community, many of whom were already "post-Christian" thinkers, and others who were looking for an excuse to jettison the moral restraints prescribed by the Bible. Evolution has not been proven by true scientific methodology, but it was accepted as the foundation of the philosophy of Humanism. Those who accept the theory generally doubt the Creation story of Adam and Eve, and this led to disbelief in a literal interpretation of the rest of the Bible as well.

Some Christians try to harmonize evolution and creation by belief in "theistic evolution," but this has the same result of undermining the authority of God's Word. During the past century many brilliant scientists who disagree with evolution have pushed back by showing that the Bible's narrative, including the Genesis flood in Noah's day, provides a better explanation of the existing fossil record. And more recently, a new discipline called "Intelligent Design" has given convincing evidence that this amazing fine-tuned universe was not an unexplainable accident, but the result of a brilliant creator.

Nevertheless, modern "higher education" embraces evolution, socialism, and a denial of biblical values. By the 1870's it was fashionable for American scholars to attend German universities. Graduating with a non-Christian worldview, these people became the leaders of the educational movement in the United States.

Meanwhile, **Psychology**, which had its origins in Greek philosophy, began employing scientific experimentation to gain new insight. In 1879 the first psychology laboratory was launched by Wilhelm Wundt at the University of Leipzig in Germany. As the field of psychology grew, Christian counselors found that it could be used to analyze spiritual needs, but it took the place of religion for many people. It began to provide good tools to determine why people were unstable, but was reluctant to give moral advice where it was needed, preferring for the patient to discover his or her own solutions. Therefore, psychologists not only failed to suggest biblical solutions, but in some cases they began to validate immoral behaviors. This problem came to a head during the eventual "sexual revolution" in the 1960's.

The Slippery Slope

During the first half of the 20th Century a number of developments affected the growth of Christianity. Theological debates left Christians divided and confused. Public education was infiltrated by agnostic and evolutionary influences. History-making inventions from the Industrial Revolution changed the way people lived. The population shifted to cities where they could find jobs and enjoy a materialistic lifestyle. New economic and governmental concepts began changing the structure of nations, including the United States. Two World Wars and the invention of nuclear weapons produced a sense of despair. And new philosophies of life lured people away from their moral foundations. The net result of all of this was a gradual descent into a more worldly type of Christianity.

Here is a brief discussion of some of the major events from 1900 to about 1950, and the effect they had on Christianity. Please notice that, throughout the two millennia of the church's existence, there were both losses and gains as the spiritual battle raged over Christianity. But, just as Jesus promised, it has never been possible for our spiritual enemy to conquer the church that Jesus built. There are overcomers in every one of the six churches we have already studied (Revelation 2:7, 11, 17, 26; 3:5, 12) and there is a similar encouragement to true believers in the Laodicean Church.

To him who overcomes I will grant to sit with Me on My throne, as I also overcame and sat down with My Father on His throne. – Revelation 3:21

Theological Upheaval

The unfortunate conclusion, even if sometimes unspoken, by those who accepted the theories of liberal theologians was that the Bible was not really the Word of God. Two strong Christian movements began near the beginning of the 20th Century: The Pentecostal Movement and Christian Fundamentalism. Both of these had a strong influence in bringing their followers back to a belief that the Bible is indeed God's inerrant Word.

Pentecostalism had roots in the founding of the National Holiness Association in 1867, and the Christian and Missionary Alliance in

1887, but it became a major force during the Azusa Street Revival that began in 1906. The emphasis was on the experience caused by the filling of the Holy Spirit, including healing and speaking in tongues. Two major denominations that eventually emerged from this revival were the Assemblies of God (1914) and the International Church of the Foursquare Gospel (1927).

Christian Fundamentalism began during the years of 1910 to 1915 with the publication of *The Fundamentals*, a set of 90 essays written by 64 different authors, chosen from various Christian denominations. Fundamentalism also had roots in the previous century. One major influence was belief in Premillennialism, a literal thousand-year reign of Christ following the Rapture of the church (see the notes on Chapter 3, verse 10). The Early Church held this belief, but it was not emphasized during the Middle Ages. The Catholic Church taught that the millennial kingdom was symbolic of the eventual result of church growth. In other words, they thought that they were already establishing the Kingdom Age. And, of course, the new liberal theologians likewise did not expect a literal future kingdom.

After the Reformation, Bible scholars from the Plymouth Brethren Church, which was founded in 1832, began to revive interest in eschatology. John Nelson Darby, one of the founders of the group, became a popular teacher. He taught "Dispensationalism," the view that there were various phases of God's dealing with mankind, and that there is a clear distinction between Israel and the church.

C. I. Scofield was a popular teacher and preacher toward the end of the 19th Century. He developed a study Bible with his notes on prophecy and Dispensationalism. The Scofield Bible was first published in 1909, and revised in 1917. It had a great influence on the growth of Fundamentalism.

One of the editors of *The Fundamentals* was R. A. Torrey, who had been a disciple of D. L. Moody. He became an evangelist, and was then persuaded to move to Los Angeles to establish the Bible Institute of Los Angeles (now Biola University and Talbot School of Theology) and to become the first pastor of the Church of the Open Door.

Fundamentalism defended orthodox Protestant beliefs, and stood against Modernism's liberal theology, Catholicism, evolution, cults and other teachings that did not accept the Bible as the inspired and inerrant Word of God.

During the course of the 20th Century most main-line denominations like the Methodists, Episcopalians, Presbyterians, Congregationalists, and Lutherans, gravitated toward Modernism. They generally practiced a "social gospel," and supported the concept of an ecumenical movement that led to the founding of the World Council of Churches in 1948 and the National Council of Churches in 1950. Most Pentecostals, Baptists, smaller groups and many new denominations that broke ties with their liberal mother-churches carried the more "orthodox" banners of Christianity. They emphasized evangelism, and joined the National Association of Evangelicals when it began in 1943.

Evangelicals grew rapidly for several decades while liberal churches suffered a serious loss of members.

Progressive Education

While Evangelicals successfully held back the church's drift toward worldliness, another spiritual battle was being fought in the realm of public education.

As far back as 1787, the Founding Fathers of the United States prescribed public education based on Christian principles. The Northwest Ordinance, which provided for the government of new territories, included this statement:

> "Religion, morality, and knowledge, being necessary to good government and the happiness of mankind, schools and the means of education shall forever be encouraged."[83]

Standard textbooks like *The New England Primer* and *McGuffey Readers* were used in schools. They combined the mastery of essential skills with moral–even biblical–standards. *The New England Primer* included rhymes like these:

> *In Adam's fall*
> *We sinned all.*

Thy life to mend,
This Book attend. [Picture of the Holy Bible]

Peter denies
His Lord, and cries.

From the third *McGuffey Reader*, the most popular and widely used textbook series for schools in America from 1836 to 1960, here is an excerpt from a section called "Things to Remember."

> *12.* Trust in the Lord, and He will guide you in the way of good men. The path of the just is as the shining light that shineth more and more unto the perfect day.
>
> *13.* We must do all the good we can to all men, for this is well pleasing in the sight of God. He delights to see his children walk in love, and do good one to another.[84]

In 1919 John Dewey, an American pragmatist, psychologist, and educational reformer, together with a group of fellow socialists, founded the New School for Social Research in New York City. He had been influenced by a view of utopian socialism even before the Russian Revolution. Because of his "progressive" philosophy, he taught that rigorous reading and writing should not be required of young students because it would inhibit their social development. He felt that the "center of gravity" was not in the teacher or the textbooks, but in "the immediate instincts and activities of the child himself." His experimental methods started to be used in private schools, and by 1940 they became the norm in public schools.[85] Little by little, public education became less academic and more social. There was a gradual shift from concepts of morality to a new definition of tolerance: acceptance of each person's beliefs as equally valid. This would become an even greater problem in the '50's and 60's when prayer and Bible reading were banned in schools.

Except for private Christian colleges and universities, higher education drifted far to the left in politics. Secular universities became mass-producers of liberal-minded, evolutionary, agnostic or even anti-Christian leaders and teachers of the next generations.

Urbanization and Materialism

Another threat to Christian devotion was posed by the life of luxury many people began to enjoy thanks to the Age of Invention which followed the Industrial Revolution. By the early 20th Century electrical power was available, enabling telephones, electric lights, and motor-driven conveniences.

The automobile was changing the way people lived. Jobs were available in the fast-growing cities where all these new products were being produced. Newspaper ads and the new medium of radio trumpeted the advantages of all the new products one should try. This drew myriads of people into urban centers. They began to experience "the good life" of materialism. They also came in contact with new temptations, such as bars, dance halls, and theaters. As mentioned before, the Bible usually casts cities in an evil light (see Chapter 1, verse 5 and Chapter 2, verse 13). Satan has control of the kingdoms of this world until it will be renovated by The Lord Jesus Christ when He returns as King of Kings (Revelation 19:11-15).

By the end of the two world wars many families enjoyed a two-income life-style. For many, this brought disruption to their family life.

Corruption of Government

Early in the new century the Supreme Court began to make decisions that weakened the interpretation of the Constitution and the Judaeo-Christian basis of law. Oliver Wendell Holms was appointed to the high court by President Theodore Roosevelt in 1902. Holms had written a book called *The Common Law* some two decades earlier that proposed that law should evolve in keeping with Darwin's doctrine of evolution.[86]

The American Civil Liberties Union (ACLU) was formed in 1916 and became champions of the modern concept of "separation of church and state." By this expression they did not mean what the Anabaptists had believed, that the church leaders should not run the government nor the government leaders control the church (see "Church /State Alliance" in Chapter 3, verse 1).

The First Amendment to the Constitution had stated, "Congress shall make no law respecting an establishment of religion, or prohibiting the free exercise thereof." But the ACLU ignored the fact that the founders were nearly all devout Christians who quoted Scripture, took their oaths on the Bible, allowed national monuments to be embellished with Bible passages, and opened their sessions with prayer. After presidential inaugurations they attended worship together. None of these things were considered by those who wrote the Constitution and the By-Laws to be violations of the First Amendment.

Over time the Supreme Court became less loyal to the original purposes of the Constitution. Lower court judges and legislators began to agree with the ACLU, and public schools often went out of their way to expunge Christian teaching and symbolism from their institutions.

World Wars

Two global wars in the span of just 31 years had a negative effect on the faith of many. World War I (1914-1918) was called "The war to end all wars." It drew all the major economic powers into the conflict, and resulted in the death of more than nine million people.

World War II (1939-1945) erupted just two decades later. The intense fighting, using improved equipment and weapons, and followed by disease and famine, killed between 60 and 85 million people. It was ended by the use of two atomic bombs.

The overall effect on survivors of these wars was a sense of insecurity and despair. For many it was a challenge to Christianity's (and all religions') hardest question, "Why would a good God allow such suffering?"

The two world wars, and the Great Depression between them, had a negative impact on missionary activity because missionaries were forced to leave troubled areas and gifts to support missions declined considerably.[87]

New Philosophies

Humanism, later called Secular Humanism, began as an organized movement in 1933 with the publication of *A Humanist Manifesto*. This document was the first of three attempts to define a human-centered belief system that did not encourage belief in a god or existing supernatural views of reality. Education pioneer John Dewey was one of the original signers of the document. The International Humanist and Ethical Union was founded in 1952, when a gathering of world Humanists met under the leadership of famous evolutionist Sir Julian Huxley.

After World War II the philosophy of **Existentialism** became popular. It grew out of the teaching of Søren Kierkegaard, who proposed that individuals validate their own existence through free and conscious acts of their will. It discounted the importance of scientific knowledge and denied the existence of objective values. Even those who did not know about the teaching of this philosophy began to place greater value on their own unique personal experience.

Another philosophical development of this changing world is known as **Relativism**. This is the attitude that there is no such thing as absolute truth or moral values. Instead, things may be true only in relation to the culture, people, or historical context of those who hold them. Therefore "my truth" is not necessarily the same as "your truth," and one is not necessarily better than the other.

This led to a new definition of "tolerance," which used to mean the willingness to treat another person well in spite of that person's beliefs or conditions. Because of relativism, tolerance now means the willingness to accept other people's ideas and beliefs as equal to our own ideas and beliefs. This is a logical absurdity, and would not work in the real world for any business person, doctor, scientist or engineer. But many people like the concept because it allows them to do what they want without guilt. They often quote what has become one of the best-known verses in the Bible:

Judge not, that you be not judged. – Matthew 7:1

When people use this verse flippantly, they might not realize that God Himself will judge them (Psalm 1:1-6; John 3:18; Romans 2:1-5;

Romans 14:12; 2 Peter 2:9; Revelation 20:11-15), and He even expects godly Christians to judge, in the sense of discerning what is right and wrong:

> ***But he who is spiritual judges all things***, *yet he himself is rightly judged by no one. For "who has known the mind of the LORD that he may instruct Him?" But we have the mind of Christ.* – 1 Corinthians 2:15-16

Lukewarm Christianity

Many major developments have occurred from the middle of the 20th Century until now that have contributed to the spiritual decline of the church. With each of these situations there were also significant positive reactions by godly Christians that helped slow the pace of the spiritual decline. Therefore, after a discussion of each of these historical steps there will also be an acknowledgement of some of the concurrent evangelical responses

Birth of Israel: The "Beginning of Birth Pains"

Jesus taught that the first phase of the end time would be characterized as a time of troublesome events that he called "the beginning of sorrows [birth pains]" (Matthew 24:4-8 –See Appendix A for Jesus' Own Outline of the Future).

This period of history will experience wars, rumors of wars, earthquakes, famines, pestilence, and more. These will be precursors of an even worse phase of world events that Jesus called "Tribulation."

Though people of past historical periods might correctly identify the events of their time as chaotic, it does seem that the many negative events in our recent history are the most likely fulfillment of this prophecy.

The **rebirth of the Nation of Israel** on May 14, 1948, was the fulfillment of the end-times prophecy recorded approximately 2500 years, earlier. It came to pass exactly as it was predicted in Ezekiel Chapters 36 and 37! In all of history there is not an equally-amazing example of the return by a people who had been driven from their land. The Jews had been scattered by conquests and persecutions for more than two millennia. In all that time they never lost their identity as God's chosen people, though in the humorous spirit of Tevye in "Fiddler on the Roof," some of them might have asked God, "But, once in a while, can't You choose someone else?"

Humanly speaking, the right for Jews to return to their historical home was the result of two major circumstances: Zionism and a post-WWII partition of the land by the United Nations. Zionism was a movement that had encouraged Jewish people from all over the world to gravitate to the Holy Land since before the turn of the century. The United Nations action came at the end of the temporary control of the area by the British in 1947, just at the time that millions of displaced and bereaved Jewish people needed a place to live. There was international approval for the partition plan because of public sympathy for the survivors of World War II's Holocaust. Six million Jews had been exterminated in just a few years. This number represented one third of all Jews in the world at the time. The U.N. action divided the Holy Land, designating parts of it for an Arab state and parts for a Jewish state.

From a Divine point of view, prophecy was fulfilled when, as soon as the Jewish people declared their independence, they were attacked by all of their neighboring nations, and yet they survived. They went on, through several other wars, to become a great nation once again.

The rebirth of Israel was actually a great encouragement to the evangelicals, most of whom had a strong interest in prophecy. However, it created an even greater gap between the two major factions of the church. The evangelicals were supportive of Israel, but the liberal denominations tended to side with the Palestinians.

It is worth mentioning that 1948, the year of Israel's rebirth, was also a big year for other news of interest to Christians. The Dead Sea Scrolls were discovered, the World Council of Churches was formed, and The Benelux agreement (Trade union of Belgium, Netherlands and Luxemburg--Forerunner of the European Union) was formed. Prophecy students have wondered if these milestones signaled the beginning of the "last generation" before the end of the Church Age and beginning of the Tribulation. After teaching His outline of the future, Jesus gave this parable:

"Now learn this parable from the fig tree: When its branch has already become tender and puts forth leaves, you know that summer is near. So you also, when you see all these things, know that it is near—at the doors! Assuredly, I say to you, **this generation will by no means pass away till all these things take place.** *Heaven and earth will pass away, but My words will by no means pass away."* – Matthew 24:32-35

There are various ideas about the length of a biblical generation (35, 40, 70 years, etc.). But the length of time between the beginning and end of this era could be much longer. Jesus said the generation will not *pass away* until everything is fulfilled. As an example, the last person born in the Civil War generation was thought to be 108 years old when he died. That means that the generation that witnessed the Civil War did not pass away for over a hundred years.

Existence of the new nation of Israel caused a resurgence of Islamic radicalism, giving birth to the modern jihadist or terrorist mentality that has increased the number of "wars and rumors of war."

The desire by many Muslims to restore Islamic control had been festering ever since the end of World War I. In 1924 the Ottoman Empire, the last Islamic caliphate (a territory controlled by a Muslim ruler), was dismantled. The Muslim Brotherhood was formed in 1928. The purpose of the Brotherhood was to unify Islamic countries and establish Sharia (Islamic law). They were responsible for the rise of Hamas among the Palestinians. They also assisted the growth of al Qaeda. In 2011, after the "Arab Spring," they assumed control of Egypt, but were removed by a military coup in 2013. They are still very active in the Middle East.

In 1979 the people of Iran removed their Shaw–the last ruler of the Persian Empire, and installed the Ayatollah Khomeini as the Supreme Leader of the country, making Iran an Islamic Republic with a new theocratic constitution. Ever since that time it has been the archenemy of Israel and supporter of terrorist causes all over the Middle East. At this time they are about to complete the process of producing nuclear weapons. If they are allowed to succeed, they will be an existential threat, not only to Israel, but to many Arab countries that follow a different brand of Islamic teaching. Iran is a Shia Islamic nation, and its people are not Arabs. Most of the Arab nations in the area follow the Sunni branch of Islam, and are concerned that Iran will overtake them by force if it becomes a nuclear power.

Evangelical Response

Evangelical leaders were supportive of the Jewish remnant. They taught that the rebirth of Israel was a striking fulfillment of Bible prophecy and that Christians should faithfully pray for "The peace of Jerusalem" (Psalm 122:6). They were also convinced that America was blessed by God because of our support for Israel. They based this on the promise in the Abrahamic Covenant that said,

> *I will bless those who bless you,*
> *And I will curse him who curses you;*
> *And in you all the families of the earth shall be blessed."* -- Genesis 12:3

It seemed obvious to those who take the Bible literally that nations that had allowed the Jews to be persecuted were forsaken by God. On the other hand, it was thought that the abundant blessings enjoyed by the United States were at least partially caused by the country's affirmation of God's Chosen People and of their new homeland. The majority of American legislators from both major political parties have been strong encouragers of the nation of Israel.

Liberal theologians did not expect literal fulfillments of prophecy, and tended to be more sympathetic to the plight of the displaced Palestinians.

Christian ministries made use of the new technologies of radio and television to support modern Israel. J. Vernon McGee, Hal Lindsey, Chuck Smith, Chuck Missler, John Hagee and David Hocking, were just a few of the media teachers who had a high regard for God's chosen people and the restored nation of Israel. Many of these prominent Christian leaders organized tours of Israel. This endeared them to the people of the struggling new nation. Israelis generally consider evangelicals their most supportive friends in the world.

The Ecumenical Movement and the Social Gospel

Ever since Satan deceived our first parents he has devised various false religions. His ultimate goal is to be worshipped by mankind (Isaiah 14:12-15; Ezekiel 28:11-19), and to that end the Bible tells us in Revelation, Chapters 17 and 18, that he will finally produce a one-world government supported by a one-world religion. The global government is symbolized by its evil leader, the Beast, and the universal religion is symbolized by a woman riding the Beast. In recent times the framework for these monstrosities has been established.

In 1945, at the end of World War II, the United Nations was formed and in the following year its first General Assembly met with 51 member nations.

Another development was The Benelux Agreement in 1948, which eventually led to the 1953 Treaty of Rome and the formation of the European Common Market. This, in turn, became the European Union in 1993.

Between these two major unions of nations and the ongoing development in more recent times of various large trade organizations such as the North American Free Trade Agreement (NAFTA), there are many ways one could imagine that a global government might emerge.

Meanwhile, in the world of various religions, significant steps have been taken toward the goal of unifying all faiths. One of these steps was the establishment of the Parliament of the World's Religions in 1893. This occurred in the World's Fair in Chicago honoring the 400th year since Columbus discovered America. D.L. Moody and most Protestant evangelicals from Europe and America refused to participate, but the Roman Catholic Church and some liberal Protestant groups did send delegates. There were a few representatives from Buddhist, Hindu, Shinto, Jain, Taoist, Muslim, Confucian, and Zoroastrian religions.[88]

This organization has grown slowly during the past century, and their meeting in Melbourne in 2009 drew thousands of representatives from 80 nationalities and more than 220 faiths for a week of dialogue about how to increase understanding and cooperation between various religions. They discussed such topics as climate change and the West's relationship with Islam.[89]

"New Age" religions try to blend all beliefs. This is exemplified by the 2012 movie "Avatar" in which everyone worships the "All Mother" goddess. She is described as "a network of energy" that "flows through all living things."[90]

As mentioned above, the World Council of Churches was founded in 1948, and serves as a common denominator for theologically liberal Christian churches.

The Liberal Church teaches a "Social Gospel." This is the practice of doing good works for the poor and oppressed. For many years they accused evangelicals of ignoring the social responsibilities prescribed by the Bible and of caring only about saving people's souls. Some of them called this emphasis, "Eating pie in the sky, in the sweet by and by."[91]

The Roman Catholic Church called for "restoration of unity among all Christians" since its Second Vatican Council during the years 1962 to 1965.[92]

In light of the choice of Pope Francis in 2012, the Catholic Church appears to be a leader in this push to bring about ecumenical unity.

Of course, the danger with the ecumenical movement is the fact that greater unity requires all parties to give up many of their distinctive beliefs. Evangelicals do not believe they can give up anything that is prescribed by God's Word.

Evangelical Response

Evangelical leaders formed their own organization for cooperation called the National Association of Evangelicals (NAE) in 1942. The group provides a partnership in such areas as government relations and world relief.

Criticism by mainline churches that evangelicals ignored physical and social needs was an unfair complaint in the light of all the good that modern evangelical missionaries had done around the world: establishing hospitals and schools, providing food and clothing for victims of disasters, teaching better ways of farming, digging wells, and improving living conditions in general. Yet it was partly true that some evangelicals in their American and European homelands did less than the liberal churches to promote civil rights, and care for the poor and downtrodden in society.

The Salvation Army, which was mentioned earlier, was a notable exception. It was established in London by William Booth in 1865. It was a ministry to the poor and needy in London. "General" Booth and his soldiers evangelized people who would not go to a church building. They preached the Gospel and at the same time, met the needs of the people. Their ministry set the tone for "home missions" work and inspired the establishment by others of rescue mission in most metropolitan centers.

Evangelicals have also been exemplary in establishing and maintaining "disaster relief ministries." One of the earliest examples of compassion in the name of Christ is the Mennonite Central Committee (MCC), which was founded in 1920 to aid hungry people, including Mennonites in Russia and Ukraine. Many other denominations have mobilized to help people all over the world after earthquakes, storms, and other disasters have occurred.

In 1950 Bob Pierce, a Youth for Christ evangelist ministering in China was so moved by observing hungry people that he established World Vision. This has become a major organization helping needy children everywhere. Later Pierce also established Samaritan's Purse, which is now run by Franklin Graham and is well known for its "Operation Christmas Child" ministry.

Two other examples of organizations that help people in disaster-stricken areas, both begun in 1978, are Mercy Ships, originally part of Youth with a Mission, and Operation Blessing, an outreach of Pat Robertson's 700 Club ministry.

Evangelicals have provided countless thrift stores and food pantry ministries, offering the Good News of salvation along with the good news that somebody cares.

There are also numerous special-needs ministries run by people who combine evangelism with social work. One sterling example is the ministry of Teen Challenge, begun in 1958 by David Wilkerson, an Assemblies of God pastor who worked with gang members in New York City. Another sacrificial ministry is Prison Fellowship, founded by Charles Colson in 1976 after spending time in prison himself for the Watergate scandal of the Nixon era.

Moral Relativism and the Sexual Revolution

In the 1960's the spiritual battle took a turn for the worse. The rebirth of Israel ushered in the generation that Jesus said would not pass away until the end time events are fulfilled (Matthew 24:34). Satan evidently began to panic and deploy his most deadly weapons against Christianity. By the '60's the world was just a prophetic step away from the Tribulation. Concerning that dreadful time Revelation says,

> *"Woe to the inhabitants of the earth and the sea! For the devil has come down to you, having great wrath, because he knows that he has a short time."* – Revelation 12:12

The opening salvo of what would eventually be called "The Sexual Revolution" was a pair of devastating rulings from an "evolving" court system. These rulings, and others that would follow, would eventually cause critics to accuse the courts of "legislating from the bench," a concept that the writers of the Constitution would have considered a violation of the separation of powers between the legislative and judicial branches of government. The first decree was the 1962 case, *Engle v. Vitale*. It **abolished prayer in schools**. In the following year, in the case of *Abington School District v. Schempp*, **Bible reading in schools was prohibited** along with other school sponsored religious activities. In time these other events would include Christmas programs, Easter vacations, and in some cases, even the renting of school facilities by Christian organizations.

The schools, which had already been greatly influenced by progressive education, were then faced with the dilemma of how to teach good behavior when the basis for ethics and morality was no longer part of their curriculum. Slowly at first, young people experienced a decline of respect for authority, and migration toward sexual freedoms. Schools began teaching sex education classes. Tolerance of various relationships was encouraged, including sex outside of marriage and homosexuality. Contraception was explained and methods of sexual activity were demonstrated.

All the while, public schools were teaching the theory of evolution as if it were a fact, leaving students with the impression that the Bible is not true.

During the '60's the growing Marijuana and LSD culture, the anti-war protests by collegians, the hippie movement with its anti-authoritarian impact, rock concerts, sexually suggestive fashions, lack of parental control and increased mobility all conspired to tempt young people. Younger and older folks alike were often lured astray by the new permissive culture. By the end of the decade the era was known as the **Sexual Revolution**.

Liberal theologians got into the act during this time also. In 1963 Anglican Bishop John A.T. Robinson wrote a book called *Honest to God*, criticizing traditional Christianity and advocating "situational ethics," a permissive way of looking at behavior. This led to the 1966 **"Death of God" theology** taught by Robinson and others. German philosopher Friedrich Nietzsche, who died in 1900, had made the claim that God was dead. Time Magazine printed a cover asking in huge letters, "Is God Dead?"

By the 1970's some of the excesses of the '60's had retreated into the background, but the new decade brought its own problems.

The Supreme Court's 1973 *Roe v. Wade* decision **legalized abortion**. This resulted in further destruction of Christian values, and caused an American holocaust far worse than the atrocities of World War II. Since then more than 55 million babies have been killed in their mother's wombs! That represents about 20% of America's population. Many other countries have similar abortion statistics, or even worse.

Immoral movies and television programs became commonplace, and even radio was corrupted by "shock-jocks." Indecent music and programs invaded the teen world in 1977 with the advent of MTV. Many young people stopped attending church programs. Music and sports personalities became their heroes. Unfortunately many celebrities were terrible role models.

During this moral melt-down a new philosophy emerged, even if most people did not know its name. It was the relativistic concept of **"Postmodernism."** As its name implies, this world view rejected the outlook of the modern period. Modernism, which had developed since the Enlightenment, taught that through science, logic and reason it was possible to identify or establish absolute truth. The postmodern mindset was based on the newer philosophy of existentialism and its emphasis on the importance of one's unique personal experience. Postmodernists say there was no universal truth: only relative truth, depending on its cultural context.

Evangelical Response

On a personal note, I had just begun my pastoral ministry in Los Angeles in 1965, and I can assure you that it was a most interesting time to be a pastor. We dealt with rampant immorality, drugs, race riots, communist rallies, anti-war protests, theological upheaval, an upsurge of interest and practice of the occult, including Satanism, rock concerts and a slow loss of interest in Christianity by young people.

Actually, it was a great time to be alive, and most of all to be a Christian, because of the valiant response by Christians to all of these challenges. Now, almost a half-century later, statistics show that the church has nearly collapsed in Europe and is in decline here in the United States. But the efforts by Christians to "keep the faith" have been impressive. We have witnessed the rise, and sometimes the fall, of outstanding churches, Christian youth programs, apologetics teachers, missionary and parachurch organizations, evangelistic mass meetings, and popular radio and television ministries.

At this point I will name some of the notable leaders of the Christian cause during the last half of the 20th century. Please accept my apology in advance for not being able to mention all of the wonderful Christian organizations and powerful teachers, preachers and writers that made inspiring contributions to the cause. The examples I give are just a sampling from the numerous faithful servants of the Lord. They do, however, represent some of the ones that made the greatest impression on me as a fellow minister and an observer of the fray.

Outstanding churches, led by anointed, Bible-believing pastors kept evangelical Christianity viable during the difficult second half of the 20th Century. Here are just a few of them: J. Vernon McGee, Jack Hayford, Lloyd Ogilvie, Jerry Falwell, John Maxwell, John MacArthur, Adrian Rogers, Haddon Robinson, Chuck Swindoll, D. James Kennedy, John Piper, Charles Stanley, David Jeremiah, John Hagee, Tim Keller and Max

Lucado. These all pastored large churches, wrote books, and used radio and/or television to reach a large audience.

One whole new family of churches grew out of the "Jesus People" revival: The Calvary Chapel movement. Chuck Smith, Greg Laurie, Raul Ries and Jack Hibbs are examples of their excellent pastors, but there are many other strong voices in this new fellowship of over 1000 churches worldwide. They also sparked the creation of the new genre of **Contemporary Christian Music** which has helped keep a large portion of the younger generation close to the Lord.

Other influential radio and television teachers who had a significant impact on evangelical Christians included Hal Lindsey, Josh McDowell, Chuck Missler, David Hocking and Jack Van Impe.

Outside the United States, the great missionary movement had produced many unbelievably big churches. Here are examples of some of them: Yoido Full Gospel Church in South Korea (480,000 members), Deeper Christian Life Ministry in Nigeria (75,000 members), Elim Central Church in El Salvador (75,000 members), Igreja de Paz (Church of Peace) in Brazil (50,000), and Hillsong Church in Australia (24,000)

At the beginning of the '60's the **Sunday School movement** was still a major force in evangelical church life. Sunday Schools were begun in England in 1780 by Robert Raikes. He had inherited his father's publishing company, and since he had a deep interest in the plight of boys in the slums, he began a school that met on Sundays because most of the boys worked in factories during the week. The schools taught reading and used the Bible. This movement was well received because there were no public schools at that time. Sunday School started in a home, and in time became a major aspect of church life in America as well as in Europe.

In the 1960's most evangelical churches had excellent Sunday Schools, with attendance figures often being higher than church attendance. They usually offered classes for all ages before the main worship service. There were Sunday School contests to continue bringing in new youngsters, and a variety of excellent teaching materials from publishers like David C. Cook, Gospel Light, Standard Press and Scripture Press. Students and teachers strove to have perfect attendance, and wore pins on their lapels showing how many weeks, months, or years they had attended faithfully.

The curriculum was designed to teach the whole Bible over the course of a few years.

Another growing method of reaching children was the phenomenon of "Good News Clubs" held in the homes of Christian families. Child Evangelism Fellowship had been established in 1937 in the San Francisco area by Jesse Irvin Overholtzer. Its focus was reaching children with the Gospel and teaching them Bible stories. Surprisingly, Overholtzer trained his original "army of evangelists to children circling the globe" in Wheeler Hall on the campus of the University of California at Berkeley.[93] Classes were held first in churches, but were then moved to the neutral environment of homes in various neighborhoods.

Various **Christian youth ministries** were strong and growing in the '60's also. Many of the churches offered a Sunday evening "Christian Endeavor" meeting for teens. They would typically have separate Jr. High and High School sessions during which various youth conducted different aspects of the meeting, leading singing, making announcements, reading Scripture, or even giving a devotional lesson from the Bible. The city-wide organization in each area would plan youth conferences, camps, and monthly "sings" at various churches.

In those days Youth for Christ was also a vigorous program of youth-led campus groups. Depending on the policies of the schools at that time, Christian groups might be allowed as campus clubs or they might be required to rent space after school for their meetings. In many schools this was a powerful weekly outreach. Large city-wide YFC rallies were typically held on Saturday nights.

In 1951 Bill Bright began a college-level youth ministry at the University of California at Los Angeles. It was called Campus Crusade for Christ (now known as CRU). On the college scene, free speech was a popular concept, so ministries like Young Life and Campus Crusade for Christ were usually able to establish a presence on campuses all over the nation, and even around the world. By employing dedicated "missionaries" to the university world, the organization grew exponentially. Bill Bright's evangelism tool, a booklet called, "Have You Heard of the Four Spiritual Laws?" became the method of choice in churches and on campuses for introducing people to Christ. Bright also created a booklet explaining how to be filled with the Holy Spirit. Churches that were in tune with Campus

Crusade enjoyed a season of solid growth both numerically and spiritually. CRU continued to grow for decades, and is now the largest missionary organization in the world.

Gifted **apologetics teachers** were front-line heroes of the faith during this phase of church history. They often came from skeptical or even atheistic backgrounds, and sought for a time to disprove Christianity, but discovered in the process that belief in the Bible and in Jesus Christ was the most reasonable position. They produced a plethora of inspiring books to undergird this generation of believers. Here are a few examples:

C.S. Lewis, a professor at both Oxford and Cambridge Universities in England, was a popular novelist, poet, and Christian apologist. During World War II he broadcast convincing messages about Christianity. In 1952 these ideas were revised and published in the book, *Mere Christianity*. This book explained Christian concepts in ways that the average reader could understand and believe. It was voted best book of the 20th Century by Christianity Today in 2000.

The Genesis Flood, a 1961 book supporting the Bible accounts of creation and the flood of Noah's time gave rise to a "young Earth" theory of creation. One of the book's authors, Dr. John Whitcomb, was a theologian committed to the view that the Bible was God's inerrant Word. The other, Dr. Henry M. Morris, had a doctorate in hydraulic engineering, which qualified him to explain the effects of a world-wide flood.

Francis Schaeffer, who had established the Christian intellectual community in Switzerland called L'Abri ("The Shelter"), published *The God Who is There*. This landmark 1968 book explained how the encroaching philosophy of existentialism had brought about a sense of hopelessness and cultural decadence. The book explained that the God of the Bible is real and is able to overcome the despair that had crept into philosophy, art, music, culture and theology.

In 1970 Hal Lindsey and Carole C. Carlson wrote *The Late Great Planet Earth*, a book about end time prophecy. It suggested that the moral decline of the culture was one of many indications that the final generation of the church was in progress. The rebirth of Israel was a major fulfillment of prophecy. In addition, the apparent increase in natural disasters, wars and rumors of wars, and the emergence of the European Economic Community (Common Market), which could become the leader of a global government, were all steps toward the demise of this Earth and the creation of a new one. It became one of the all-time, best-selling, non-fiction books, selling some 35 million copies.[94] It was also made into a movie that was a big success. The book and the movie encouraged multitudes to believe the Bible and turn to Christ.

Josh McDowell, an evangelist with Campus Crusade for Christ, spoke to collegians all over the world, and released his 1972 apologetics handbook, *Evidence that Demands a Verdict.* It was ranked 13th in Christianity Today's list of most influential evangelical books published after World War II.[95] Since then McDowell has authored or co-authored more than one hundred other books to defend the Bible and the person and work of Jesus Christ to a generation that desperately needed that knowledge.

Parachurch organizations assisted churches by providing specialty ministries that were of interest to most Christians, but were not practical for each local assembly of Christians to do on their own. The youth ministries and disaster agencies listed above were good examples of parachurch organizations. **Inter-denominational mission boards** were also in that category, although most of them had seen their work decline by the 1960's.

Ministries like Christian Films, Moody Institute of Science, and Gospel Recordings used the latest technologies for recording and distributing Christian media. In this way they served the needs of missionaries and of the church at large.

Some parachurch organizations like Focus on the Family and the Institute for Basic Youth Conflicts were formed to help Christians deal with family problems.

Another category of parachurch organizations was formed to counteract the decline of biblical moral standards. The Moral Majority helped elect a conservative President, Ronald Reagan. The Traditional Values Coalition stood against the rapidly increasing acceptance of homosexuality and other non-biblical practices. Operation Rescue picketed at abortion clinics, and many of their members were jailed for their convictions.

Evangelistic mass meetings were a major factor in the battle for souls. They were often called "crusades," until the latter part of the 20th

Century when the word "crusade" stirred up mental images of war between Christians and Muslims during the Middle Ages.

Before the 1960's individual churches often hosted "revival meetings," using the talent of itinerant evangelists. A series of meetings would be held over the course of a few days. The events might be conducted in the church building or in tents erected for the purpose. Interestingly, the era of revivals was partly defined by advances in technology. They became popular when electric lights were new and people didn't have many options for night-time entertainment. They phased out gradually with the advent of television, when the best entertainment was on the little black and white screen in one's own living room.

Billy Graham began his evangelistic ministry in 1947. By 1949, with the help of the Hearst newspapers, his giant tent meeting in Los Angeles was wildly successful. In May of 1957 he conducted an extended crusade in New York's Madison Square Garden that was so popular that the promoters kept extending it until September of that year. More than two million people attended, and fifty-six thousand came forward to give their lives to Christ. This was also the first major crusade broadcast to millions of television viewers across the nation. I was one of those viewers who were totally amazed at what God was doing. Graham continued his evangelistic preaching all over the world for almost six decades.

There were other great evangelistic movements from the1960's onward. Reinhard Bonnke, a German Pentecostal evangelist reached crowds of up to a million people in Africa. Greg Laurie held Harvest Crusade events in Southern California and branched out to many other areas.

Christian radio, television and films made the Gospel available throughout the world during these troubled years. As noted earlier, during the missionary period of the church, these ministries had been employed to reach areas where missionaries could not go. As these technologies improved, so too did their reach and impact. In 1960 Pat Robertson founded the Christian Broadcasting Network (CBN), and in the early 1970's Paul and Jan Crouch began what would become the Trinity Broadcasting Network (TBN). As the secular media became more violent and sexually permissive, these, and other Christian networks provided a wholesome alternative and a powerful vehicle for proclaiming the Gospel.

In retrospect, the evangelical response to the sexual revolution and other moral decay in the culture was valiant, and did much to control the problem, but it was still not enough. The next three decades continued the journey toward a "lukewarm," ineffective Christian era.

The Plot Thickens

An analysis of the current slice of history, beginning about 1980, is difficult because we are still going through it.

Like the Laodicean church, whose members did not realize that they were gradually conforming to their changing moral climate, many who claim to be Christians in our generation practice a worldly mixture of biblical concepts and personal opinions. This results in their acceptance of the lower moral standards of these times.

In 1990 Pollster George Barna published his book, *The Frog in the Kettle*. In it he tried to warn Christian leaders of this dangerous trend toward compromise with the decaying culture. Since then he has written numerous other books and articles, and has been called "the most quoted person in the Christian Church today."[96] In spite of his efforts, and the warnings of the numerous other Christian leaders mentioned so far in this commentary on the Book of Revelation, Barna's own polls show that it is becoming increasingly difficult to distinguish the practices of "born-again" Christians from those of the average person in our culture.[97]

Most developments in recent decades have the potential to be either good or bad, depending on how they are used. There are many examples: the use of nuclear power; the way wealth is spent; and the way technological advances are employed; can all be either blessings or curses.

Our first parents chose to have the "knowledge of good and evil" (Genesis 2:15-17; 3:1-7). They already had knowledge of the good, but they suffered greatly when they disobeyed their Creator and learned what it was to experience evil. This tension between good and evil is also reflected in Jesus' condemnation of the Laodicean Christians (and of our current Church age) of being spiritually lukewarm.

In these days the human race is unstable and the church is in decline. Here is a brief consideration of these two issues.

World-wide Turmoil

Most of the world's population is experiencing **political and economic woes**. Several international organizations are trying to bring people together for the sake of peace and better economy. The United Nations, with its branches, like the World Court (International Court of Justice), professes to promote harmony and prosperity. In reality it is much too divided and weak to be able to accomplish these goals. The globe is seriously divided over political and economic theories and religious differences. Unwise monetary policies and lack of wise leadership is epidemic.

At this time the U.S. President is not trusted enough at home or abroad. Russian President Vladimir Putin was named "the most powerful person in the world" by Forbes Magazine,[98] but he is known to be a cold and cunning leader from the old Soviet era. There is too much corruption in politics everywhere, often caused by the untouchable super-rich who help place people in government and then control their actions.

Most of the world's economy has been in a recession in recent years. Europe is especially impacted, and the United States is trying to recover by borrowing and spending more than some experts think coming generations can ever hope to repay.

Wars have always plagued our fallen human race. There are about 40 wars being fought on our globe.[99] Some of them are civil wars, usually caused by religious differences.

Much of the current conflict originates in the Middle East where a rising tide of Islamic fervor is focused on exterminating Israel. This unrest is exacerbated by the differences between Sunni and Shia Islam. In that arena the greatest threat is the fact that Iran is on the verge of producing nuclear weapons, and is led by a supreme leader whose theology predicts that a great crisis will cause their messiah, the Mahdi, or the Twelfth Imam, to appear and save the world.

Ever since the 9/11 attacks on the Pentagon and New York's Twin Towers, Islamic terrorism has been a dreadful fact of life globally.

In addition, another "cold war" seems to be building between the U.S. and Russia, and China is building its military rapidly, causing the whole world to take notice.

Cyberwar is new kind of combat that will be fought over the Internet, and threaten any country without warning. Cyber-attacks could interrupt the flow of data and destroy or paralyze power grids, oil and water systems, transportation, and other basic infrastructures.

Cyberwar is one byproduct of the quantum leap in technology, known as the "information explosion." This **increase of knowledge** was predicted by the prophet Daniel, even though he did not understand its meaning at the time. Michael the Archangel told him that in the end time, "...many shall run to and fro, and knowledge shall increase" (Daniel 12:4). Since the introduction of the first personal computers in the late 1970's, computing and the Internet have grown exponentially to the point where the average smart phone has more power than the mainframe computers of a few decades ago, and nearly infinite knowledge is available to all via the Internet. There are, of course, countless advantages to having such power and convenience. A whole book could be devoted to the various applications and abilities that this new world of inventions has given us, and more innovations are being added every day.

However, returning to the earlier concept of new things being used in either a good or a bad way, numerous dangers and distractions entered through this fascinating portal of technology. Online pornography is a temptation to many, and when it is viewed on smart phones it is even more difficult for parents to monitor. Unwise use of texting, and "sexting" inappropriate messages and pictures is another pitfall. Listening to explicit music poses an additional danger. The use of violent video games is a factor in real-life tragedies. Bullying online causes some people to commit suicide. Excessive time spent on social media programs and entertainment and/or video sources is a serious waste of time.

Perhaps most significantly, this technology will make the predicted world-wide economic dictatorship, and the "Mark of the Beast" possible (Revelation 13:11-18).

Unfortunately, **immorality** has also found many ways to affect (and infect) this generation. The progressive element in education and government endorses or allows a catalog of behaviors that have always been considered sinful by Bible-believing Christians. Some of these are abortion, euthanasia, graphic sex education, homosexuality, premarital experimentation, smoking, drinking, use of marijuana, and gambling. The entertainment industry pokes fun at the values of evangelicals and conservatives, and calls them "haters" for voicing their concerns. The Bible says,

> *Woe to those who call evil good, and good evil;*
> *Who put darkness for light, and light for darkness;*
> *Who put bitter for sweet, and sweet for bitter!*
> *Woe to those who are wise in their own eyes,*
> *And prudent in their own sight!* – Isaiah 5:20, 21

True Christians who are led by the Holy Spirit should show genuine love and concern for those who have different life-styles. We should realize that all of us are sinners (Romans 3:23), and that the sins other people commit are not worse than our own transgressions (Matthew 5:17-48). But condoning sin is not the loving thing to do. The Lord is not only a loving God, but He is also holy, righteous and just (Exodus 15:11; Psalm 99:9; Psalm 119:137; Psalm 89:14). In His righteousness He warned that the penalty for sin is death (Genesis 2:17; Ezekiel 18:4; Romans 6:23). Sin results in spiritual death, which is separation from God (Ephesians 2:1).

Jesus often went out of His way to reach out to people who were caught in the trap of sin. In the well-known case of the woman brought to Him in adultery, He said, "He who is without sin among you, let him throw a stone at her first." In His great love He was able to offer forgiveness because He was also going to satisfy the demands of justice by dying for her. He did not deny that she had sinned. In fact, He said, "Go and sin no more." (John 8:7-11).

Those of us who have found eternal life in Christ (John 3: 3-8; John 3:16; 2 Corinthians 5:17) know that we must not allow sin to reign in our lives (Romans 6:12-19). Instead we are expected to be repentant and confess our sin (1 John 1:9) so that the Lord can restore us and help us be more like Him. If we have sincere love for friends or relatives who are sinning, we will do our best to help them acknowledge their need and give their lives to the Lord (Galatians 6:1-5).

Non-confrontational Christianity

The issue arises, "What was the Church doing during this period of serious moral decline? Was it able to stop the holocaust of abortion, or the export of pornography, or the plague of human trafficking? Was it even able to keep its own young people engaged and provide good answers to their hard questions?

The Church did help stem the tide of evil, which would have been much worse without the presence of born-again believers. But surveys show a steady decline of godly influence and an increase in the **biblically-illiterate population**. One such survey, conducted by The Bible Society showed that 46% of adults surveyed did not know that the story of Noah's Ark came from the Bible, but about half of them thought that the Hunger Games were biblical. One third said that "Harry Potter" could be a biblical story. About 30% of the children interviewed did not know that the story of the Nativity was from the Bible.[100]

With an ever-increasing population and a declining interest in church, innovative pastors found various ways to boost their attendance, but some of their experiments yielded mixed results. Bill Hybels of Willow Creek Community Church near Chicago, and other pastors as well, began to offer **seeker-sensitive services** in 1975. Church services employed attractive, even entertaining, methods to build attendance by people who presumably did not attend church. The message was a simplified Gospel, carefully given in a way that would not be considered harsh or judgmental. It was purposely non-confrontational and positive. This approach was relatively successful in introducing people to Christ, but not so good in the discipleship area. For greater growth, new converts were encouraged to attend week-night training sessions. After more than three decades, a survey of seeker-sensitive churches revealed that many Christians failed to grow spiritually in that atmosphere. In 2007, in Bill Hybels' own words, too many Christians expected the church to keep feeding them when they should have become self-feeders. He admitted that he had made a mistake and would have to change the way he and his church were doing things.[101]

By the early years of the 21st Century there were scores of **megachurches** in the United States. Many of them had followed the

Willow Creek model, or the pattern set by Rick Warren's Saddleback Community Church in Southern California, and had experienced the same results. On the good side of the issue, these massive churches had indeed influenced great numbers of people to place their faith in Christ. On the negative side, some of these ministries tended to collect people who were not interested in true biblical discipleship. An unhealthy number of them considered this kind of church the best "bargain" from a consumer's point of view--presenting the most interesting program in town at whatever day or hour was most convenient for them and the most fun for their children. In the process the audience heard **politically correct messages**, and were rarely confronted with anything controversial, like abortion or homosexuality, divorce, or anything that would discourage them from attending. Congregations that were not taught "the whole counsel of God" (Acts 20:26-28) were not inclined to oppose the cultural shift that was going on, nor to influence their own family members to follow biblical principles.

Surveys showed that while the megachurches were still growing, the number of Christians was declining. The 2012 Pew Forum on Religion and Public Life survey indicated that the number of American Christians declined 5% during the previous five years, and even Evangelicals dropped 2%. In essence, some of the megachurches were increasing at the expense of the smaller churches. Meanwhile the "Nones," people who do not identify with any religion, grew 5%![102]

I want to stress that I am not against megachurches as such. There are a number of great Bible-teaching megachurches, in the United States and abroad that do take a stand on controversial issues, and do have a high percentage of mature and growing Christians. Even in the case of the more non-controversial churches there are many spiritual victories, and the Lord knows the hearts of the dedicated pastors, and the good that is done by many of them. However, some of the pastors who had the greatest opportunity for speaking out against the onslaught of evil missed their opportunity and failed to be watchmen on the wall:

> But if the watchman sees the sword coming and does not blow the trumpet, and the people are not warned, and the sword comes and takes any person from among them, he is taken away in his iniquity; but his blood I will require at the watchman's hand.'

"So you, son of man: I have made you a watchman for the house of Israel; therefore you shall hear a word from My mouth and warn them for Me. When I say to the wicked, 'O wicked man, you shall surely die!' and you do not speak to warn the wicked from his way, that wicked man shall die in his iniquity; but his blood I will require at your hand. – Ezekiel 33:6-8

Unfortunately there was another impediment to the progress of the Church during these years. There were several high-profile **pastoral scandals**, involving church leaders. The Catholic Church has been criticized for decades because of numerous cases of pedophilia by some of its priests. Among Protestant clergy there have always been occasional moral failures, but some of the highly publicized problems of the past few decades turned many away from the church. Without going into details, some very famous Christian leaders were accused of financial misconduct, including Christian television pioneer Jim Bakker, and Robert Schuller, who had built the famous Crystal Cathedral. Two of the most prominent ministers accused of sexual misconduct were television evangelist Jimmy Swaggert and Ted Haggard, pastor of a megachurch in Colorado and head of the National Association of Evangelicals.

Another negative development during the past few decades was the **alienation and lack of interest by young people** in the Church. Another recent survey by the Barna Group revealed that "nearly six in ten (59%) young people who grew up in Christian churches end up walking away from either their faith or from the institutional church at some point in their first decade of adult life. The unchurched segment among Millennials (born between 1984 and 2002) has increased from 44% to 52% in the last decade.[103]

A controversial solution to the problem of reconnecting young people to the Church is the growth of the so-called "**Emergent Church.**" The jury is still out on how much of this movement is good and how much is bad. It is good in the sense that its leaders try to understand and relate to the thinking of the postmodern generation. But in the process they seemed to de-emphasize the Bible as the literal Word of God, causing some leaders, like Rob Bell, to question such basic biblical concepts as heaven and hell. Leaders in the movement lean toward universal salvation. They also borrow heavily from Catholic liturgy and mysticism.

One last major push during this stage of history is **ecumenism**: the cooperation and even coalition, of religions. As seen in the earlier mention of the World Council of Churches and the Parliament of World Religions, this is not a new idea, but it is gaining ground as never before. The issue of abortion, and more recently of contraception as part of the national health care system, is bringing many Protestant and Catholic activists together to fight for their common causes.

A similar effect was experienced in California when the Mormon-led Proposition 8 ballot initiative was created to define marriage as the union of one man and one woman. For their mutual advantage, Mormons and Evangelicals worked hand-in-hand.

It is increasingly fashionable in some churches to have representatives of various major religions offer prayers and meditations. **"Chrislam"**, a working relationship between Christians and Islam, gives the impression that we all worship the same God. This erroneous concept is supported by some high-profile evangelical leaders.

The New Age movement is quietly gaining ground as a sort of common denominator among various beliefs.

Perhaps most significant in this matter of ecumenical union is the possibility that Pope Francis, who is incredibly popular on the world scene, will be an advocate of the movement.

Evangelical Response

Many of the powerful ministries that sprang up during the Missionary Age continue their work, but with a gradually declining effect. We have already considered the fact that there was **successful missionary work** in every period of Church history. This was characterized as an "open door:" a situation made possible by the Lord Jesus Christ in each age. In this last, Laodicean stage of history the missionary enterprise can be considered an "Open Door of Escape." In this third millennium after Christ, missiologists explain that this ought to be the time for a great spread of the Gospel to Asia. The strongholds of Communism, Buddhism, Hinduism, and Islam are in view, and amazing developments are being reported, such as the growth of the Chinese underground church to an incredible estimated number of 100 million believers. That same Chinese Church has the vision of a "Back to Jerusalem" campaign to take the

Gospel to the rest of the Asian world.[104] There are also many reported occurrences of Jesus appearing to Muslims in countries where missionaries are not allowed.[105]

A newer development in missions work is the phenomenon of organized campaigns to plant additional churches in large areas already evangelized, and often with cooperation between various denominations. One example of this effort is Multiplication Network Ministries. This organization is currently working in more than 30 countries in Latin America, Africa, Europe and Asia, with the goal of helping existing denominations plant outposts of the Kingdom in every community.

In this generation there are still many **outstanding churches**-- places where believers are "spiritually hot," not just lukewarm like the Laodiceans. But with the passage of time a growing percentage of church leaders have failed to teach the whole Bible and to affirm that it is literally God's infallible Word. Christians looking for this kind of church often report difficulty finding one.

When moving into a new area, concerned Christians could not depend on past denominational experience. They needed to visit various churches and observe how much emphasis these ministries placed on missions, evangelism and discipleship. They also evaluated what kind of ministry the prospective congregation offered for children and youth.

While the Sunday School movement declined steadily, the need for adult Christian instruction and discipleship was replaced in part by **small groups**, like "Experiencing God, "The Truth Project," and women's bible studies from teachers like Kay Arthur and Beth Moore. Most of these groups met weekly or bi-weekly in the evenings. They provided some level of Bible instruction, fellowship, and usually included a time of prayer together.

For children, **"Good News Clubs"** made a dramatic come-back, not so much in people's homes, but rather on school property during non-instructional time. This was the result of an encouraging Supreme Court decision in 2001 that "the school could not deny equal access to the Club for any time that is generally available for public use."[106] Matt Staver, President of Liberty Counsel, used this ruling to encourage many Christian organizations to stand up for their First Amendment rights.[107]

Some of the larger evangelical churches provided or recommended **Christian schools**. Most of these schools follow basic Christian doctrine and fundamental methods of education. Parents who chose a Christian school were normally very concerned about the curriculum that was used. Two examples of basic curriculum employed by these schools are A Beka Book and Accelerated Christian Education.

These private schools are careful to include all of the state-required subjects, but in controversial issues, like the origin of the human race, they give preference to the biblical view while explaining the pros and cons of the secular perspective that is taught in the public arena. Christian schools also emphasize good study habits, Christian ethics, character development, knowledge of the Bible, and appreciation of the biblical world-view. Most Christian schools belong to the Association of Christian Schools International (ACSI). Many are also accredited by the secular Western Association of Schools and Colleges (WACS).

Homeschooling is another popular solution to the dilemma of providing a good education in a Christian environment. A variety of effective methods and materials are made available to dedicated parents who can spend the time supervising their children's education. The entire industry of homeschooling has become very efficient in mixing study time at home with some time in public schools and enough social interaction with other homeschoolers to balance their educational experience.

Students from Christian schools and homeschooled children usually have higher scores on standardized education tests than their public school counterparts.

A variety of **new parachurch organizations** have sprung up during these years of spiritual and moral turmoil. Some of them are family-oriented like "Focus on the Family." They began a daily radio broadcast in 1980 featuring their founder, Dr. James Dobson. It was a daily dose of encouragement about marriage, raising children, and the right to life.

Men got a huge boost in the 1990's because of the Promise Keepers movement. For many years this organization offered stadium events gathering tens of thousands of men to hear powerful messages on how to be a godly husband, father and leader. The apex of this effort was a rally in 1997 when more than a million men assembled on the Mall in Washington D.C. The event, called "Standing in the Gap," was the largest gathering of men in American history. It was the closest thing to a national revival that I ever witnessed—an ocean of men singing and praying, with our faces to the ground!

Women also had large stadium events to build their faith. Starting in 1996 an event called "Women of Faith" was held yearly in various major venues.

Pro-life organizations have done their best to hold back the tide of abortions during this era. Two of these are The Family Research Council and The American Family Association. An interesting technological development that has helped their cause is the improved ultrasound imagery of the baby in the womb. Expectant mothers often decide against abortion after seeing their child moving or sucking its thumb.

For people with homosexual tendencies there is Exodus International and some Christian-based counseling ministries to help people understand the issues and to make wise decisions.

Celebrate Recovery has spread rapidly with its assistance to people with all kinds of dependencies. Group meetings are offered in the facilities of a great number of churches.

Some very effective legal organizations give assistance to Christian churches and individuals when their civil rights are violated by secular activists. Three heroic examples are Liberty Counsel, founded in 1989 by Matt Staver, the American Center for Law and Justice, established in 1990 by Pat Robertson, and led by Jay Sekulow, and Alliance Defending Freedom, founded in 1994 by Alan Sears.

The **apologetics field** has gained outstanding new organizations and spokesmen to face the challenges of "defending the faith." The Ravi Zacharias International Ministries was begun in 1984 to promote the ministry of this brilliant speaker and writer who is effective in defending traditional evangelicalism.

A new field of scientific study known as "Intelligent Design" was introduced in 1991 by Phillip E. Johnson, a retired UC Berkeley law professor and author. He wrote the book, *Darwin on Trial,* in which he presented convincing evidence that Darwinian evolution had failed to prove itself, and that modern scientific methods call for belief in a Creator. He was a co-founder of the Discovery Institute's Center for Science and

Culture, which has become the well-spring of many great authors and speakers on the subject.

In the 1990's Biola University and Talbot School of Theology (my alma mater) established an Apologetics Department, led by Craig Hazen, and featuring many notable apologists, including J.P. Moreland from Biola and William Lane Craig from Talbot. They sponsor special "Defending Your Faith" events with popular speakers like Lee Strobel (*The Case for Christ*, 1998), Greg Koukl (Stand to Reason), and representatives of the Intelligent Design movement. The department publishes *Philosophia Christi*, the premier journal of Christian philosophy. The Biola/Talbot nexus was rated the top apologetics school, but there are several others with growing influence.[108]

The so-called "Young Earth Creation" theory has maintained its momentum also with the addition of ministries like Ken Ham's "Answers in Genesis" in 1994, and the opening of their Creation Museum in Petersburg, Kentucky in 2007. A debate in 2014 between Ham and "Bill Nye, the Science Guy," drew millions of viewers on the Internet, and stimulated discussion of the biblical point of view.

It is not possible to properly acknowledge all the great contributions made in this apologetics field, but a few others should be mentioned in passing: Ray Comfort, and his "Way of the Master" radio and television ministry, Dinesh D'Souza, author of *What's So Great about Christianity?*, and Jay Smith, who has the unique and difficult role of exposing the errors of Islam and the advantages of Christianity. He does this at Speakers' Corner, a free-speech area in London's Hyde Park, even though he has been physically attacked for his beliefs.

While young people were suffering the negative influence of some of the vulgar music and immoral lifestyles portrayed on MTV, **Contemporary Christian** artists became more skillful in their craft of devotional and inspirational music. In some ways they have become the new evangelists to their generation. One example among scores that could be cited is "Glorious Day" by Casting Crowns. It is an old hymn with great theology. The way they sing it appeals to the younger crowd:

One day when Heaven was filled with His praises
One day when sin was as black as could be

Jesus came forth to be born of a virgin
Dwelt among men, my example is He
Word became flesh and the light shined among us
His glory revealed
[Chorus]

Living, He loved me
Dying, He saved me
Buried, He carried my sins far away
Rising, He justified freely forever
One day He's coming
Oh glorious day, oh glorious day

One day they led Him up Calvary's mountain
One day they nailed Him to die on a tree
Suffering anguish, despised and rejected
Bearing our sins, my Redeemer is He
Hands that healed nations, stretched out on a tree
And took the nails for me
[Chorus]

One day the grave could conceal Him no longer
One day the stone rolled away from the door
Then He arose, over death He had conquered
Now He's ascended, my Lord evermore
Death could not hold Him, the grave could not keep Him
From rising again
[Chorus]

One day the trumpet will sound for His coming
One day the skies with His glories will shine
Wonderful day, my Beloved One, bringing
My Savior, Jesus, is mine
[Chorus]

Glorious day, Oh, Glorious day

Ever since the invention of the printing press, **Christian books** have been instrumental in maintaining the faith and spreading the Gospel. The most outstanding Christian series toward the end of the 20th Century was the 16-volume *Left Behind* novels by Tim LaHaye and Jerry Jenkins. These depictions of the end time became the all-time best-selling Christian novels.

The Internet has become a popular alternative to reading books during the last decade of the 2000's. Conventional wisdom says that the Internet, smart phones and electronic readers will never completely replace printed books. Nevertheless, most book publishers, and whole chains of Christian and secular bookstores have disappeared. The good news is that every imaginable version of the Bible, and all the Bible study tools, commentaries, and even audio and video teaching on Bible subjects, are now freely available to all via our phones and computer connections. One only needs to "Google" *online Bibles* to get a list of these powerful sites, including the Blue Letter Bible, Bible Gateway, and many others. One may search for "Bible Prophecy" to get our site, *Prophecy Central,* and hundreds of other Christian depositories of information. Or enter just part of a verse you wish to find, and the Internet will show you the chapter and verse!

Every church, mission, ministry, and any individual Christian who has something to share is now able to have a website, a blog, and pages on social media. This is a previously unimaginable privilege and opportunity. And if the Lord doesn't return soon, the Internet will just become an even more amazing resource!

Everything considered, the zeal and involvement of born-again Christians during this difficult period of time has been commendable, even if it does fall short in some ways. Like the Laodiceans, we, as a whole, cannot be considered "hot" or highly successful in our response to the negative influences of our age. Thankfully, however, we are not completely "cold" either. We care, and we are still involved, but something is lacking. In Jesus' opinion, we are "lukewarm."

Individual Christians can be "on fire for the Lord," and many are. Individual local assemblies of believers might be making a huge impact on their part of the world with the Gospel. Even large areas of the globe can be aflame with love for the Lord and effective in reaching this generation. This has been true in every age.

But Christianity as a whole cannot be described in this glowing way at this time. There are too many who do not know the Lord personally. This is why, as we will see, Jesus invites the Laodiceans to open the door of their lives to Him (Revelation 3:20). Too many are trying to improve the world and build the Kingdom by their own good works without the power of the Holy Spirit in their lives. (See the discussion of "Kingdom Work" in Chapter 1, verse 9; and Chapter 2, verse 16. See also the "Filling of the Holy Spirit" in Chapter 1, verses 5 and 10, and Chapter 3, verse 1.)

As we will see when we get to the final verses in this letter to the Church at Laodicea (Revelation 3:18-22), the church does not need to remain in its tepid condition. It is possible for lukewarm Christians to respond to the Lord's chastening and repent! And those who do not know Christ personally are invited to accept Him as Savior. A promise of future blessing is given to the "overcomers." These things should inspire hope and encourage Christians to be optimistic about the future. In the meantime, Jesus expects us to "occupy" (do business) until He comes (Luke 19:11-13).

I read something recently that suggested that those who are expecting a literal return of Christ to set up His kingdom are experiencing an "abortion of hope" because they ignore the responsibility to make things better. Supposedly we are obsessed with "doom and gloom," and just want to survive until Jesus returns. The exact opposite should be true, for Paul called the promise of Christ's return "the blessed hope" of the believer (Titus 2:13).

There is no need for pessimism here. If believers will respond properly, they can be revived. We are praying for one more revival to reach this generation of young people with the Gospel. Too many of them do not know what the Bible teaches. They don't know what they need to do in order to have a right relationship with Christ. There is every reason to expect that the Lord will send another great awakening in the end time just as He did before the flood in Noah's days and before judgment on Nineveh in Jonah's days. (See notes on revival in Chapter 3, verse 2.)

Returning to the last few verses of Jesus' message to the Laodiceans, we are reminded that all is not lost for this halfhearted church.

There is a path out of their complacency. And perhaps, most encouraging to us, these improvements may be applied to our own generation. They may, in fact, be put to use in our own churches, and in our own lives!

Counsel

I counsel you to buy from Me gold refined in the fire, that you may be rich; and white garments, that you may be clothed, that the shame of your nakedness may not be revealed; and anoint your eyes with eye salve, that you may see. As many as I love, I rebuke and chasten. Therefore be zealous and repent. Behold, I stand at the door and knock. If anyone hears My voice and opens the door, I will come in to him and dine with him, and he with Me. To him who overcomes I will grant to sit with Me on My throne, as I also overcame and sat down with My Father on His throne.

"He who has an ear, let him hear what the Spirit says to the churches.""" – *Revelation 3:18-22*

Jesus told them, *"I counsel you."* Even though advice is given to each of the seven churches , and we have called those segments "counsel," this is the only place where the actual Greek word *symbouleuo* or "counsel" is used in the book. Its literal meaning in Greek is "to make a resolute plan together." This is the sort of thing one does when seeking the advice of a business consultant or a financial planner. It is a picture of the Lord Jesus—the Son of God, taking the time to sit down with a struggling family member to map out a plan of success.

Here is Jesus' advice to them. First since they were spiritually poor, they should *"buy from Me."*

This is encouraging because it shows that their condition is not incurable. They may be lukewarm now, but there are steps they can take to be restored to the normal "hot" condition of spiritual fervor.

Furthermore, the things they need are readily available, but only from Jesus (eternal life--John 10:10, purpose--Matthew 4:19, truth--John 14:6; and everything else they might need--Philippians 4:19), and through the Holy Spirit (indwelling and assistance--John 14:25-26; 15:26; 16:5-15;

power--Acts 1:8; spiritual gifts--1 Corinthians Chapters 12-14; filling/control--Ephesians 5:18-21; freedom and victory--Galatians 5:16-18; spiritual fruit--Galatians 5:22-26).

Three commodities are recommended by Jesus to the Laodiceans. As mentioned at the beginning of the notes about this letter, the city was famous for its banking, its garment industry, and its production of a healing balm for the eyes. As He did so often when He taught his disciples in Galilee and Jerusalem, Jesus used objects and situations that were well-known to illustrate spiritual truth.

The first thing they (and we) should obtain from Jesus is *"gold refined in the fire, that you may be rich."* Gold is the nearly universal standard of wealth. In our own American history, our currency, the dollar, was based on gold. Its value was equal to a fixed quantity of gold. This gold was kept in fortified vaults like the one at Fort Knox, Tennessee. For that reason the dollar was considered the most stable currency worldwide. Now, of course, since the establishment of the Federal Reserve System, there is no direct relationship between gold reserves and the dollar, so it is subject to fluctuation and inflation.

Gold is symbolic of deity in the Bible. In the Tabernacle (Exodus 38:24), and the later Temple (2 Chronicles Chapters 3 and 4), God prescribed the use of large amounts of gold because, being the most valuable material available, it symbolized His own presence there. Similarly, when the Magi brought gifts to Jesus, the Gold was an indication that they understood His deity (Mathew 2:11).

The apostle Peter used the imagery of gold refined in the fire as an illustration of mature faith (1 Peter 1:6-7).

Jesus also offered to provide *"white garments, that you may be clothed, that the shame of your nakedness may not be revealed."* Our sin leaves us spiritually naked and soiled. When Adam and eve first sinned, their new knowledge of evil destroyed their innocence and caused them to realize that they would need some sort of covering because their thoughts were no longer pure. They fabricated coverings from leaves, but God made them a more durable garment of animal skins (Genesis 3). This appears to be the first time an animal had to be slain. It was a foreshadowing of the sacrificial system that would be instituted until Jesus would come as the

301

"Lamb of God who takes away the sin of the world" (John 1:29). Only His sacrifice will suffice to pay for sin:

> *"Come now, and let us reason together," Says the* LORD,
> *"Though your sins are like scarlet, They shall be as white as snow;*
> *Though they are red like crimson, They shall be as wool".* – Isaiah 1:18

Near the beginning of this Book of Revelation we saw that one of the descriptions of Jesus was "Him who loved and washed us from our sins in His own blood." (See chapter 1, verse 5.)

White garments were given to those who believe in Jesus in Chapter 3, verse 5, and we will learn more about this in our future study of Chapter 4, verse 4; Chapter 7, verses 9 through 14; and Chapter 19, verse 14. White garments symbolize the gift of cleansing from sin through the sacrifice of Jesus Christ.

Next Jesus prescribes this: ***"and anoint your eyes with eye salve, that you may see."*** People do not always realize when their vision is impaired. Dim and distorted perception may seem normal to those who have always had limited vision, or who have gradually lost their sight.

I once suffered a painful but temporary eye injury. While working my way through college, I had a job in a machine shop. One day, while using a wire buffer on a piece of metal, and since I did not wear protective glasses, a tiny piece of metal from the wire wheel flew into my left eye. It was immediately painful, but it was so small that we could not actually see it. I did finally have to go to an eye doctor who found it and removed it surgically. For days I had a bandage on my eye, and every time I moved my eyes it felt like the accident was happening again. Thankfully, I healed quickly, and the whole episode became past history.

Today, I have a different problem, brought on very slowly by the process of aging. There was no sudden pain or even noticeable change from year to year, but I can no longer read the fine print, and it seems every electronic gadget has words and labels that I can't distinguish from Egyptian hieroglyphics. When I compare this progressive loss of sight with the painful but temporary problem of the past, I think that this gradual loss might even be worse than the earlier eye injury unless I do something about it.

Jesus healed several blind folks, and He did it a different way every time (Matthew 20:29-34; Mark 8:22-26; Luke 18:35-43). He claimed Isaiah's description of Messiah (Isaiah 61:1-2) for Himself, and added that He would give sight to the blind (Luke 4:18). He not only restored physical vision, but He gave spiritual sight to those who believed in Him (Mark 4:11-13; John 9:38-40). Spiritual sight transforms everything in our lives. It reminds us constantly that an all-powerful and loving God is at work in the world around us. We perceive the glories of Creation, the beauty of our relationship with the Lord, and the wonders of His provision.

The Savior had criticized the Laodiceans severely, but it was not done to harm them. He said, ***"As many as I love, I rebuke and chasten."*** Who can deny the love of the One who died to pay for their sins? He had told His disciples:

> *"I am the good shepherd. The good shepherd gives His life for the sheep. . . As the Father knows Me, even so I know the Father; and I lay down My life for the sheep. . . Therefore My Father loves Me, because I lay down My life that I may take it again. No one takes it from Me, but I lay it down of Myself. I have power to lay it down, and I have power to take it again. This command I have received from My Father."* – John 10:11-18

> *Greater love has no one than this, than to lay down one's life for his friends.* – John 15:13

Parents instinctively know that if they love their children they must discipline them. Proper correction will literally save their children's lives:

> *"My son, do not despise the chastening of the LORD,*
> *Nor be discouraged when you are rebuked by Him;*
> *For whom the LORD loves He chastens,*
> *And scourges every son whom He receives."* – Hebrews 12:5b-6

Jesus, who had already told the Laodiceans what they had done wrong in the past, now instructed them what they could do to change their future: ***"Therefore be zealous."*** This is the only occurrence in Revelation of the Greek word *zeloo*, meaning "to be envious" or "to be eager." Our English words "jealous" and "zealous" both come from this word and are nearly identical. They have very different meanings depending on the context. The noun form of this verb is *zelos*, which means "eagerness, zeal, or rivalry." It is an *omamatopoeic* term that was created to mimic the sound of boiling water. Furthermore, is comes the root word *ze* that means "hot enough to boil." This is a most-interesting expression to find in this letter to the lukewarm Laodiceans. The Lord had wished that they were hot—or even cold, so that they would realize they were not hot. Now he tells them they can have this burning emotion of enthusiasm for spiritual things.

However, if they would like to be zealous, they would need to *"repent."* Repentance is a change of thinking about one's behavior. (See the notes on this in Chapter 2, verse 5.) It is a prerequisite to revival. Every real revival has begun with some form of heart-felt sorrow for spiritual failure. Only then, when the evil thoughts and habits are recognized as the poison that they are, and are honestly expelled, will the life-giving Spirit of God take fresh control of the sinner's thoughts.

Will some people ever be able to say that they deserve salvation because they sought so diligently for the truth and finally found the right way to God? The apostle Paul said the answer is "No!"

> *As it is written:*
> *"There is none righteous, no, not one;*
> *There is none who understands;*
> *There is none who seeks after God.*
> *They have all turned aside;*
> *They have together become unprofitable;*
> *There is none who does good, no, not one."* – Romans 3:10-12 (Psalm 14:1-3)

In every case, it is God who takes the initiative—designing and offering a plan of salvation, though it cost Him the sacrifice of His Only-begotten Son (John 3:16). And once Jesus was here on Earth, the Gospels tell us that He went looking for followers, and called them one by one! Now that He has ascended back to Heaven, He still extends the invitation: *"Behold, I stand at the door and knock."*

During all the years of my ministry, this has been my favorite verse for encouraging seekers to accept Christ. On several occasions I have been questioned by well-meaning Christians about the use of this passage because it was addressed to members of a church. I would just remind them, "Yes, but it was a church full of unsaved people!" Some of the Laodiceans were undoubtedly true believers, but many obviously were not. The majority might have assumed that they would be all right because they were as good as most of their friends.

I had been just like that at one time. I attended church as a pre-teen and teenager, and actually liked it, but if anyone had ever said to me, 'Are you sure you are going to Heaven when you die?" I would have just said, "I hope so. I hope I have been good enough." Actually, no one ever asked me, but one day someone did share with me the plan of salvation, and soon after that I accepted Christ as my Lord and Savior.

What happens when one hears Jesus knocking and asks Him into his or her life? Jesus explained: *"If anyone hears My voice and opens the door, I will come in to him and dine with him, and he with Me."* There is no requirement to be "good enough." Jesus called people just where they were. Some were fishing on the Sea of Galilee, some were tax collectors or obvious sinners. Some were diseased or demon possessed. But all of them symbolically opened the door of their lives to Him.

Not only would Jesus sit and eat with those who invited Him in, but He would take up residence with them. Because He is God the Son, and therefore omnipresent, He can say to each of us,

"I am with you always, even to the end of the age." – Matthew 28:20, and,

"I will never leave you nor forsake you." – Hebrews 13:5

However, there is one serious misunderstanding about this matter of receiving Christ, or of "opening the door" to Him.

There are dual dangers here:, and both of them are most serious:

1- False assurance of salvation: It is regrettable that some who call themselves Christians have just gone through the motions of repeating a prayer of confession and faith in Christ, then they have gone on to live a basically unchanged life. In the Church of Laodicea, and in our own worldly age, this is too often the case. Some call it "cheap grace," or "easy-believism." Jesus said, "By their fruits you will know them." (Matthew 7:15-

20). Most tragically, some of these people will think they were true believers, but will be rejected by the Lord, who will have to say to them, "I never knew you" (Matthew 7:21-23).

2 - No assurance of salvation: On the other hand, there are sincere Christians who are not able to look back to a time in their life when they knew for sure that they did accept God's gift of eternal life by believing in Jesus and in His sacrifice for them (John 3:16; Romans 5:6-11; 1 John 5:9-13), decided to become His disciples (Matthew 4:18-22; John 1:12; Matthew 28:19-20), repented of their sin (Acts 17:30; 2 Corinthians 7:10; 2 Peter 3:9), openly declared their faith in Him (Acts 2:38; Romans 10:9-10), and as a result, became a "new creations in Christ" (John 3:3; 2 Corinthians 5:17).

Opening the door of our lives to Christ is just one way among many of picturing the act of faith that occurs when one truly decides to follow Christ. The result is a union with Jesus (John 15:4-5; 17:11, 21-23; Romans 6:5-7;) that one only begins to realize when he or she first believes, but progressively is perceived as *Christ in us* (Romans 8:10; 2 Corinthians 13:5; Galatians 2:20; Colossians 1:20; Revelation 3:20), and even more amazingly, as being *in Christ* (Romans 6:3, 11, 23; 8:1-2; 1 Corinthians 1:30; 2 Corinthians 5:17; Galatians 3:27-28; Colossians 1:2; 1 Peter 5:14; Ephesians 1:1, 3, 10; 2:6-13, etc.)!

Wonder of wonders, Jesus not only dwells with us, but He will allow us to live and reign with Him! ***"To him who overcomes I will grant to sit with Me on My throne, as I also overcame and sat down with My Father on His throne:"***

> *This is a faithful saying:*
> *For if we died with Him,*
> *We shall also live with Him.*
> *If we endure,*
> *We shall also reign with Him. –* 2 Timothy 2:11-12

> *Blessed and holy is he who has part in the first resurrection. Over such the second death has no power, but they shall be priests of God and of Christ, and shall reign with Him a thousand years. –* Revelation 20:6

In spite of its problems, the Laodicean Church did have many "overcomers." There is always a remnant in every age. (See the notes about this expression in the introduction to Chapter 2 and Chapter 3, verse 26. All true Christians are overcomers and will remain true to Christ to the end!

"He who has an ear, let him hear what the Spirit says to the churches." (See the notes about this expression in Chapter 2, verse 7.)

Final Thoughts about an End Time Revival

If you have read this far, you probably have the same earnest longing that I do for a great revival in our days. Is such a desire realistic? Yes, because God is not willing that any should perish (2 Peter 3:9). In the book of Jonah we learn that even in such an evil place as Nineveh, the capital of Israel's enemy, the Assyrians, God wanted those who had never heard the truth to have the opportunity to believe and be saved. The prophet Jonah did not want the Assyrians to have that privilege, so he fled from God. After he had been caught, and then released from the great fish, the Lord sent him to Nineveh, and he did warn the people there to repent and turn to God. To his amazement, a great revival broke out, and huge numbers believed in the Lord. Nineveh was still eventually destroyed for its evil history, but at least those who would believe in God were given the opportunity to believe.

Earlier, in Noah's time, God not only told him to build an ark, but also to preach righteousness to the people. In their case, the Bible says, their thoughts were "only evil continually" (Genesis 6:5). None of them repented and believed except for Noah's own family.

Our generation is complex. There are places like parts of Central and South America, Korea, and parts of Africa where there are revivals going on now with amazing numbers of believers winning others to Christ. In China the underground church has grown exponentially and is spiritually strong in spite of persecution. Europe and North America, the bastions of the truth during the Missionary Age, have slowly grown apathetic. It is worse in Europe, where many of the churches have become taverns or mosques, but it seems that the United States is following in their footsteps.

How does God see our present world? We can be sure He still loves all of His creatures. Through His Son He has already provided salvation for all who will receive it.

Like the Laodicean Church, there is still an opportunity for lukewarm Christians to be revived. But will we? Our young people desperately need to know the truth about Jesus, and a great many of them do not understand the Gospel.

We cannot schedule a revival, nor do anything great to make it happen. But we can repent of our worldliness and pray:

If My people who are called by My name will humble themselves, and pray and seek My face, and turn from their wicked ways, then I will hear from heaven, and will forgive their sin and heal their land. --2 Chronicles 7:14

Critics might point out the fact that this verse was given in Solomon's days to the Chosen People. But can anyone doubt that God would treat His adopted children in the Church (John 1:12; Romans 8:15; Galatians 4:5; Ephesians 1:5) the same way? Writing to the Corinthians, Paul made it clear that the things that happened to Israel are examples to us (1 Corinthians 10:6-11).

To put it another way, if we care about the souls of people—including our own relatives and friends, how can we not earnestly desire for them to come to know the Lord? How could we not pray for the right circumstances in their lives to point them to Christ? Why would we not pray for another mighty revival for their sake?

In conclusion, here are some of the promising developments of this present time that could lead to a world-wide revival, or to many smaller renewals. In future years, if we are still here, we will look back and notice whether or not they produced the desired result. If not, we will compose a new list and publish an updated commentary.

Missionary activity – (See the extensive notes about the Missionary accomplishments of the Church in Chapter 3, verse 8). Even though missionary work has declined, there are tens of thousands of highly-trained, incredibly-devoted missionaries still taking the Gospel to the masses using all the methods that have been produced in the past, and employing advanced technology to finish the task of providing Scriptures to people everywhere. Most of the best results in our generation are the work of indigenous leaders in nearly every country of the world. Who knows when something very powerful might begin in some inconspicuous place that would lead to a wild-fire of revival and evangelism!

Heroes of the Faith – People love heroes, especially in sports and entertainment. There are many dedicated, courageous Christians in government, the media, education, science, and other fields. Some of them might have the platform to influence great numbers of young people for Christ. Time will tell.

Prayer movements – There are many prayer movements today. Some of them are led by young people. This is especially significant since bright young people and young adults have been leaders in past revivals, and it is primarily for their sake that we desire to experience such a renewal. Historically, major revivals have often come from college youth movements.

Christian music – Just as most the great hymns of yesteryear were the product of revival movements, so inspiring new music, performed by exceptional young artists, are making an incredible impact on people today.

Christian movies and videos – The Jesus Film Project (mentioned in Chapter 3, verse 8), which has been seen by more than 6 billion viewers, is still being shown to approximately 3.8 million people per year in more than a thousand languages.

Actually some of the highest-grossing movies on the big screen have been Bible epics or faith-based stories. In 2004 Mel Gibson shocked the movie industry by making the blockbuster "The Passion of the Christ." It became the highest grossing R-rated film in the United States. (It was rated R because of the violence our Lord suffered.) The most popular 2013 TV series was "The Bible," with more than a million viewers. Mark Burnett and Roma Downey, the producers of that series have now released the biblically-accurate and moving "Son of God." And they are planning on a follow-up series in 2015 on NBC called "A.D.: After the Bible." An independent film, "God's Not Dead," had surprising success at the box office and delivered a powerful Gospel message for young people and young adults. Several other Bible or faith-based movies are in process, and the trend is seen as a surprise movement from Hollywood.

Television and Radio keep improving with new applications and technological advancements. TBN, CBN, Sky Angel, Daystar and other TV satellite networks reach most of the planet with Christian programming.

Trans World Radio (TWR) is the largest media ministry, and it is still expanding. They project that by 2015 they will be able to deliver Christian content to nearly 60 percent of the people in the world in their own language.

Salem Broadcasting is another extensive provider of Christian content, but there are hundreds of smaller networks and Christian stations that also feed the mind and spirit of Christians. Some of these programs are Christian talk radio. These informative broadcasts help inform Christians of important events that could lead to revival, and mobilize the Christian community for action when necessary.

As mentioned above, **The Internet** has become the preferred source of information for many people. Web based videos now rival television's viewing audience. An almost unfathomable number of videos are available via YouTube and other providers using smart phone service and the Internet. Some of these "go viral" and can suddenly and unexpectedly be seen by millions of viewers. Many of these spontaneous successes have been Christian stories or messages.

Books– Solomon said "Of making many books there is no end" (Ecclesiastes 12:12). Printed books are less popular at the moment, but Amazon.com had started a new free book publishing service to stimulate the production of new literature. This upsurge will not just appear on paper, but will be electronically transmitted instantly and inexpensively to computers and smart phones all over the world.

A new thing--something we have not yet considered--might be the most likely form that the Lord, the ultimate creative genius of the universe, will use to launch an end time revival. The Bible story is a continuous progression of new things from God's own hand. The Creation, the Flood, the call of Abraham, the birth of Isaac when Abraham was 100, Joseph's rise to power in Egypt, the burning bush, the Exodus, manna in the wilderness, supernatural conquests, the prophets dreams and visions, the star that led the Magi, the human birth of the Son of God, Jesus miracles, the apostle's miraculous ability to speak in other languages on the Day of

Pentecost, and so many other innovations demonstrate the endless variety of God's dealing with mankind.

The whole chapter of Isaiah 43 reminds believers of God's creativity. Here are just two verses from that chapter:

> *"Do not remember the former things,*
> *Nor consider the things of old.*
> *Behold, I will do a new thing,*
> *Now it shall spring forth;*
> *Shall you not know it?*
> *I will even make a road in the wilderness*
> *And rivers in the desert.* — Isaiah 43:18-19

What will the Lord do in our times to bring about a revival? Will we be part of it? Please join me in asking the Lord to allow us to be involved in whatever He is going to do!

Appendix A
Jesus' Own Outline of the Future
The Olivet Discourse

Jesus had much to say about things that are yet to come. But before He gave His own outline for the future, He made a striking prediction of something that would happen within just a few decades.

> *Then Jesus went out and departed from the temple, and His disciples came up to show Him the buildings of the temple. And Jesus said to them, "Do you not see all these things? Assuredly, I say to you, not one stone shall be left here upon another, that shall not be thrown down." –* Matthew 24:1-2

Looking across the Kidron Valley, from where He was on the Mount of Olives, Jesus called attention to the magnificent Temple built by Herod the Great. It was considered one of the most magnificent buildings in the world at that time. He said that in spite of its amazing size and grandeur, it would be utterly destroyed. This prophecy was fulfilled less than 40 years later in 70 AD, when the Roman army captured Jerusalem and completely dismantled the Temple. In this way Jesus validated His vision of future things.

When the disciples wanted to know more, Jesus gave them a simple outline of things to come. It doesn't include everything that will happen, but it gave them (and us) a timeline we can use to sort out various future events that we study.

Four Periods of Time

1-Beginning of Birth Pains

> *And Jesus answered and said to them: "Take heed that no one deceives you. For many will come in My name, saying, 'I am the Christ,' and will deceive many. And you will hear of wars and rumors of wars. See that you are not troubled; for all these things must come to pass, but the end is not yet. For nation will rise against nation, and kingdom against kingdom. And there will be famines, pestilences, and earthquakes in various places. All these are the*

312

beginning of sorrows. – Matthew 24:4-8

Jesus warned about false messiahs, and predicted an increase in wars and rumors of wars, as well as famines and earthquakes before the beginning of the Tribulation. The list of signs given in the parallel passage in Luke's Gospel includes plagues, fearful events, and signs in the heavens (Luke 21:9-11).

Natural disasters, famines, and plagues are always with us, but they seem to be greater in some years than in others. Over-all, these conditions do seem to be increasing.

Another important event that Paul revealed is the "Rapture"–or "catching away" of true believers at the end of the Church Age. Again, Jesus did not mention it in His sermon about the future because the whole concept of the Church was a "mystery," which had not yet been revealed. This period of time, just before the beginning of The Tribulation is the logical place for the Rapture to occur. It also corresponds to the end of the Church Age foretold in Revelation (Chapters 2 and 3), and the point in the vision at which the apostle John was told to "Come up here," (Chapter 4, verse 1) to describe the rest of the events of the future, starting with the Tribulation.

2-The Tribulation

> *"Then they will deliver you up to tribulation and kill you, and you will be hated by all nations for My name's sake. And then many will be offended, will betray one another, and will hate one another. Then many false prophets will rise up and deceive many. And because lawlessness will abound, the love of many will grow cold. But he who endures to the end shall be saved. And this gospel of the kingdom will be preached in all the world as a witness to all the nations, and then the end will come.* – Matthew 24:9-14

When Jesus spoke of "tribulation," He was referring to a seven-year covenant that Daniel foretold.[109] We know this is true, because in verse 15 He mentions the "abomination of desolation" that marks the breaking of that covenant by the evil ruler who is to come:

Then he shall confirm a covenant with many for one week;
But in the middle of the week
He shall bring an end to sacrifice and offering.
And on the wing of abominations shall be one who makes desolate,
Even until the consummation, which is determined,
Is poured out on the desolate." – Daniel 9:27

The first half of these seven years of turmoil will be characterized by a growing polarization between good and evil, with believers being severely persecuted.

The apostasy that we are already seeing during this present time will be an even greater problem during the Tribulation because, as Jesus said, "lawlessness will abound." Once Christians have been removed in a great exodus at the Rapture, there will undoubtedly be a multitude of new believers. Many who have heard the Gospel, but had not hardened their hearts against it, will suddenly realize that what they had heard was true, and that some of their friends and family have been taken to be with Jesus, just as they had said. The evil leadership of the world at that time will give other explanations—perhaps, that UFOs have removed the narrow-minded troublemakers from the Earth. Many of those who have heard the Gospel might realize the truth and give their lives to Christ.

However, new Christians during the Tribulation will be persecuted for their faith. They will be killed or driven underground where they will hide from the authorities. It will be a very difficult time for them.

After the Rapture, people who called themselves Christians, but who had never truly accepted Christ as savior, might still attend their cold, liberal churches where the Bible is not really taught. Their churches will begin to band together with others who have no spiritual life, and even with other religions. But these people will not have a true love for God, and because of the evil, lawless, trends in society, they will drift further away from the truth.

Increased lawlessness will be a by-product of the absence of godly Christians from places of influence in the world. In the Rapture, true Christian legislators, judges, teachers, and others who influence culture will be taken away, and the new believers of the Tribulation period will not be allowed to ascend to those positions. Therefore, whatever restraint

Christian leaders have now will be gone and morals will become progressively more corrupt.

During this first half of the seven-year Tribulation, the apostle John predicted the torments of "The Four Horsemen of the Apocalypse" (Revelation 6:1-8): The false messiah, a great world war, terrible famine, and death by various means.

Jesus promised that the Gospel will be preached to all the Earth during this time. This probably relates to John's vision of angels preaching the Gospel all over the world and warning everyone not to receive the Mark of the Beast (Revelation 14:6-11).

3-The Great Tribulation

"Therefore when you see the 'abomination of desolation,' spoken of by Daniel the prophet, standing in the holy place" (whoever reads, let him understand), "then let those who are in Judea flee to the mountains. Let him who is on the housetop not go down to take anything out of his house. And let him who is in the field not go back to get his clothes. But woe to those who are pregnant and to those who are nursing babies in those days! And pray that your flight may not be in winter or on the Sabbath. For then there will be great tribulation, such as has not been since the beginning of the world until this time, no, nor ever shall be. And unless those days were shortened, no flesh would be saved; but for the elect's sake those days will be shortened.

"Then if anyone says to you, 'Look, here is the Christ!' or 'There!' do not believe it. For false christs and false prophets will rise and show great signs and wonders to deceive, if possible, even the elect. See, I have told you beforehand.

"Therefore if they say to you, 'Look, He is in the desert!' do not go out; or 'Look, He is in the inner rooms!' do not believe it. For as the lightning comes from the east and flashes to the west, so also will the coming of the Son of Man be. For wherever the carcass is, there the eagles will be gathered together. – Matthew 24:15-28

Jesus gave a preview of the horrifying events at the middle of the seven years of the treaty. According to the Book of Revelation, the first half would have already been a time of distress since true believers would have been persecuted and driven underground or killed. But then, the Beast will have an image of himself set up in the "Holy Place" in the newly rebuilt Temple in Jerusalem. This is the "Abomination of Desolation" predicted by Daniel, and it will lead to the institution of a world-wide economic dictatorship and the dreaded "Mark of the Beast" (Daniel 9:27; Revelation 13).

At that point many Jewish people will realize that the new world dictator is evil. Those who live near Jerusalem will need to flee immediately into the wilderness. The Old Testament prophecy of Isaiah 63:1-6 indicates that God will defend them during this awful time in the area of Bozrah, near the ancient city known as Petra in modern Jordan.

As the dreaded seven years of tribulation and "great tribulation" come to a close, the Beast will realize that his world empire is crumbling. In frustration he will unite all nations in their mutual opposition to Jesus Christ, and will gather a great army from all over the world to participate in the Campaign of Armageddon.

Jesus' will return in power and great glory, destroying His enemies and gathering the faithful together to enjoy His restored kingdom. His Glorious Return will be like the lightning in the sky. When He comes "every eye will see him," and He will come as "King of Kings and Lord of Lords" (Revelation 1:7; 19:11-16).

4-After the Tribulation

> *"Immediately after the tribulation of those days the sun will be darkened, and the moon will not give its light; the stars will fall from heaven, and the powers of the heavens will be shaken. Then the sign of the Son of Man will appear in heaven, and then all the tribes of the earth will mourn, and they will see the Son of Man coming on the clouds of heaven with power and great glory. And He will send His angels with a great sound of a trumpet, and they will gather together His elect from the four winds, from one end of heaven to the other."* — Matthew 24:29-31

After the Campaign of Armageddon, Jesus will gather true believers who remain and allow them to enter His Millennial Kingdom, where He will reign for 1000 years over a restored "Eden-like" Earth

(Revelation 20:1-6). Non-believers still alive after Armageddon will also be gathered and bound for future judgment (Like the weeds of the parable in Matthew 13:24-30).

Appendix B
Apostate or Worldly

The Greek noun *apostasia*, meaning "departure" or "defection" is only used twice in the New Testament. One of these instances is Acts 21:21 where it means a "departure" from Moses.

The other occurrence of the word is in 2 Thessalonians 2:3, where it is translated "falling away:"

> *Now, brethren, concerning the coming of our Lord Jesus Christ and our gathering together to Him, we ask you, not to be soon shaken in mind or troubled, either by spirit or by word or by letter, as if from us, as though the day of Christ had come. Let no one deceive you by any means; for that Day will not come unless* **the falling away** *comes first, and the man of sin is revealed, the son of perdition, who opposes and exalts himself above all that is called God or that is worshiped, so that he sits as God in the temple of God, showing himself that he is God.* – 2 Thessalonians 2:1-4 (NKJV)

One of the main uses of the English word "apostasy" is to describe the process of falling away from one's former faith or beliefs. There certainly are New Testament prophecies that indicate this sad state of mind will be prevalent in the end time (Matthew 24:12; 1 Timothy 4:1-3; 2 Timothy 3:1-8; 2 Timothy 4:2-4).

2 Thessalonians 2:1-4 could possibly mean that vast numbers of Christians will have lost their faith. However, it is more likely that it refers to another event: the Rapture of the Church.

First, the return of Jesus to gather believers to Himself is the stated subject of this passage (verse 1).

Second, the definite article (the word "the") is used before "falling away" to indicate that it is a particular, known event.

Third, it makes sense because when the Rapture occurs, the ultimate defection from Christianity will follow, since true believers have been taken, and only false Christians remain. These professing Christians, who have never accepted Christ and are not filled with the Holy Spirit, will either realize their mistake and accept Christ, or they will harden their hearts against the truth. If they accept Christ, they will be executed or driven underground. If they harden their hearts and believe the lies of the Beast (Revelation 13) they will become part of the one-world religion, including the worldly church. This organization will be the spiritually adulterous woman who rides the Beast (Revelation 17). This global religion will endorse and enable the Beast to be an evil world dictator.

The verb form of the word, *aphistemi*, is used 14 times in the New Testament, and it is usually translated "depart." It is only found in three places where it refers to the end time:

> *But He will say, 'I tell you I do not know you, where you are from.* **Depart** *from Me, all you workers of iniquity.'* --Luke 13:27

> *Now the Spirit expressly says that in latter times some will* **depart** *from the faith, giving heed to deceiving spirits and doctrines of demons,*--1 Tim. 4:1

> *...useless wranglings of men of corrupt minds and destitute of the truth, who suppose that godliness is a means of gain. From such* **withdraw** *yourself.* --1 Tim. 6:5

A better description: "Worldly"

In this commentary we have chosen to describe the condition of the Laodiceans as "worldly," although "apostate" would also be an accurate depiction. On our Prophecy Central site we have maintained a section for years on "Apostasy," where we trace the degeneration of society, caused by the decline of church's godly influence.

However, the more common biblical term for backslidden Christians is "worldly." New Testament references to the "world" may mean the physical created universe, or the Earth. However, the context often dictates that it refers to the evil "world system," corrupted by the Fall, and dominated by Satan.

Here are some of these passages:

Satan is the "god" of this age.

> *Again, the devil took Him up on an exceedingly high mountain, and showed Him all the kingdoms of the world and their glory. And he said to Him, "All these things I will give You if You will fall down and worship me."*
>
> *Then Jesus said to him, "Away with you, Satan! For it is written, 'You shall worship the LORD your God, and Him only you shall serve.'"*– Matthew 4:8-10

> *Now is the judgment of this world; now the ruler of this world will be cast out.* – John 12:31

> *I will no longer talk much with you, for the ruler of this world is coming, and he has nothing in Me.* – John 14:30

> *in which you once walked according to the course of this world, according to the prince of the power of the air, the spirit who now works in the sons of disobedience,*--Eph. 2:2

> *We know that we are of God, and the whole world lies under the sway of the wicked one.* – 1 John 15:9

Jesus' kingdom is not of this world. He will overcome the world.

> *Jesus answered, "My kingdom is not of this world. If My kingdom were of this world, My servants would fight, so that I should not be delivered to the Jews; but now My kingdom is not from here."* – John 18:36

> *...of judgment, because the ruler of this world is judged.*- John 16:11

The evil world system is hostile to Jesus and His followers.

> *"If the world hates you, you know that it hated Me before it hated you."* – John 15:18

If you were of the world, the world would love its own. Yet because you are not of the world, but I chose you out of the world, therefore the world hates you. – John 15:19

These things I have spoken to you, that in Me you may have peace. In the world you will have tribulation; but be of good cheer, I have overcome the world. – John 16:33

They are not of the world, just as I am not of the world. – John 17:16

Do not love the world or the things in the world. If anyone loves the world, the love of the Father is not in him. For all that is in the world—the lust of the flesh, the lust of the eyes, and the pride of life—is not of the Father but is of the world. And the world is passing away, and the lust of it; but he who does the will of God abides forever. – 1 John 2:14-17

I beseech you therefore, brethren, by the mercies of God, that you present your bodies a living sacrifice, holy, acceptable to God, which is your reasonable service. And do not be conformed to this world, but be transformed by the renewing of your mind, that you may prove what is that good and acceptable and perfect will of God. –Romans 12:1-2

But God forbid that I should boast except in the cross of our Lord Jesus Christ, by whom the world has been crucified to me, and I to the world. – Gal. 6:14

...in which you once walked according to the course of this world, according to the prince of the power of the air, the spirit who now works in the sons of disobedience,--Eph. 2:2

...teaching us that, denying ungodliness and worldly lusts, we should live soberly, righteously, and godly in the present age,--Titus 2:12

Adulterers and adulteresses! Do you not know that friendship with the world is enmity with God? Whoever therefore wants to be a friend of the world makes himself an enemy of God. – James 4:4

Do not love the world or the things in the world. If anyone loves the world, the love of the Father is not in him. For all that is in the world—the lust of the flesh, the lust of the eyes, and the pride of life—is not of the Father but is of the world. And the world is passing away, and the lust of it; but he who does the will of God abides forever. – 1 John 2:14-17

We know that we are of God, and the whole world lies under the sway of the wicked one. – 1 John 15:9

Recommended further study:

"The Rapture in 2 Thessalonians 2:3" -- by Thomas Ice --
http://www.raptureready.com/featured/ice/TheRapturein2Thessalonians2_3.html

"New Testament study of the word 'apostasy'" -- by Stella Paterson --
http://www.ekklesia4him.net/Apostasy_study.pdf

"Apostasy in the Christian Church" – by Matt Slick --
http://carm.org/apostasy-christian-church

Endnotes

[1] John MacArthur, *The MacArthur New Testament Commentary: Revelation 1-11*, [Chicago: Moody Publishers, 1999], pp. 9-11.

[2] Roman Religion Gallery, Nigel Pollard, BBC, Accessed April 10, 2014, http://www.bbc.co.uk/history/ancient/romans/roman_religion_gallery_06.shtml.

[3] Hal Lindsey, *There's A New World Coming*, [Santa Ana, CA: Vision House Publishers, 1973], p. 52.

[4] A pdf file of Hislop's book is available at http://arcticbeacon.com/books/Alexander_Hislop-The_Two_Babylons-1853-MER.pdf.

[5] William Barker and William Ainsworth, *Lares and Penates of Cilicia*, 1853, pp. 232-234.

[6] Alexander Hislop, *The Two Babylons*, Ibid., pp. 189-190.

[7] "Pontifex Maximus," Encyclopedia Britannica, accessed April 10, 2014, http://www.britannica.com/EBchecked/topic/469749/pontifex-maximus.

[8] Alexander Hislop, ibid., pp. 191, 204.

[9] Ron Graff, *2012: The Year the World Didn't End,* pp. 75 ff. Free download of the entire hypertext book [pdf format] at http://Bible-prophecy.com/books/year2012/year2012.pdf.

[10] "Thyatira," International Standard Bible Encyclopedia, accessed April 10, 2014, http://www.bible-history.com/isbe/T/THYATIRA/.

[11] ISBE, ibid.

[12] "Thyatira," Wikipedia, accessed March 8, 2014, http://en.wikipedia.org/wiki/Thyatira.

[13] C.S. Lewis, *The Four Loves,"* Goodreads, accessed April 15, 2014, http://www.goodreads.com/work/quotes/14816053-the-four-loves.

[14] "The Oracle at Delphi," PBS, accessed April 10, 2014, http://www.pbs.org/empires/thegreeks/background/7_p1.html.

[15] Raymond E. Brown, Priest and Bishop: Biblical Reflections (New York: Paulist Press, 1970 , accessed April 10, 2014, http://christiananswers.net/q-sum/sum-r005k.html.

[16] Hippolytus of Rome, *Apostolic Tradition*, p. 21 (c. AD 215).

[17] "Infant Baptism," Apologetics Press, accessed February 12, 2014, http://www.apologeticspress.org/APContent.aspx?category=11&article=2709.

[18] "Assurance of Salvation?", Catholic Answers, accessed April 15, 2014, http://www.catholic.com/tracts/assurance-of-salvation.

[19] Catholic Encyclopedia --http://www.newadvent.org/cathen/04517a.htm.

[20] "Pope Siricius," Wikipedia, aaccessed March 10, 2014,

https://en.wikipedia.org/wiki/Pope_Siricius, and
https://en.wikipedia.org/wiki/Clerical_celibacy.

[21] "Sacrifice of the Mass," Catholic Encyclopedia, accessed April 10, 2014,
http://www.newadvent.org/cathen/10006a.htm .

[22] "Transubstantiation," Wikipedia, accessed April 10, 2014,
http://en.wikipedia.org/wiki/Transubstantiation#Middle_Ages.

[23] "Second Council of Nicaea," Wikipedia, accessed March 9, 2014,
http://en.wikipedia.org/wiki/Second_Council_of_Nicaea.

[24] "Otto I, the Great," Catholic Encyclopedia:, accessed April 10, 2014,
http://www.newadvent.org/cathen/11354a.htm.

[25] "Marozia," Wikipedia, accessed April 10, 2014,
http://en.wikipedia.org/wiki/Marozia.

[26] "Pope John XII," Catholic Encyclopedia, accessed April 10, 2014,
http://www.newadvent.org/cathen/08426b.htm.

[27] "Filioque," Wikipedia, accessed April 15, 2014,
http://en.wikipedia.org/wiki/Filioque.

[28] "East–West Schism." Wikipedia, accessed April 10, 2014,
http://en.wikipedia.org/wiki/East%E2%80%93West_Schism.

[29] "Dictatus Papae," Wikipedia, accessed March 16, 2014,
http://en.wikipedia.org/wiki/Dictatus_papae.

[30] Ibid.

[31] "List of Apologies Made by Pope John Paul II," Wikipedia, accessed May
16, 2014,
http://en.wikipedia.org/wiki/List_of_apologies_made_by_Pope_John_P
aul_II.

[32] "Ecumenical Councils," Catholic Encyclopedia, accessed April 11, 2014,
http://www.newadvent.org/cathen/07790a.htm#IIIA.

[33] "Infallibility," Catholic Encyclopedia, accessed April 10, 2014,
http://www.newadvent.org/cathen/07790a.htm#IIIB.

[34] Ibid.

[35] "Questions & Answers Concerning Indulgences," accessed May 17, 2014,
http://law2.umkc.edu/faculty/projects/ftrials/luther/lutherindulgences
.html.

[36] "Indulgences," Wikipedia, accessed April 12, 2014,
http://en.wikipedia.org/wiki/Indulgence#cite_note-48.

[37] "Indulgences," Wikipedia, accessed April 12, 2014,
http://en.wikipedia.org/wiki/Indulgence#cite_note-Covolo-44.

[38] "John Huss," Christian History, accessed April 10, 2014,
http://www.christianitytoday.com/ch/131christians/martyrs/huss.html?s
tart=2.

[39] Mark Galli, "The Crusades: From the Editor – The Good, the Bad, and the
Ugly", Christianity Today, 10/1/93.

[40] "Spanish Inquisition," Wikipedia, accessed April 10, 2014,
http://en.wikipedia.org/wiki/Spanish_Inquisition#Torture.

[41] "Did Eric Rudolph Act in a "Tradition of Christian Terror?," Christian History, accessed February 11, 2014, http://www.christianitytoday.com/ch/news/2003/jun13.html.

[42] "Bible Possession Once Banned by the Catholic Church!," accessed March 8, 2014, http://www.aloha.net/~mikesch/banned.htm.

[43] Ray C. Stedman, *God's Final Word: Understanding Revelation*, [Grand Rapids: Discovery House Publishers, 1991], p 65.

[44] "Margaret Thatcher, "IMDb, accessed April 10, 2014, http://www.imdb.com/character/ch0028330/quotes.

[45] "Indulgence," Wikipedia, accessed February 17, 2014, http://en.wikipedia.org/wiki/Indulgence.

[46] Questions & Answers Concerning Indulgences- University of Missouri, Kansas City school of Law, accessed March 4, 2014, http://law2.umkc.edu/faculty/projects/ftrials/luther/lutherindulgences.html.

[47] Ibid.

[48] "The Protestant Heritage," Encyclopedia Britannica, accessed April 10, 2014, http://www.britannica.com/EBchecked/topic/1354359/The-Protestant-Heritage/225161/The-community-of-the-baptized-and-the-political-community.

[49] "Martyrs," Global Anabaptist Mennonite Encyclopedia Online, accessed April 10, 2014, http://www.gameo.org/encyclopedia/contents/M37857.html.

[50] "Anabaptist," Encyclopedia Britannica, accessed May 1, 2014, http://www.britannica.com/EBchecked/topic/22160/Anabaptist.

[51] "Dirk Willems A.D. 1569," Martyr's Mirror, accessed March 8, 2014, http://www.homecomers.org/mirror/dirk-willems.htm.

[52] F Tupper Saussy, *Rulers of Evil*, [Ospray Bookmakers, 1999], p. 33.

[53] Saussy, ibid, p. 46.

[54] "Ignatius of Loyola," Wikipedia, accessed April 10, 2014, http://en.wikipedia.org/wiki/Ignatius_of_Loyola.

[55] "The Jesuit Extreme Oath of Induction," Grace-Centered, accessed February 14, 2014, http://www.gracecentered.com/christian_forums/catholic-forum/the-extreme-oath-of-the-jesuits/.

[56] "Association of Jesuit Colleges and Universities," accessed April 10, 2014, http://www.ajcunet.edu/institutions.

[57] "On the Most Holy Sacraments of Penance and Extreme Unction," The Council of Trent, accessed March 22, 2014, http://www.thecounciloftrent.com/ch14.htm.

[58] "Council of Trent," Encyclopedia Britannica:, accessed April 10, 2014, http://www.britannica.com/EBchecked/topic/604238/Council-of-Trent.

"Council of Trent," Catholic Encyclopedia:, accessed April 10, http://www.newadvent.org/cathen/15030c.htm .

"Prayers for the Dead," Catholic Encyclopedia:, accessed April 10, 2014, http://www.newadvent.org/cathen/04653a.htm.

59"Sardis, The Dead Church," Grace to You, accessed February 22, 2014, http://www.gty.org/resources/sermons/66-11.

60 "Ignatius of Antioch," accessed March 17, 2014, http://en.wikipedia.org/wiki/Ignatius_of_Antioch.

61 *To the Philadelphians*, Chapter 6, verse 1. Accessed May 17, 2014, http://www.earlychristianwritings.com/text/ignatius-Philadelphians-lightfoot.html

62 Catholic Near East Magazine, Spring, 1978--Accessed April 10, 2014, http://www.cnewa.org/default.aspx?ID=124&pagetypeID=4&sitecode=hq&pageno=1.

63 'a Short Biography of Patrick," Heaven Sent Revival, accessed April 10, 2014, http://www.pentecostalpioneers.org/Patrick.html.

64 "Timeline of Christian Missions," Wikipedia, accessed April 18, 2014, http://en.wikipedia.org/wiki/Timeline_of_Christian_mission.

65 "Christianity among the Mongols," Wikipedia, accessed March 4, 2014, http://en.wikipedia.org/wiki/Christianity_among_the_Mongols.

66 Tom Holland, *In the Shadow of the Sword*, [New York: Anchor Books, 2012], p. 274.

67 *Timeline of Christian missions* – See date 1549, Wikipedia, accessed May 1, 2014, http://en.wikipedia.org/wiki/Timeline_of_Christian_missions.

68, Ibid.

69 "Congregation for the Evangelization of Peoples," Wikipedia, accessed February 13, http://en.wikipedia.org/wiki/Congregation_for_the_Evangelization_of_Peoples.

70 "Timeline of Christian Missions," Wikipedia, accessed April 20, 2014, http://en.wikipedia.org/wiki/Timeline_of_Christian_missions#cite_note-166.

71 United Bible Societies, accessed March 9, 2014, http://www.unitedbiblesocieties.org/.

72 United Bible Societies, accessed April 10, 2014, http://www.unitedbiblesocieties.org/sample-page/.

73 "The Ten Best-selling Books of All-time," accessed May 2, 2014, http://home.comcast.net/~antaylor1/bestsellingbooks.html.

74 Patrick Johnstone, Operation World, [Grand Rapids, Michigan: Zondervan Publishing House, 1993], p. 643.

75 "Timeline of Christian Missions," accessed April 10, 2014, http://en.wikipedia.org/wiki/Timeline_of_Christian_missions.

76 "Cru," Wikipedia, accessed March 8, 2014, http://en.wikipedia.org/wiki/Cru_(Christian_organization).

77 "Jesus Film Project," Wikipedia, accessed April 10, 2014, http://en.wikipedia.org/wiki/Jesus_Film_Project.

78 "Laodicea," Easton's Bible Dictionary, accessed April 10, 2014, http://www.biblestudytools.com/dictionary/laodicea/.

79 "Laodicea on the Lycus," Wikipedia, accessed April 10, 2014,

http://en.wikipedia.org/wiki/Laodicea_on_the_Lycus.

[80] Ray C. Stedman, *Ibid.*, pp. 97-98.

[81] Ray C. Stedman, *Ibid.*, p. 99.

[82] Thomas Ice, "The Rapture in 2 Thessalonians 2:3", accessed May 18.2014, http://www.raptureready.com/featured/ice/TheRapturein2Thessalonians 2_3.html.

[83] "Text of the Northwest Ordinance," Archiving Early America, accessed April 10, 2014, http://www.earlyamerica.com/earlyamerica/milestones/ordinance/text.h tml.

[84] "McGuffey's Readers," Dear Christian Parents, accessed March 30, 2014, http://www.dearchristianparents.com/mcguffeys_readers.html.

[85] "How Progressive Education Gets It Wrong", Hoover Digest, accessed April 10, 2014, http://www.hoover.org/publications/hoover-digest/article/6408.

[86] "The Decline of Western Civilization," accessed April 10, 2014, http://bsimmons.wordpress.com/2006/11/09/the-decline-of-western-civilization-a-historical-time-line-now-add-nov-7th-2006/.

[87] "Mission (Christianity)," Wikipedia, accessed February 5, 2014, http://en.wikipedia.org/wiki/Mission_(Christianity).

[88] "World Parliament of Religions," Christianity.com, accessed April 10, 2014, http://www.christianity.com/church/church-history/timeline/1801-1900/world-parliament-of-religions-11630638.html.

[89] Accessed March 1, 2014, http://blogs.reuters.com/faithworld/2009/12/08/guestview-faiths-meet-at-parliament-of-world-religions/.

[90] Accessed April 10, 2014, http://www.goodfight.org/a_v_avatar_one_world_religion.html.

[91] Accessed February 6, 2014, http://www.phrases.org.uk/meanings/282700.html.

[92] "Decree on Ecumenism," Vatican, accessed April 10, 2014, http://www.vatican.va/archive/hist_councils/ii_vatican_council/docume nts/vat-ii_decree_19641121_unitatis-redintegratio_en.html, last accessed on 5/1/2014.

[93] "History of the Good News Club," accessed March 28, 2014, http://www.goodnewsclubs.info/history.htm.

[94] "List of Best-selling Books," Wikipedia, accessed May 1, 2014, http://en.wikipedia.org/wiki/List_of_best-selling_books#cite_note-43.

[95] "Josh McDowell," Wikipedia, accessed April 10, 2014, http://en.wikipedia.org/wiki/Josh_McDowell.

[96] George Barna, accessed May 1, 2014, https://www.barna.org/about/george-barna#.U2LqKmcU8dU.

[97] "New Marriage and Divorce Statistics Released," Barna Group, accessed April 10, 2014, https://www.barna.org/barna-update/article/15-familykids/42-new-marriage-and-divorce-statistics-

released#.U2LkjGcU8dU.

[98] "The World's Most Powerful People," Forbes, accessed April 10, 2014, http://www.forbes.com/sites/carolinehoward/2013/10/30/the-worlds-most-powerful-people-2013/.

[99] "The World at War," GlobalSecurity.com, accessed March 8, 2014, http://www.globalsecurity.org/military/world/war/.

[100] Accessed May 1, 2014, http://www.wnd.com/2014/02/poll-hunger-games-harry-potter-are-biblical/.

[101] Accessed April 10, 2014, http://www.youtube.com/watch?v=x3tmi8nK9wM.

[102] "'Nones' on the Rise," Pew Forum, accessed February 25, http://www.pewforum.org/2012/10/09/nones-on-the-rise/.

[103] "Five Reasons Millennials Stay Connected to Church," Barna, accessed March 16, 2014, https://www.barna.org/barna-update/millennials/635-5-reasons-millennials-stay-connected-to-church#.Uv0KtWePIdU.

[104] "Back to Jerusalem," accessed May 2, 2014, http://backtojerusalem.com/v3/.

[105] "Jesus Appears to Muslims in Dreams, Conversions and Testimonies," Beliefnet, accessed April 10, 2014, http://www.beliefnet.com/columnists/watchwomanonthewall/2013/02/jesus-appears-to-muslims-in-dreams-conversions-and-testimonies-video.html.

[106] "Good News Club v. Milford Central School," Wikipedia, accessed March 32014. http://en.wikipedia.org/wiki/Good_News_Club_v._Milford_Central_School.

[107] Accessed April 10, 2014, http://www.cefct.org/linked/legal%20brief.pdf.

[108] "The Top Ten Graduate Schools in Apologetics," accessed May 7, 2014, http://www.thebestschools.org/blog/2012/01/03/top-10-graduate-programs-apologetics/.

[109] See Chapter 10 (online) of Sir Robert Anderson's *The Coming Prince*. This prophecy is recorded in Daniel 9:20-27. The prophecy is actually about "seventy weeks of years." The first 69 weeks represent 483 years (69 X 7) beginning with the decree issued by Artaxerxes Longimanus in the twentieth year of his reign, authorizing Nehemiah to rebuild the fortifications of Jerusalem. It ends on the very day that Christ offered himself to be King of the Jews, but was rejected by his enemies. There is a gap between the 69 weeks and the 70th week. During this gap the mystery of the Church Age unfolds. After the Rapture of the Church, the final seven years of the prophecy will take place. Accessed May 2, 2014, http://philologos.org/__eb-tcp/chap10.htm .

www.ingramcontent.com/pod-product-compliance
Lightning Source LLC
Chambersburg PA
CBHW071405090426
42737CB00011B/1363